Two Jamaicas

The Role of Ideas in a Tropical Colony

Two Jamaicas

The Role of Ideas in a Tropical Colony
1 8 3 0 – 1 8 6 5 ⅌

Philip D. Curtin

Harvard University Press, Cambridge
1 9 5 5 ⅌

© Copyright, 1955, by the President and Fellows of Harvard College

❧ Distributed in Great Britain by
Geoffrey Cumberlege, Oxford University Press, London

Library of Congress Catalog Card Number 55–10969
Printed in the United States of America

To
PHYLLIS CURTIN

Preface

In 1859, after a visit to the West Indies, Anthony Trollope remarked, "Those who are failing and falling in the world excite but little interest; and so it is at present with Jamaica." [1] Since then, the West Indian islands have come to occupy a still smaller place in world affairs, and the decades following slave emancipation — the "dark period" of Jamaican history — have attracted no more interest from later generations than they did from contemporaries. In the eighteenth century the islands had played an important role in the rivalries of European powers. For both the French and the British, they were the most valuable of overseas possessions, and therefore their history was important as a part of European history. Later on, during the struggle over slave emancipation, the British West Indies had an important place in the domestic politics of Great Britain. But the crisis over the Jamaican constitution that brought down the Melbourne government in 1839 marks the end of serious West Indian influence on British politics. The history of the islands in the period that followed has been relegated to a chapter of Imperial history called, "Minor Colonies." The history of the individual islands has fallen under the rubric of "local history," of interest principally to those who want to know the background of the place in which they live or the administrator who wants to know what lies behind his current problems.

Viewed simply in the light of their direct influence on the world at large, there is some justice in this decline of interest in the islands. Even the specialist in the British Empire is right, in one sense, in turning to the more hopeful development of the dominions that would be the core of the present Commonwealth. In the middle of the twentieth century, however, the European world is confronted by a widespread revolutionary ferment in the tropical colonies that were once ruled complacently as a minor aspect of "white man's burden." From

Indochina to the Gold Coast, colonial peoples have accepted what the Europeans offered them — a superior technology, more efficient government, sometimes a new religion, and, for a minority, elements of a European education. They have also lost what the Europeans took from them — their older social and governmental organization, their traditional economy, and the sanctions of sentiment, religion, and custom that formerly held their society together.

Only a few decades ago, optimistic theorists about colonial policy seemed to believe that this process would go forward to the point where subject people accepted European "civilization" in its entirety, and "barbarism" had completely disappeared. The less optimistic took consolation in the fact that, at the very least, the "tutelage" of European nations was a benefit in itself. It is now obvious that neither was correct. One result of the impact of European ideas has been the growth of local nationalism. This development has made indefinite "trusteeship" impossible, except through the use of overwhelming military force. At the same time, European ideas and European ways have not been accepted *in toto*. Colonial peoples have taken part of the offering and rejected the rest. They have dropped some of their indigenous ideas and institutions, but others have shown an amazing vigor. It now seems likely that the present ferment will result eventually in the formation of new societies where neither the European nor the indigenous will have survived in its entirety. Instead, there will be an amalgam of both — a product of the adjustment of a diverse inheritance to the problems of a world where colonialism, as it was formerly practiced, is no longer possible. It is also clear that the process of adjustment and cultural synthesis will be very different in different colonial areas. There is no need to look further than the two sides of Africa, where the Ashanti of the Gold Coast and the Kikuyu of Kenya have embarked on different courses.

Since each generation finds its historical questions set, to an extent, by its current problems, the history of the West Indies in the nineteenth century is brought into a new focus by the experience of Africa in the twentieth. Elements of African and of European culture had confronted each other for more than two hundred years in the Caribbean. Then, beginning in the late eighteenth century, the existing relations between the two races and the two cultures were broken. Both the white colonists and their former slaves had to pick up the broken strands of their social and economic development and try to put together a new kind of tropical society. For Jamaica, the years between 1830 and 1865 were years of crisis and readjustment — a process not too different from the present ferment of the newer tropical colonies. With the perspective of time, therefore, the role of ideas in a Caribbean colony during the years following the emancipation takes on an importance far beyond that of local history.

This is not to say that a single case-study could establish a pattern of universal validity for other colonial societies. Even in the nineteenth-century British Caribbean, each colony tended to go its separate way after emancipation and to find its own solution to the problems of a free-labor society in the tropics. The history of Jamaica is used here not because it was typical but because it was the largest of the British islands and the one for which historical sources are most adequate. History does not repeat itself, in any case — not, at least, the totality of historical experience in any given time and place. The role of ideas in nineteenth-century Jamaica can be expected to be vastly different from the role of ideas in another colony at another time.

But the fact that a given society is colonial opens special problems in its intellectual history — problems that would have little meaning in a metropolitan society. Such problems, emerging from a study of nineteenth-century Jamaica, concern the origin and transfer of ideas. The ruling Jamaicans were European in culture and education; therefore, they might be expected to turn to England for a solution to their problems. At the same time, Jamaican society was very different from British society, and British ideas could hardly be applicable to Jamaican conditions. Mother country and colony differed in respect to climate, geography, social structure, and the cultural background of the majority of the people. Nevertheless, the ruling classes were united in a common language, a common education, and by the circulation of individuals as new men "came out" from England and others returned. The transfer of ideas was potentially very easy between the two societies which were, in most respects, extremely different from each other. The problem is whether ideas

developed in one kind of environment can be transferred whole
to a different kind of society.

This problem of the transfer of ideas cannot be raised without
reference to the Marxist contention that ideas grow out of the
mode of production and the relations between classes in any
society. The acceptance of this thesis would lead a priori to the
expectation that British ideas would be accepted in Jamaica only
with the greatest of difficulty. The Jamaican ruling class would
be expected to develop an ideology of their own. This ideology
would explain and justify their special position in the colony,
and it would differ as much from the British ideas of the period
as the structure of Jamaican society differed from that of Great
Britain.

In examining the history of a small colony — the history of
ideas or otherwise — there is a special problem. Since a small
colony is closely dependent on the mother country, its history
can be seen from either of two directions — as a special area of
British history, or as that of a separate society with a life of its
own. The first of these approaches has been dominant in the historiography of small colonies, and the cause of this tendency is
not hard to find. Travelers, missionaries, government officials,
and even absentee proprietors have tended to consider a colony
like Jamaica as though it were a tropical segment of Great
Britain, a sort of detached plantation whose wealth or poverty,
good or bad management was to be reported back to the "home
office" where all decisions would be made, correcting the errors
and exploiting the possibilities. It was only natural for historians
to take on the attitudes of their principal witnesses.

This view is partly accurate for the history of any small
colonial dependent. Jamaica belonged to an imperial system.
It produced crops that were largely consumed off the island. Its
working class was originally alien, imported from other tropical
trading posts. Its ruling class was also alien, living a life they considered one of temporary exile. Both its political institutions
and slavery, the principal social institution, were devised by Europeans and imposed for European ends.

This view is only partly accurate, however. While admitting
that the history of a West Indian colony cannot be written in an
exclusively Caribbean context, to see it exclusively in the con-

text of Imperial policy also misses the point. Jamaica is an island, and this fact is important. It constituted a small, relatively homogeneous environment, cut off by water and politics from its nearest neighbors and by distance from the center of the Empire. A common environment and common political institutions gave Jamaicans of all origins a common set of problems, no matter how divergent their interests, or how temporary their stay on the island. Government officials were shifted from one colony to another, but a new governor arriving in Jamaica took on the problems of his predecessor, was informed by the same local individuals, and sent in very much the same sort of report to the Colonial Office in London. Since these reports formed the basis of central policy, it was not nearly as central in origin as it has often been considered. There was, of course, a tendency for harassed Colonial Office personnel to think of policy in terms of groups of small colonies — to think of the West Indies rather than Jamaica. And in fact, as well as in the mind of Whitehall, Jamaica was only one of a number of colonies passing through a similar experience of revolution and readjustment in this period. Thus the problem of Jamaican policy was only one facet of a more complex imperial problem. If we were dealing here with, say, Grenada, this difficulty would be a serious one. Jamaica, however, was so much the most important of the West Indian colonies that policies originating in that island were more often applied thoughtlessly to the others than the reverse. While there are pitfalls in either approach, the history of Jamaica will be treated, where possible, as the history of a separate society with a life of its own.

One final word of warning is necessary. The sense in which this is a study in the history of ideas should not be misunderstood. If intellectual history is taken to be the history of Great Ideas or Great Books, then the kind of history that follows must be called something else. Nineteenth-century Jamaican ideas are not often worthy of notice for their own sake, and the principal interest is not in the intellectual effort of the exceptional person. It is in the outlook of the ordinary man, even though this must often be approached through the works of the not-so-ordinary men who left some record of their beliefs.

In the course of preparing this study, I have accumulated a

considerable debt to many individuals and institutions. I am especially grateful to Professor David Owen of Harvard University for his many helpful suggestions at all stages in the preparation of the work. Mrs. Chase Duffy and Mrs. Isabelle Satterthwaite read the manuscript and made many useful comments. It would be impossible to list all the friends in Jamaica who helped make research there both pleasant and profitable, but the staff of the Reference Library of the West Indies deserves a special word of praise. Of its members, I should especially like to acknowledge the help of Mr. J. R. T. Ettlinger, Miss Beryl Fletcher, Miss Phyllis O. B. Caws, and Miss Joy Fennell. Outside the range of research in libraries, I owe a special debt to Mr. Stanley A. G. Taylor, for helping me to see many connections between the history of Jamaica and the land itself. Finally, I should like to thank Miss Ann Louise Coffin for her careful editing of the manuscript.

March 1, 1955   P. D. C.

Contents

ILLUSTRATIONS

PART I ᴣᴥ

THE EVE OF REVOLUTION
Jamaica in the 1830's

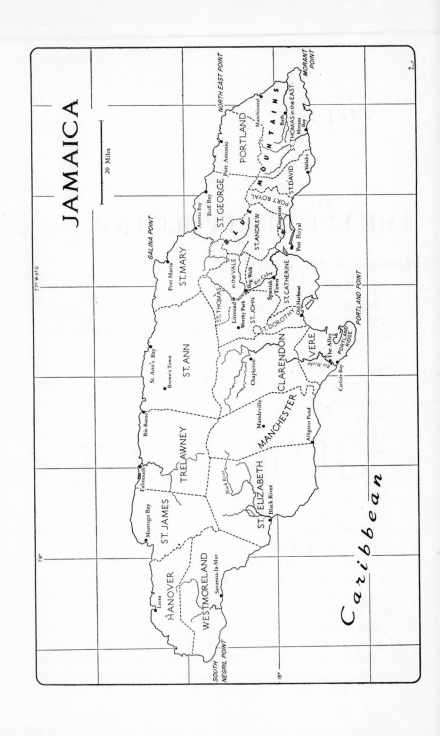

JAMAICA

20 Miles

I

A Planting Economy

THE END OF THE EIGHTEENTH CENTURY and
the beginning of the nineteenth formed a period of radical
change in Western Europe. With the American and French
revolutions, the growth of nationalism in the Napoleonic Wars,
and the British Reform Act of 1832, the forms of eighteenth-
century monarchy changed into new political forms, closely
recognizable as the beginnings of Western democratic states.
In economic affairs, a similar series of changes, often grouped
together as the "Industrial Revolution," brought with it the
first large-scale change to a modern industrial society. Taken
together, and paced by corresponding changes in ideas, these
movements amounted to a general revolution in the European
way of life and the European way of thinking about society,
politics, and the relations of human beings to one another.

In these movements the term, "European," also meant the
wider world beyond the European peninsula. The general revolution extended to all areas where Europeans lived and to all
areas where Europeans controlled subject peoples. Indeed, the
first of the specifically political revolutions was the revolt of
Great Britain's North American colonies. The revolt of the
slaves in Saint Domingue and the dissolution of the Spanish
Empire were other facts of the general political change, and the
emancipation of the slaves in the British Empire brought with
it a social revolution in each of the British West Indian colonies. The Jamaican revolution of the 1830's, therefore, can be

seen as a tiny part of a much broader series of changes within the European-dominated world.

It can also be seen as an element in the breakup of the South Atlantic System, a regional economic, political, and social order of which Jamaica had been a part. In the 1830's, the basic outlines of the South Atlantic System had been in existence for two centuries. It began early in the seventeenth century, when the seaboard nations of northwestern Europe seized the smaller Caribbean islands which had never been effectively occupied by Spain. Through a process of borrowing some techniques from the Spanish and Portuguese empires and developing others that were new, the northern maritime nations set up a new kind of overseas empire. The Spanish and Portuguese in the preceding century had conquered some non-European societies and traded with others. In the process they had planted sugar in tropical colonies and had begun the African slave trade to America. The newness of the seventeenth-century empires in the Caribbean lay in the fact that they were almost exclusively planting societies oriented toward the single end of supplying Europe with tropical staples.

It would not be quite accurate to call the South Atlantic System a single entity, since it was sealed off, in theory at least, in watertight national compartments. For Britain the individual elements were a series of trading posts on the coast of Africa, some of the islands in the lesser Antilles, Jamaica, and the complementary temperate colonies of North America, which supplied provisions for the slaves, manufactured rum for the slave trade, and provided part of the shipping that was essential to the system. As a national entity, this far-flung trading system has been known to history as the Old Colonial System. For the French there was a similar collection of complementary colonies, with African posts, Martinique and Guadeloupe in the lesser Antilles, and Saint Domingue in the western part of Hispaniola, to occupy the place of Jamaica. Temperate American colonies played a smaller part in the French system than in the British, but in their essentials the two systems were the same. With greater variations the Spanish colonies in the Caribbean and the Portuguese in Brazil formed a part of the system, while the Dutch and the Danes also participated in some phases.

Throughout the eighteenth century, the South Atlantic System had an important place in the economy of Western Europe, and rivalries between France and England often took on the aspect of colonial wars, one component of which was the effort to enlarge one national compartment of the System at the expense of the rival empire. Even small islands were considered valuable prizes, as the ruins of expensive stone fortifications on the West India islands still testify. Beginning in the 1770's, however, the South Atlantic System began to decline. The decline was not immediate, but spread over half a century. The American Revolution destroyed the unity of the old "triangular trade" in slaves, sugar, and provisions between the North American colonies, the West Indies, and the African coast. The French Revolution brought with it the loss of Saint Domingue, the most valuable of the French colonies. Changes taking place outside the South Atlantic System were still more important. By the end of the Napoleonic Wars, the West Indian colonies were not, perhaps, less intrinsically valuable than they had been seventy or eighty years earlier, but the increase of European productivity and the opening of newer avenues of trade had already made them relatively less important to their respective mother countries.[1]

The South Atlantic System is only a general pattern of European colonialism when seen from the outside or in retrospect. Its decline appeared to the Englishmen of the time as the decline of the British Empire, and the loss of Saint Domingue was, for the French, a purely national disaster. To the Jamaican planter, the decline of the Old Colonial System appeared first as an exorbitant price for salt fish and timber from Canada, when the cheaper supplies from New England were cut off by the American Revolution. The successful slave rebellion in Saint Domingue in 1791 showed him that a similar danger existed for Jamaica, but it also brought a higher price for sugar and a period of temporary prosperity. The abolition of the British slave trade in 1807 was a much more obvious blow — the South Atlantic System was an artificial creation in the sense that the planting colonies could neither supply nor reproduce their own labor force.[2] But even more than an economic disaster, abolition of the trade was a portent of the force of aroused humanitarianism in Great Britain — evidence of the important intellectual changes in Europe since the more tolerant eighteenth century. Against this danger, however, there could be set the record sugar crop of 1805. The Jamaican planter was hardly in a position to know that this crop would not be equaled again on his island until 1936, and then under vastly different conditions. Nor could he realize that his colony was being bypassed and left behind in the rapid development of the European economy. Following the peace of 1815, the signs of economic decline began to be more obvious, but it was still possible for Jamaicans to see developments, now recognized as a secular economic decline, as a mere depression of the sugar trade. Jamaica was still one of the most important colonies in a diminished Empire. It still produced about half of the total British sugar entering trade. It still retained some of its old reputation as a source of easy wealth for any Briton with a little ability and a little luck. And perhaps this reputation was no more undeserved in 1820 than it had been fifty years earlier. Even in the eighteenth century the "West Indian lottery" had been a precarious source of prosperity for the individual planter, whatever its value to the Empire as a whole. A few might make fortunes, but there were always the uncertainties of war and weather, which periodically brought the cry of "ruin" from the West India interest.[3]

By 1830, however, the height of Jamaican prosperity had sensibly passed. Spanish America and other previously untouched areas began to produce sugar for the European market, and the West Indies began to lose their competitive position. Sugar from the British islands was protected by prohibitive tariffs within the British market, but sugar of West Indian produce was also refined in Great Britain for sale on the Continent. In this market British West Indian sugar met the competition of new foreign sources, and even within the home market the West Indies competed with new suppliers from Mauritius and East India. The price of sugar in London, though it was still high enough for some planters to show a profit, was generally much lower than the wartime levels.[4] As early as 1816 Jamaican plantations were being "thrown up" and allowed to grow up in brush and to become, in the Jamaican expression, "ruinate."[5]

Not only the economic difficulties of sugar growing, but an

increasing fear of the British humanitarian campaign for the
amelioration and abolition of slavery tended to bring a general
decrease in Jamaican property values, estimated at a 33 per cent
loss between 1815 and 1831.[6] In the 1820's the cry of ruin was
raised again and more loudly than ever. The Rev. George
Wilson Bridges, rector of the parish of St. Ann, wrote, as his conclusion to a long study of Jamaican history:

> The streams of blood which flow down the pages of history
> through the first fifteen years of the present century, are now
> stopped, and the world once more enjoys calm repose. But peace
> and justice have been long since banished from Jamaica; all her
> institutions are withered, and her ruin has been accelerated by
> storms and earthquakes. The trunk is at length bent to the ground,
> and although the hurricane has passed away, it can rise no more, —
> its vegetation and its life have fled.[7]

This still represented only a hyperbolic fear of the future,
rather than a reasoned estimate of the contemporaneous situation. Jamaica had not yet lost her supremacy as the wealthiest of
West Indian colonies or as one of the most prized of all British
overseas possessions. She was still one of the "richest jewels of
the British crown." [8] The prestige of the governship of Jamaica
was second only to that of India and Canada, and it would remain so for twenty years more. The hope for new prosperity,
like the prestige of the colony, was to live long beyond the period
when it had any basis in reality.

*   *   *

Life in Jamaica about 1830 was still set solidly in the framework of the Old Colonial System. Just as the system as a whole
centered on the Imperial trading center in London, the life of
the island centered on the island trading center at Kingston. And
by virtue of its economic supremacy Kingston was also the social,
intellectual, and cultural center of the colony. As the chief port,
it was the window on the outside world — a world where most of
the Jamaican ruling class would rather have found themselves.
Although a subsidiary of London, the real center of the plantation economy, Kingston was at least the middleman between
that center and the individual estates. This position made King-

ston much more "the town" than St. Jago de la Vega, or Spanish Town, the official capital of the colony.

Kingston in the 1830's was a dirty, hot, bedraggled tropical town set at the foot of a long sloping plain against the backdrop of the Blue Mountains. It was the most important town in the British West Indies, but not in appearance. Never a beautiful town, by 1830 it had such an air of having lost its self-respect that visitors were even more struck by the impression of neglect and faded prosperity than the economic situation warranted. As early as 1816 a visitor had written: ". . . if any person will imagine a large town entirely composed of booths at a race course, and the streets merely roads, without any sort of paving, he will have a perfect idea of Kingston." [9] This effect was accomplished partly by the prevailing wooden construction of the principal buildings, partly by the fact that tropical architecture in West Indian towns was much more open than an Englishman would expect, partly by lack of civic pride, and partly because most of the principal inhabitants used the town only as a place of business, preferring to live in the country, higher up the plain toward the mountains of St. Andrew. When it rained, water poured through the streets, gradually washing away the roadway and eventually bringing the street level below that of the surrounding foundations. When it was dry, the trade wind blew up a constant cloud of dust from the streets and added this to the general atmosphere of fallen fortune. In 1834 another traveler wrote that Kingston had ". . . the aspect of a ruined city that has been recently abandoned. It is impossible to form an idea of an inhabited town so desolate and so decayed." [10]

Kingston's fortunes in the 1830's were certainly in decline, but the decline had not yet become the catastrophe it would become a few decades later. With a population around 35,000, Kingston was a large town by West Indian standards. As a port, it still cleared the better part of the trade between Britain and Jamaica, and in the 1830's this was still an important trade, not only for Jamaica but for the economy of the empire as a whole.[11] In addition to sugar and coffee, Kingston had a large share of the new trade between Britain and the liberated countries of Latin America. Legal and illegal together, this entrepôt trade probably amounted to about half of Kingston's total business.[12]

When it declined in the 1840's with the coming of steamships, direct trade, and competition from the more favorable entrepôt at St. Thomas in the Danish West Indies, the loss was a principal cause of Kingston's decline – quite apart from the general decline of the planting economy.[13]

The fact that Spanish Town was the official seat of government gave it a special position among the smaller towns of Jamaica. By 1830, the intended magnificence of the Georgian square of yellow brick public buildings had faded a bit, and they were now presumptuously ornate for the rather rundown village of five thousand people that surrounded them. Only fifteen miles across the plain from Kingston and on the main road to everywhere in the island except the two southeastern parishes, the capital served as a sort of official annex to the port area. A planter coming in from the country would commonly visit both. Spanish Town even had some advantage over Kingston as the social center, being the home of the governor and the officialdom — not that they actually lived in town if they could help it, any more than the Kingston merchants did. Still, it was the official center, and from November to Christmas and occasionally into the new year there was a bustle of activity for the annual meeting of the island legislature. This was often a slack period for sugar planting, and the planters coming in for the meeting of the Assembly made what might be called the Spanish Town "season."

Besides Kingston and Spanish Town there were a dozen smaller towns scattered along the coasts of the island. These were the parish towns, places where sugar was shipped in season from a "barquadier" with a few warehouse buildings attached. They were centers of parish affairs built around the court house and the militia muster. Some of these were far enough from Kingston to constitute separate centers of commercial affairs. On the north coast Falmouth and Montego Bay competed for the leadership of the "northside," with a common jealousy for Kingston, Spanish Town, and the "southside." Next in size were a group of smaller ports, which acted as local centers for a smaller area. In this group were Savanna-la-Mar and Black River at the southwest, Morant Bay at the southeast, and St. Ann's Bay and Port Antonio at the north and northeast. There were many other, smaller "bays," some of them nothing but beaches for shipping sugar or coffee in lighters.

The towns, however, were only small concentrations of people on the rim of the land itself. The life of the country was beyond the towns in the great estates that made the existence of the towns possible, and there was a great deal of Jamaica even beyond the estates. The 148 miles from east to west along the spine of the island is not a great distance, even by nineteenth-century standards of transportation, and it is only 52 miles across Jamaica from north to south at the widest point, yet in 1830 most of this area was still inaccessible, still unoccupied, and, in fact, not susceptible to occupation by the sugar economy.[14] Much of the mass of the Blue Mountains in the east, sending out confused systems of ridges, or the limestone hills over the rest of the island, pocketed with numerous valleys having no surface drainage, was simply a no man's land without access by roads or even trails and without inhabitants except a few bands of maroons — former runaway slaves who had managed to free themselves after open war against the English in the eighteenth century.

As a result of Jamaican geography, the sugar economy occupied only a small part of an island that was still largely undeveloped. The rest, however, was far from being a no man's land in the sense of having no legal owner. In fact, the practice of granting large patents of land against the payment of a small quitrent had gone so far by the 1830's that more land had been patented than existed.[15] Many of the grants were in the mountains and had never been cultivated. Some had been used a few years and then allowed to become ruinate. Much of the best sugar land was on the flat plains of the south coast, in the parishes of Vere or Westmoreland, where the land was heavily populated and one cane-piece bordered on the next. But most estates through the island — in the accessible interior valleys, like St. Thomas-the-Vale, along the north coast, or in river valleys were based on very large grants, only part of which was usable for sugar cultivation. These estates contained some flat land, but they also ran off into the "mountain" or "back lands," where the boundaries between one estate and another were unsurveyed and unimportant to the proprietors.

Coffee, which grows best at high altitudes, had been carried further into the interior of the island, but here again the plantations cultivated only a small fraction of the land grant and tended to be concentrated in especially favorable areas, like a part of the Blue Mountains and in the Red Hills. Thus, while Jamaica had been occupied by the English for more than a century and a half, and even though it was not a large island, it was cultivated intensively in selected areas and not at all in others. It still had a potential "frontier" in the American sense.

*　　*　　*

Since the beginning of English occupation in 1655, a very complex system of cultivation had grown up, established by long tradition and now, in the 1830's, set in its ways and seemingly unwilling or unable to meet a changing world situation. The West Indies were spoken of as "sugar islands," but Jamaica was not so exclusively a sugar producer as some of the other Caribbean colonies. Nevertheless, she was still a sugar island in the prestige of the sugar grower and in the overwhelming proportion of sugar and rum in Jamaican exports.[16]

The basic unit was the sugar estate, and in 1834 there were about 650 estates on the island, ranging in size from eight hundred to two or three thousand acres.[17] As much as 650,000 acres would thus have been devoted to sugar estates, but this figure is deceptive.[18] Just as the estates covered only a small part of the island, the cane covered only a small part of the estate. Probably not more than 100,000 acres were actually planted in cane. Most of the estate land was in pasture, waste, or provision grounds worked by slaves in their off hours. On a good estate of two thousand acres, four hundred, or even less, would be the cane fields clustered close around the sugar works.[19]

With expensive labor and cheap land, planters might be expected to apply the labor more extensively; but this was not possible. Sugar is a labor-intensive crop, and planters were forced to apply the available labor to the best land, leaving the rest unused. Much of it was not suitable for sugar in any case, but there were other factors also making for concentration. Mills were small, and cane was heavy and difficult to transport from a distance, but the key problem was labor. As long as slavery lasted, planters could concentrate it where they wanted it, and concentration on only a part of the estate was an adequate solution for the labor shortage. With emancipation, the problem of keeping labor concentrated on some land while the rest was cheap and empty would become serious.

Through the years, the commercial side of sugar planting had become routine, basically similar for all estates. It was a seasonal business. The planters' year began and ended on August 1. By that date the previous crop was shipped and the books were closed. Each estate in Jamaica had a close credit connection, usually as a mortgagee, with a mercantile house in London, Liverpool, Bristol, or Glasgow. In the fall the planter sent out his order for supplies needed during the coming season. This was usually a credit transaction, with the British merchant taking a mortgage that was renewed from year to year. The merchant forwarded the supplies so as to arrive at the beginning of the cane-cutting season, the "crop," which began after Christmas. By granting credit the British merchant bound the planter to buy supplies and ship his rum and sugar through the lending house on a commission basis.

When the connection was begun — and it had been running for a number of years on most Jamaican estates — the mortgage might have been equal to the value of the property. By the 1830's, however, the general fall of property values often made the mortgage higher than the value of the estate. The merchant, however, still received interest on the original loan, plus a monopoly on the estate's business, and the opportunity to charge non-competitive commissions. It was often more profitable for him to drift along than to foreclose and run the estate himself or sell at a loss. Even for the profitable estate the web of credit was difficult to avoid, and the system was an expensive drain on whatever profit there might be.[20]

The agricultural side of sugar planting was also seasonal. Plantation life revolved around the "crop." About the time of the annual Negro festival at Christmas, sugar estates changed from their normal agricultural operations and became part-farm, part-factory. For two or three months or longer the estate was at a high pitch of tension. The labor force that was sufficient for the usual work of plantation maintenance during the rest of the year was put under a tremendous strain by the necessity of getting the cane cut, transported to the mill, ground, and boiled to fill the great hogsheads of raw sugar or "muscavado" that would be shipped during the spring and summer. When the cane was ripe the mill had to be kept going twenty-four hours a day in order to grind the sugar when the yield was highest — otherwise part of the crop was lost. On a medium-sized estate with about two hundred slaves of all ages, thirty-five or forty people were needed in the sugar works alone.[21] This was a large number of able-bodied workers to lose, when the major job of cutting cane and transporting it to the mill was still to be done.

There was another period of especially arduous work during the planting season. The cane was set out during the relatively wet weather of the fall or spring. Planters planned a combination of the "spring plant" and "fall plant" in order to bring two crops of cane, one that would be ready for the beginning of "crop" and another that would come along as the first was finished. All fields were not planted each year, since shoots from the old plants, called "ratoons," could be left to come up by themselves. In three to five years, however, they had to be dug up and replanted, since the yield decreased each year.[22] To help with the heavy work of planting, it was possible to hire gangs of slaves from jobbers who kept them for this purpose, but jobbing gangs were too expensive to be a satisfactory solution to the seasonal labor shortage. This problem, which was serious enough under the slave system, was also to become more difficult with emancipation.

By 1830 the routine of sugar growing was fixed in a mold of tradition and habit that went back to the eighteenth century and beyond. In its resistance to change the planting economy was similar to the English agricultural system before the enclosures of the eighteenth century. When the planters complained of depression, they met the criticism from England that they were using backward methods. This was indeed the case. The West Indians had lagged behind the English agricultural improvements. Their system was technologically backward, and it was wasteful of labor. Since it was hard to calculate labor costs under slavery, planters were slow to see the value of labor-saving devices. Even the plow had not yet replaced the hoe as the chief instrument for planting cane.

The planters' defense was to claim that their system was adapted to tropical conditions and could not be altered. In one sense there was some justice in their case. The old system was so firmly embedded in the habits of the planting class and their slaves that change was extremely difficult. Neither the normally absentee proprietor, nor his creditor, the merchant, nor the resident planters were in a position to make innovations. And even if they had had the power to make radical changes or experiments in planting they had still to contend with tradition and habit on the estate itself.

*   *   *

The Jamaican estate of 1830 had become a very complex organism. Each position carried with it the traditional skills for doing the traditional job, and estate personnel were divided into ranks and grades that tended to make the estate a microcosm of the larger Jamaican society. The gradations of this miniature society were even marked out in the physical layout of a typical estate.

The most imposing structure was the great house, home of the proprietor when he was in residence, symbol of his authority, and home of his representative when he was not. Proprietors tried to build on a height where possible, to take every advantage of the breeze. Often it was the situation and not the building that gave the great house its air of command. The architecture, in any event, was usually simple and open. The ground floor was not used, except for storage and occasionally for workrooms. The second floor contained all the living quarters and was approached from the front by a double flight of outside stairs, passing on either side of an archway leading straight through to the back of the house. The invariable feature of the second floor was a wide hall, the principal living area, running the length of the house with bedrooms opening onto it from either side. The roof was tall and pitched on all four sides, and the outside walls of the second floor were either partly or entirely made of jalousies, a form of permanent venetian blind. These could be closed down in wet weather, and in dry weather they let the trade wind sweep through the house without admitting the glare of sunlight. There were many variations on this design, but even the great mansions in stone, like Rose Hall in Trelawney, kept very close to the basic pattern.[23]

The deserted great houses one sometimes sees today in the old sugar area of Jamaica cannot be taken as the continuing symbol of a paternalistic regime of great landed proprietors, who presided over the welfare of their estates and their slaves. There were the proprietors and the great houses, but the one was not often the inhabitant of the other — no longer, at least, by the 1830's. Jamaican estates were usually founded in the seventeenth or eighteenth century by a slave-owning patentee who was on the spot, but as the estate became prosperous the proprietor's children were sent "home" for their education, and they stayed in England if they could afford to. Their affairs in Jamaica were managed by agents, and their visits to Jamaica were brief and infrequent.[24] By 1800 land ownership by absentees had become the pattern throughout the British West Indies, and the tendency toward absenteeism seems to have increased in Jamaica until the 1830's. Probably two-thirds or more of all Jamaican plantations under cultivation at that time were owned by absentees and the proportion was higher among sugar estates than among other properties.[25]

Much of the cultural and intellectual poverty, and some of the economic decline of Jamaica in the nineteenth century can be laid at the door of absenteeism. The process is obvious. The most successful proprietors left the island, and the political, social, and cultural life of the colony remained in the hands of those who were less successful. Success in sugar planting is not a universally valid test of social value, but in a predominantly planting society it has some meaning. More important, absenteeism tended to drain off those with leisure and money to spend on public affairs, men who had education and interest in arts and letters, and who, in the last analysis, had to make the decisions that would have improved the outmoded agricultural methods of the sugar economy. Furthermore, the pattern of colonial life that held out return "home" as the final measure of success could hardly make for a society whose ruling class had a permanent interest or permanent roots in the colony. Even though only a small proportion of the planters managed to become absentee proprietors, absenteeism as a goal in life tended to make the planting class a group with little interest in improving the quality of public affairs in Jamaica — a country they intended to leave as soon as possible.[26]

In the absence of the proprietor, his representative with power of attorney occupied the great house, and with it the chief place in the Jamaican social order. The "planting attorneys," as they were called, formed a class of professional representatives. An attorney might manage one estate, but more often he held attorneyships from several different proprietors and managed more — sometimes as many as fifteen or twenty. It was the attorney's duty to hire the overseers and manage all the proprietor's affairs in the colony. In return for this, the attorney received a customary fee of 5 or 6 per cent of the sale price on each crop shipped, the use of the estate great house and servants if he needed them, and immense opportunities for illegal and semi-legal practices that would increase his income. The attorney's fee was an enormous drain on the income from the property, and the method of payment was not one to encourage an interest in the long-term productivity of the estate. Still, the planting attorneys were the wealthiest men in Jamaica and the most powerful. An attorney with a wide clientele might have an annual income of eight to ten thousand pounds currency.[27] This was not only more than the average proprietor enjoyed, but it was also less subject to variation in bad times. Sugar was always produced and shipped, whether it paid its way on the London market or not.[28]

Although the attorney had the principal command in the sugar economy, he was not necessarily a professional planter and he might not visit all his estates more than once or twice a year. The chief operating official, the principal white man in residence, was the overseer. Although he received neither the income nor the social status of the attorney, his authority on the estate was immense, and he was moderately well off financially with an income as high as two hundred pounds currency a year.[29] He also had the use of the great house in the absence of both attorney and proprietor — that is, most of the time. If not, he was supplied a house and servants. It was the overseer's

job to make the day-to-day decisions about plantation routine
and to see to the discipline and efficiency of the subordinate
supervisors — both white and black. This meant, in normal
circumstances, that he had complete and rather autocratic control over everyone on the estate.[30]

The subordinate white estate workers usually lived in a
separate barracks near the great house in conditions that made
no pretensions to luxury. These men were principally bookkeepers, but on some estates there were also white masons and
carpenters. The skilled workers were relatively well off in
Jamaica, sometimes making as much money as the overseer himself.[31] The bookkeeper, on the other hand, was the apprentice
planter, the white proletarian of the planting society. He had
usually come out from England to make his fortune —with
neither skill nor experience. The only quality he had to sell
was a white skin. His principal job on the estate was to meet
the requirements of the Deficiency Laws, which called for a
set ratio of whites to Negroes on each estate. These originally
had been passed by most West Indian colonies in order to encourage the immigration of whites, but by the 1830's their only
purpose was to keep able-bodied Europeans on the plantations
to serve in the militia and discourage slave insurrections.[32]

In this capacity, the bookkeeper's duties had nothing to do
with keeping books, and, as a missionary of the period wrote, it
more likely had to do with "keeping swine." [33] His pay was as
little as possible, usually not more than eighty pounds currency
a year and keep. As a member of the ruling caste, he had enormous authority over the slaves, but very little responsibility.
He had to go into the field with the slaves to see that the work
was being done, and he had to stand watch in the boiling house
or issue stores, in order to protect the estate's property. Actual
supervision of the work, however, was usually in the hands of
the Negro drivers in the field or the Negro boatswain and head
boilerman in the sugar works. These men took their orders
directly from the overseer and reported to him each evening on
the work accomplished. In time the bookkeeper's authority
might be increased. As he learned more about planting, he could
rise into the ranks of the overseers, often within three to five
years, but the security of his position depended on the whim of

the overseer, who could fire him without notice. If he could move upward, he could also move downward into the ranks of the "walking buckras," the whites who had lost their jobs and their horses and wandered from estate to estate, looking for work or a handout.[34]

An additional feeling of impermanence was given to the lives of all the white planters by the traditional pattern of family life. The proprietor or the successful attorney might have a wife from England or might have married a creole white, but below this social level the European wife was an extravagance, which neither the planter nor the estate could afford. Mainly because of the expense of keeping European women on the premises, but also, it was said, because a black mistress made a convenient spy of Negro affairs, the general policy of planting attorneys was to hire only unmarried men as overseers and bookkeepers. The bookkeeper was expected to find himself a "housekeeper" from among the slave women, while the overseer could either do the same or find a permanent "housekeeper" from the free colored class. By the 1830's the custom of sexual union with the slaves was so well established that a new bookkeeper who failed to take a mistress was likely to meet with distrust for his holier-than-thou attitude.[35]

Since children followed the condition of the mother, the children of these unions were legally slaves, but in practice the planters usually secured the manumission of their children. In this aspect the Jamaican social system differed sharply from the practice of other slave areas like the American South. Since there were few white women to prevent the open recognition of colored children and their eventual freedom, Jamaica was divided into three, rather than two, racial castes. There were not simply whites and Negroes, but white, colored, and black. Although, the sexual union of master and slave did little to increase the mutual understanding between the two races on the plantations, it created a new class of racially mixed freemen — a group which heavily outnumbered the whites in the 1830's.

At a distance from the great house and the bookkeeper's barracks was the Negro village. This was laid out along irregular paths, each Negro or couple having a small piece of land, probably less than a quarter of an acre, and a hut of his own construction surrounded by trees — mango and coconut, ackee and breadfruit. The trees improved the appearance of the village, but this was not their purpose. The slaves had to grow most of their own food in their spare time — that is, after plantation hours, on Sundays, and on alternate Saturdays outside of "crop." They were allowed to use almost any uncultivated land they needed for this purpose, in addition to their allotment in the village.

The provision ground system of slave feeding was an important institution in Jamaica and one in which Jamaica differed from some of the other islands. Except in areas of contiguous cane fields, like the parish of Vere, all plantation slaves had provision grounds. It meant extra work, but it also gave the slaves experience in working on their own account — they could sell the surplus in the market. As a result, the slaves were skilled at a type of work they liked better than plantation work at regular hours under stern discipline. Their "property rights" in their grounds and the proceeds from the sale of provisions were usually respected by the planters. Thus there was a chance for differences of economic status even among plantation slaves.

This was not the only difference of status among the slaves, however. The chain of command of the estate did not stop with the whites, but continued through the slave group to make a whole series of gradations from the attorney to the field hand. There was, of course, a sharp break between the black and white castes, but the range of distinction between the head driver and a female field Negro was as great as that between the attorney and a new bookkeeper. Nor was the break between white and black quite as sharp as the difference between the slave and the free indicates. Legal status aside, the two races approached each other in the skill and responsibility of the Negro leaders.

The authority of the drivers was immense. These men were the permanent leaders of the other slaves: they were specially picked for intelligence, ability, and knowledge of planting. The head driver was considered the "life and soul of an estate," the slave equivalent of a first sergeant.[36] He and his subordinates were in charge of the slave gangs, each of which worked as a unit while the driver stood by with the long cart whip round his neck — the badge of office and the means of summary punishment. Usually there were three gangs. The great gang, made up of all able-bodied adults, was given the hardest manual labor. The smaller second gang contained children over twelve and the weaker adults, such as nursing mothers and old people who could still do light work. The young children were organized in the third or small gang, which worked under a woman driver as a device for discipline and training in the plantation routine.[37]

Next in authority to the drivers were the various skilled slaves in charge of special departments on the estate — in a sense, departmental foremen in charge of small, specialized gangs. There was commonly a head wainman, a head muleman, and a head cattleman. The most skilled slave on the estate, however, was the head boiler. He and the boatswain, the driver assigned to the sugar works, had general charge of the manufacturing process, and the quality of the finished product depended on their ability. Roughey's *Planter's Guide* gives an almost impossible list of the requirements of a good boiler:

> He should always be a person who has an intimate knowledge . . . the way the cane has been raised and treated; the kind of soil it grows upon; if the soil has been high or low manured; the age of the cane; the species it is of; whether it has been topped short or long in cutting; if it has been arrowed, bored, or rat-eaten; giving by the perspicuous view, a thorough knowledge of the lime tempering the cane-juice requires; the time it may take to concoct, inspissate, and be fit to skip into the coolers. He must be impartial in his mode and time of potting the sugar from the cooler into the hogshead, so that it stands the hogshead well, cures properly, lets off the spumy, spurious molasses, without embodying it in the sugar, thereby giving it an open, free grain. He should be an economist in the boiling of sugar, without being a miser to the distilling house. He must be honest, sober, industrious, and keep the junior boilers to their work. Such are the qualities, I presume, requisite for a head boiler on a sugar estate.[38]

The drivers and skilled workers were anxious for the authority these positions gave them; and once they had achieved it, they exercised it with as much rigor and brutality as the whites above them. At the same time, the other slaves accepted them as the natural leaders of the community and occasionally appealed to them to adjust differences between slaves in a kind of extra-legal court of arbitration.[39] Their power originated in its delegation from the master, but it also rested on the acceptance of their leadership by the other slaves.

*   *   *

The sugar estate, because of the prestige of the crop itself and because of its economic importance to the island, tended to set the pattern for the operation of other plantations. Some plantations, indeed, were only the necessary complement of the estates. Because of the heavy use of cattle for transportation, turning sugar mills, and manure, the breeding pen was important to the Jamaican economy and the class of pen-keepers were second only to the estate owners in prestige. The pens were so important that they occupied an area about one-third that of the sugar estates. Planting attorneys managed pens as well as estates, and it was a common practice to combine the ownership of an estate with that of a pen and run the two as a joint enterprise. As a result of the close ties between the two, the forms of estate organization, like the three-gang system, were adapted to the smaller labor force of the cattle pen.[40]

Although less important than sugar, when taken together, the minor staples — coffee, pimento (allspice), ginger, arrowroot, and woods — were an important segment of the Jamaican economy. Coffee was second only to sugar as a plantation crop, and, though the capital investment in machinery was not so large, it also had to be partly processed before being shipped. The seasonally heavy demand for labor during the picking season meant that the coffee planter and the sugar planter had similar labor problems. Coffee, however, had become important only in the 1770's and reached its peak production in the 1820's, when sugar had already begun to decline; but with the new problems of the thirties, the fall of coffee was even faster than that of sugar.[41] None of the other minor staples was quite so definitely a plantation crop as coffee. They could be grown as a sideline for a sugar or coffee plantation, by small settlers, or even in the slaves' provision grounds.

*   *   *

This survey of the Jamaican planting economy has so far

neglected the aspect that most attracted the attention of contemporaries. This was the question of slavery. Without going
into the arguments as to the quantity or quality of cruelty
practiced on the slaves of the West Indian islands, it can be admitted, from our distance in time, that slavery was indeed cruel.
It was a system of forced labor, and forced labor necessarily in-
volves unpleasantness for those who are forced. In the West
Indies it probably went beyond this, since absolute power over
a captured people of a strange culture was given to a few uneducated men far from home. The slaves were increasingly protected by law from the grosser forms of abuse, but abuse was still
easy and detection was difficult. On balance, West Indian slavery
may not have been any more cruel than the contemporaneous
labor system in other tropical countries, but this was not the
question in the early nineteenth century. It was cruel, and it
was pointed out in Britain as a moral wrong. In the end it was
destroyed because it was an evil of a sort that seemed intolerable
to the British electorate of the 1830's.

Whatever the future of slavery might be, it had left a profound
mark. Jamaica, as a society, was not only molded by the plantation economy, it was created by it. In the seventeenth century
the decision was made, unconsciously, but made none the less,
to grow tropical staples on this newly acquired and virtually
uninhabited West Indian island. Within limits set by the social
and political techniques of the time, the price of this decision
was the establishment of some kind of forced labor — indentured
Europeans, African slaves, or native Indians, if there had been
any left. This was the only known way of keeping relatively
large numbers of people at work on relatively small pieces of
land, when these people are surrounded by plenty of good,
unoccupied land.[42]

The result was the plantation system and with it slavery —
two institutions that are not necessarily joined but which had
been historically linked in Jamaica from the beginning. One of
the principal questions posed by emancipation was whether the
plantation system could still exist without the coercive labor
system that first made it possible.

II

African Jamaica

The Slave and His Allies

ALTHOUGH JAMAICAN SOCIETY of the early nineteenth century was unified with a peculiar single-mindedness in
the business of producing sugar and coffee, the unity hardly
penetrated beyond the common economic endeavor. Jamaicans
were divided legally into the three castes of free whites, colored
people with limited privileges, and Negro slaves. Of the three
divisions, the white and colored people had something in common as the heirs of European culture as it existed in Jamaica.
The Negroes stood apart as a separate group, not only because
they were slaves, but because their cultural heritage was still
largely African.

The caste separation of the blacks from the rest of society has
helped make an uneven historical record in Jamaica. The blacks
were illiterate and left no record of their own. The white and
colored writers who left some record of Negro culture were cut
off, as members of a higher caste, from knowing much about
Negro life and, as members of an alien culture, from understanding much of what they knew. They were more interested
in indoctrinating the blacks with essential European techniques
for saving souls and planting estates, than in understanding the
culture of the Africans. The result is a sketchy, one-sided record,
mainly touching Negro life only where it touched the life of the
other castes. This defect necessarily carries over into any attempt
to reconstruct a picture of the culture of the Jamaican slaves.

However incomplete the record of Negro culture, the work

of recent anthropologists has broken down the older idea that
the African was brought to America culturally naked, to be
given whatever castoff cultural equipment the planting society
thought fit for him.[1] The black Jamaicans of the early nineteenth century had a set of ideas, sentiments, habits, irrational
responses, and preconceptions. All of these went to form the
background from which the Negroes would act during the coming revolution, and afterward in building a new society based
on free labor.

         *   *   *

   In many ways Negro culture was more truly native to Jamaica
than European culture, although both were alien. Unlike the
whites, the blacks' voyage from their homeland was strictly a
one-way affair. Once in America, the only contact with Africa
was the reinforcement of later arrivals, and, after the abolition
of the slave trade in 1807, the flow of Africans to Jamaica was
very much reduced. The last years of the trade, however, were
the heaviest period of slave imports, 63,045 new slaves coming
into Jamaica between 1801 and 1807. As a result the proportion
of African to creole slaves in 1807 was high, and, even though
this generation was beginning to pass away by the 1830's, there
was still a sizable minority who remembered Africa.[2]
   Although the African tradition was strong, it was not a single
cultural tradition. The slaves brought to Jamaica had belonged
to different tribal or national groups in Africa. The strongest of
these numerically were the Kramanti or "Coromantyn" — the
Ashanti-Fanti people of the Gold Coast — and the Ibo of the
Niger delta. Each group had cultural characteristics which were
recognized by the whites and influenced the market price of
individual slaves. The Kramanti were considered stronger, and
thus better workers, but prone to rebellion, and therefore
dangerous. The Ibo, on the other hand were supposed to be
tractable, but deceitful and given to suicide if ill treated. The
Mandingo, from the region between the Niger and the Gambia,
also were brought to Jamaica in fairly large numbers and always
attracted attention because many had been exposed to some
Moslem teaching in childhood. They were considered more
peaceable than the Kramanti, but less industrious than the Ibo.

Other groups were the "Pawpaws" from Dahomey and a few Congo and Angola Negroes from south of the Bight of Benin, but they came in smaller numbers and probably had less influence on Jamaican culture.[3]

This diversity of national origin was an important factor in making Jamaican Negro culture American rather than purely African. The great majority of Jamaicans had come from West Africa; their differences were only regional variations of a common culture area.[4] Since the whites were not anxious to force Europeanization any further than was necessary for plantation work, the slaves were left to educate their own children. Consequently there developed a new culture, compounded of the diverse elements of the African heritage and some European elements — always tending to emphasize these elements that were common to all groups. This process of cumulative adaptation and amalgamation of Negro cultures had continued for a century and a half. By the 1830's the Afro-Jamaican culture was solidly established, and it was passed on to each new generation as it had long been passed by a process of assimilation to new arrivals from Africa.

One example of the adaptation of the African cultures to Jamaican life was the Negro equivalent of marriage. The planters had little interest in the sexual mores of the slaves. The slaves made whatever sexual union they chose, and these were usually more permanent than simple promiscuity. The Jamaican Negro normally had a "wife," perhaps more than one. This family made a social unit that had nothing to do with the blessing of the established church. In the management of the slave's private provision grounds, the wife had charge of certain matters, especially marketing. She cooked the meals for the head of the family, waited on him, and ate by herself.[5] While the Jamaican woman would accept this situation with its heavy responsibilities and lack of legal permanence, she was unwilling to accept Christian marriage. By the time the missionaries arrived on the scene, Afro-Jamaican "marriage" was too well established to be easily changed. Jamaican women tended to consider Christian marriage a mark of subordination and slavery to the male.[6] In the long run, this turned out to be one of the most deep-seated of Jamaican Negro attitudes.[7]

Negro speech in the Caribbean shows the same process of adaptation. In Jamaica, as in the other colonies, the newly arrived slaves had to talk to one another and to their masters. In West Africa they had shared common grammatical forms. To this they added the most convenient vocabulary, that of the ruling class. The result was a new dialect which is still spoken in Jamaica.

Against the major tendency toward a unified creole culture, there were also some social ties remaining from Africa and the passage to America. Although these ties tended to fade out later in the century, in the 1830's slaves born in Africa still thought of themselves as a distinct group from the creole Jamaicans. On estates where the African-born were of the same tribal origin, the rivalry with the creole slaves could be especially strong — each group presenting its grievances separately to the overseer.[8] Another mark of the passage from Africa was the strange bond between "shipmates," who had made the middle passage together. In Jamaica this was considered almost as strong as blood relationship, and it passed from one generation to another — a young man felt that the "shipmate" of his father was his own relative as well.[9]

*   *   *

The reaction of the white Jamaicans was different toward different elements of Negro culture. This attitude was, of course, the result of their own European cultural preconceptions. The planting class, before emancipation, considered music and dancing innocuous and even to be encouraged. Ceremonies that seemed to be connected with religion or magic were considered harmful and suppressed as much as possible. But the line between the secular and religious in music and dance was none too clear to the blacks themselves; consequently, the ruling class was ineffective in its attempt to suppress one while allowing the other.

During the Christmas holiday, three days were allowed by law as a Negro festival. The slaves were encouraged to celebrate, and the celebrations were often reported by travelers and missionaries as an interesting item of local color. Plantation discipline relaxed throughout the island, and slaves were allowed to visit from one estate to another; though the militia was also called into active duty to prevent trouble. Over the years the celebration took on customary forms, with at least a superficial resemblance to the carnival in Louisiana and Brazil. In all the major towns, and many of the smaller places, the participants divided into two teams, the reds and the blues, and organized competing parades. Young girls of either faction prepared elaborate costumes, sometimes furnished by their masters, and paraded through the streets in "sets," each trying to outdo the other in magnificence.[10]

Another part of the Christmas festival had a more religious connotation. This was the John Canoe dance. The chief performer wore a traditional headdress in the form of a model boat looking something like a stylized Noah's ark. With this contraption on his head and a wooden sword in his hand, he performed a dance through the streets of the town accompanied by a group of followers and musicians with *goombay* drums, gourds filled with the seeds of the Indian shot plant, and other African rhythmic instruments.[11] Although the planters considered this harmless fun, and the missionaries objected mainly because of the rum-drinking involved, the John Canoe dance was, in fact, very closely associated with the survivals of African religion and magic. The figures represented in the houseboat-headdress, the phraseology of the songs, the instruments — all were very similar to those of the African cult groups that were otherwise driven underground.[12]

Throughout the year the chief Negro entertainments were of African derivation. The most important were dances. One of these is described in impeccable language by a missionary, writing in 1843 and recalling the years before emancipation.

Their nightly dances or plays, which were frequent and general, were of a character the most licentious. They were usually accompanied by a band of the most rude and monotonous music, composed of instruments of African manufacture. The assemblage on such occasions consisted of both sexes, who ranged themselves in a crude circle round a male and female dancer, and performed to the music of their drums.

The songs were sung by the other females of the party, one alternately singing, while her companions repeated in chorus; the singers and dancers observing the exactest precision as to time and measure. On some occasions the dances consisted of stamping the feet, accompanied by various contortions of the body, with strange and indecent attitudes; on others, the head of each dancer was erect, or occasionally inclined forward; the hands nearly united in front; the elbows fixed, pointing from the sides; and the lower extremities being held firm, the whole person was moved without raising the feet from the ground. Making the head and limbs fixed points, they writhed and turned the body upon its own axis, slowly advancing toward each other, or retreating to the outer parts of the circumference. Their approaches to each other, and the attitudes and inflexions in which they were made, were highly indecent, the performers being nearly naked.[13]

The pattern here is clearly African. The instruments, the same as those for the John Canoe processions, were common in the West African area, and so was the pattern of leader-and-chorus singing.[14] Furthermore, the drumming, dancing, and singing were not only secular and "licentious." They could also be put to religious use.

*   *   *

In discussing present-day Negro culture in Trinidad, Melville and Frances Herskovits have developed the idea that any people has a culture focus, defined as "those aspects of the life of the people which hold greatest interest for them." They feel that the cultural focus of the Negro in Trinidad, and in the Americas as a whole, has been in the field of religion.[15] In nineteenth-century Jamaica, it was this side of Negro life that was most frequently reported by white observers. The Herskovits' recent investigations indicate that the religious emphasis is not simply a reflection of the interests of the missionaries who did most of the reporting but an emphasis placed on religion by the Negroes themselves.

It was in religion that Europeans worked hardest to influence Negro culture in the nineteenth century, and it is in religion that the survivals of African patterns are most noticeable in twentieth-century Jamaica. This is in line with the Herskovits' notion of the culture focus. They believe that the culture focus is the area in which a change imposed from the outside is most difficult. They believe, also, that a new and alien culture is likely to be accepted in the focal area only after it has been reinterpreted to bring it into accord with traditional forms. Although the Herskovits' theory was not developed with specific relation to Jamaica, it provides a promising explanation of the major role played by religion in the slaves' adjustment to freedom.

Negro religion, in the mind of the early nineteenth-century white planter or missionary, was extremely vague, though both planter and missionary opposed it. Practices that should properly be called magic — the personal attempt to intervene in the natural world by calling the supernatural to one's private aid — and religious beliefs and practices of a more general nature, were often lumped together as "obeah." Or, at times, a distinction was made between magic and religion by calling the first "obeah" and the second "myalism." [16] The confusion was natural. The practice of magic was usually secret for professional reasons, and it was also illegal in Jamaica. Because religious worship was necessarily more open, it was easier to suppress. Thus, while the techniques of magic could be passed down from one generation to another with little loss, religious ideas at the level of theology could hardly be preserved in the environment of slavery. Religious techniques thus survived in different forms in different parts of the island, and they tended to merge gradually into the techniques of magic. By the 1830's many of the original distinctions between African religion and magic were probably lost to the Negroes themselves.

On the side of magic, or the practice of obeah, the derivation from West African practices is clear. The West Africans laid great importance on the fetish as a means of controlling the supernatural world.[17] In Jamaica obeah men made charms for many purposes. These charms were not intrinsically valuable, but they served to control the spirits. They were one way of making the shadows, or "duppies," act either in favor of the obeah man's client, or against his enemies. In the latter case, if the spirits alone were not effective, an obeah man could use poison to help out. The obeah man could also be called on to undo the work of another magician. Essentially obeah was neither good nor bad: it could be used either way.[18]

Obeah was one reflection, in the world of magic, of the most general religious belief of the Jamaican Negro. His world was peopled by spirits of all sorts, the duppies of the dead, and even of the living. Judging from West African religion, these were the remains of a much more complex pantheon — a whole social organization of gods, with special names, functions, and individuality.[19] In other Caribbean countries some elements of this pantheon survived, but, at least in the incomplete record of the early nineteenth century, it had disappeared in Jamaica. What remained was a cult of the ancestors, the duppies of one's immediate forebears, and manipulation of the spirits of the dead in general.

In West Africa the worship of the gods was organized in cult groups, often esoteric, which used drums, dancing, dreams, and spirit-seizure as part of organized worship. An aspect of this survived in Jamaica in the myal cult, and more theology may have survived with it than the record shows. In spite of the white Jamaicans' tendency to think of myal practices as "white magic" opposing the "black magic" of the obeah man, this was not altogether the case.[20] The obeah man was a private practitioner, hired by his client for a specific purpose, while the myal man was the leader of a cult group devoted to organized religious activity. Like the obeah man, he tried to control the supernatural world of the shadows, but protection from obeah was only incidental to his work. Myal practices were also designed to prevent duppies from doing harm, to help people recover their lost shadows, and generally to propitiate the world of the spirits. Myal practice was especially associated with dances performed before the silk-cotton tree, one of the favorite haunts of the duppies.[21] The dances were designed to lure back the duppies of those who had lost them — a complicated procedure involving sacrifices of chickens, drumming, dancing, spirit-possession of a person in a trance, drugs, and other elements very close to African religions.[22]

Many of the same remnants of African religion also held on in Jamaica in the Negro funeral ceremonies, designed to make sure the duppy of the dead man would accompany him to the grave and not stay around to annoy the living. At one time this was taken by the whites to be a Negro equivalent of a European

wake, and thus permissible, but after 1831, night funeral ceremonies were suppressed, as other religious ceremonies had
been.[23]

As one would expect, the record left by the white reporters
of Negro culture is most complete in describing religious ceremonies, much less complete on religious beliefs, and negligible
in tracing the influence of these beliefs on Negro society; but
some of the social implications of Negro religion were too
obvious to be missed altogether. The religious sanctions supporting the obeah and myal men gave them a position in the
community above the prestige of the ordinary slave. They were
personages with whom the common man had to deal with a
mixture of respect and fear. Alongside the secular leaders of the
plantation hierarchy, they offered an additional, religious fund
of leadership. The authority of secular and religious leaders
alike was enhanced by the prevailing attitude of respect for the
old. This was a strong sentimental attachment with the Negroes,
and it went back to the religious position of the men who were
almost-ghosts, about to join the world of the spirits. Even in life
they began to enjoy some of the veneration that should be shown
to ancestors.[24] The fact that some slaves were already in positions
of traditional leadership, backed by the sanctions of religion
helped to guarantee that, on emancipation, the slave community
would be able to act on its own, rather than blindly following
the lead of the whites, whether planters or missionaries.

The Negro preoccupation with the spirits of the ancestors had
a further important consequence. It led to a special attachment
for the family burial place — the home of the friendly duppies
of one's ancestors and the only sure hold on a spirit world that
was otherwise unfriendly, or at best neutral. Thus ancestral
grave-dirt was especially effective in obeah charms. This attitude
created in the slaves one of the few attachments for the estates
where they had worked.

*   *   *

Obeah, myalism, and preoccupation with the spirit world were
Negro religious manifestations not noticeably touched by European culture. They stand at one end of a religious spectrum
showing a coloration varying from African to European. Before

1830, very few blacks indeed were to be found at the European end of the spectrum. They were not welcome in the Church of England before emancipation, except in rare cases, and, though large numbers of slaves were baptized, it was simply a formality unaccompanied by instruction.[25] The eighteenth-century Established Church was a white man's church, and it was to remain so long after emancipation. The general religious revival in Britain, which was to be a driving force behind emancipation, did not bring a large number of missionaries from the dissenting sects until the 1820's. Long before this, elements of Christianity had come to Jamaica and mixed with African ideas and practices.

The Afro-Christian sects in Jamaica date from the end of the war of the American Revolution, when several hundred United Empire Loyalists emigrated from the United States by way of New Providence, bringing their slaves. Some of these slaves had been converted to Christianity in the North American colonies, since the prejudice against the religious instruction of slaves was not as strong there as in the West Indies. Once in Jamaica they became unofficial missionaries. By the 1830's, their teaching had spread to many different parts of the island, being transformed in the process into a combination of orthodox Christianity and an African cult group.

The most prominent of the original group of Afro-Christians was George Lisle, or Leile, a freedman who came to Kingston in 1783, having belonged to a Baptist planter in Virginia. He preached around Kingston for several years, keeping his congregation as orthodox as possible. He even built a chapel with the help of some of the more religious white population. Like other Negro preachers, he was often in trouble with the authorities on charges of teaching sedition, but he managed to keep going.[26] This was the beginning of the Native Baptist movement.

Lisle's chapel was only one variety of Native Baptist congregation. Another kind was founded by George Lewis, a true heretic who purposely rejected the whites' version of Christianity in favor of his own, more African, variety. He had been born in Africa and taken to Virginia as a slave. After the American Revolution he was brought to Kingston, where his mistress let him work as a peddler in return for a monthly fee. He mixed peddling with preaching along his route in the parishes of Manchester and St. Elizabeth and spread his doctrine through the southwest part of the island.[27]

Other variations began with sections of Lisle's congregation, which became unorthodox through illiteracy and misunderstanding. The two most important of these were founded by George Gibb and Moses Baker. Gibb, another Americanized African went into the northside parishes around St. Mary, while Baker was taken by his master, a Quaker, to Flamstead Estate in St. James, where he was allowed to teach the other slaves. Gibb and Baker departed from Lisle's orthodoxy in much the same direction. The organizational basis of both cults was the "leader system," an adaptation of the English Wesleyan practice of dividing the church members into classes for teaching. Possibly the Native Baptists picked it up from the few white missionaries who were already at work in Jamaica, but more likely it was part of their American training. In any case, the leader system underwent some strange transformations. The class-leaders became something more than simply the teachers of the new converts. They were the real spiritual guides, taking a position equivalent to leadership of a myal cult group, and their power over the classes was authoritarian to the point of tyranny. They could refuse baptism to an applicant or expel rebels from the church — an important power that could be extended beyond simply religious matters. Emphasis on the position of the leader weakened the powers of men like Gibb and Baker over their organizations, and the loosely federated classes tended to break off under an individual leader and form the nucleus of new cult groups.[28]

The characteristic doctrinal departure from orthodoxy in the early Native Baptist groups was the emphasis on "the spirit" and a corresponding neglect of the written word. Most of the leaders could not read in any case, and the shift accorded with the remnants of African religious attitudes. The followers of both Baker and Gibb were required to be possessed of "the spirit" before baptism was administered. This meant that "the spirit" had to descend on the applicant in a dream, which was then described to the leader. If the dream were satisfactory, the applicant could enter the class. There evolved a regular technique and ceremonial for bringing on spirit-possession, which included a fast according to a set canon followed by a trip into the bush alone at night to wait for the spirit to descend.

The ceremony of baptism by immersion also took on a new importance and became an elaborate initiation for the new member. It was no longer a symbol, but the extension of Grace itself and thus led to practices that the white missionaries condemned as antinomianism. It led, as well, to the subordination of Christ as the chief religious figure and an emphasis on John the Baptist. This was only natural, since John had been the "leader" who admitted Christ to baptism, though it was also shocking to the European missionaries.[29]

The Afro-Christian synthesis was a natural development in the slave society of the late eighteenth and early nineteenth centuries. Given the isolation of the estates, the insulation of the Negroes from white culture, and the prestige of the masters' gods, it was an easy step to elevate Christ and John the Baptist into the remnants of the African pantheon. Even under the impact of constant missionary influence, some sort of Afro-Christian unorthodoxy would have been likely. In Jamaica there was no widespread orthodox teaching until the 1820's, either by the dissenters or by the Established Church. Thus the Native Baptists were given forty years without serious competition. During this period a reinterpretation of Christianity was created, organized, and spread throughout the island. By 1830 the doctrine and organization of the Native Baptists had become a thoroughly integrated part of Negro culture — another religion competing with the Christianity of the European missionaries.

The influence of the Afro-Christian sects was important in non-religious matters as well. The Negro, in coming to America, had completely lost his political and social organization. This gap was partly filled by the plantation hierarchy and partly by the myal and obeah men, but the Native Baptist leaders took on positions of even greater authority and leadership, since they controlled the superior power of Christianity which seemed to protect the whites so effectively. At least in some places, and perhaps generally, the economic and religious sanctions of leadership tended to reinforce each other. The drivers, boilers, masons, and other plantation officials became the leaders in the Afro-Christian cults. This development was to be expected, since the plantation officials were chosen for the qualities of leadership and intelligence that enabled these same men to build their religious authority.[30]

* * *

The Negroes were not entirely dependent on their own community for leadership. The white missionaries were self-appointed leaders of the blacks, both before and after emancipation. The missionary had a peculiar place in Jamaican society: he was simultaneously a member of the white caste and an ally of the slaves. In this dual capacity, he was only partly accepted by the Negroes and he was rejected by the white caste as a deserter and an enemy of white society. Both the dissenters and the evangelicals within the Church of England were obvious allies of the British humanitarian movement: they were also organizing the slaves and teaching them religion, and this was considered "sedition" to a planting society. There was more justice in the planters' complaint than the missionaries would admit. The coming emancipation was to be a revolution for Jamaica, and the missionaries were the Jamaican representatives of the revolutionary party overseas.

This is not to say that all ministers of the gospel were in favor of emancipation. On the contrary, most ministers of the Church of England were staunch supporters of the *status quo*. The only exception was a small group of evangelicals who made their appearance in the 1820's. By 1831, however, there were only nine catechists of the Church Missionary Society, and the Bishop of Jamaica would push missionary activity only as far as he could go without offending local church and planter opinion. This was not far.[31]

The Church of Scotland was also essentially a white man's church, with kirks only in Kingston and Falmouth. Missionary Presbyterianism was represented by a group of ministers, united in the Scottish Missionary Society, who had been working in the northwestern parishes from the early 1820's. Presbyterianism was thus divided in a way that paralleled the division between the parish clergy and the C.M.S. One group was clergy to the whites, the other to the blacks.[32]

By the 1830's the Wesleyan Methodist Missionary Society had

the largest dissenting congregations on the island, built up through a gradual extension of their activities since the 1790's. In 1831 they had eleven circuits centering in the port-towns of the island. By that date they had become a two-caste church. They were the special sect of the colored people in the towns, and their carried on missionary activities to attract the blacks on the estates as well.[33] As in England, the Methodists were more conservative than the other dissenters. They tried to attract the white planting class by avoiding all political issues, especially anything that could be interpreted as an attack on slavery, and by maintaining a strict caste segregation in their chapels.[34] This attempt, however, was unsuccessful. The planting class continued distrustful of any missionary work among the slaves, and the policy led, in later years, to serious difficulties among the Wesleyans themselves.

Two other sects were almost entirely devoted to the conversion of the slave population, with little attempt to attract either whites or browns. These were the Baptists and the Moravian Brethren. The Moravians had been working slowly in a limited area since the middle of the eighteenth century. Their work was more stable than that of other sects, but they were still a small group in the 1830's.

The Baptists were in something of a special position. They were able to profit from the preparatory work of the Native Baptists, and thus, in spite of later arrival in the field, their membership in 1831 was quickly overtaking that of the Wesleyan Methodists. The work of orthodox English Baptists had, in fact, begun as the result of a direct appeal from Moses Baker, who wanted English help in keeping his congregations together. The first official mission was begun in 1814, using Baker's converts near Falmouth as a nucleus. In 1816 a second mission was sent to answer the appeal of Native Baptists at Old Harbour.[35]

From the beginning the official Baptists took over the leader system and the classes of their predecessors. In the 1820's the system was elaborated and extended through the work of William Knibb and Thomas Burchell. The class and leader system made it possible for Burchell to expand his mission station at Montego Bay to the point where he alone could run a church of 1600 members in full communion and 3000 inquirers — and this congregation spread along a circuit that required 103 miles of riding each week.[36] As a means of controlling the large congregations, tickets were issued to each person, indicating whether he was an "inquirer," "candidate," or "member." The tickets were renewed quarterly, when each slave made his financial contribution, and without a ticket he could neither attend service nor approach the communion table. It was an admirable device. It simplified the collection of money, and the threat of revocation gave the minister a means of discipline over the converts. The ticket, which was issued only by the European missionary, helped him to circumvent the power of the class-leaders and weld the federated class system into a more unified congregation.

The leader, however, was still the key figure. He had the power of denying admission by giving a bad report, since, with such large congregations, missionaries were forced to rely on the leaders' reports for information about the members.[37] Thus, the Native Baptist movement, which was originally an accommodation of Christianity to the African heritage, was reincorporated in the official Baptist Church through the ticket-and-leader system. In allowing this, the European Baptists were themselves moving toward the Afro-Christian synthesis, and they were doing so in ways they hardly understood themselves. The ticket, for example, was closer to the African heritage than the ministers realized — closer, at least, than they would admit. The planters' accusation that missionaries were selling "passports to heaven" was not far from the truth. To the illiterate African the ticket was a fetish — a white man's fetish, and therefore a fetish of superior power. It was the Christian equivalent of the fetishes carried by Negroes in the Gambia region of West Africa, where even among non-Moslem Negroes a few words from the Koran on a scrap of paper were credited with special powers.[38] The Baptist ticket in Jamaica was similar: it bore the member's name, the signature of the parson, and was inscribed around the edge with mottos like "Pray for your Children" and "Pray for the Grace to live near God." [39]

The Baptists were not the only Christian missionaries who edged toward Africanism by using the ticket-and-leader system. The Wesleyans also used it, and the Church of England tried it for a time in Barbados, though never in Jamaica. The Scottish Presbyterians experimented with Negro elders in their new Jamaican churches, but they rejected the plan, fearing it would put too much power in the hands of the slave aristocracy of drivers and former Native Baptist leaders.[40] The problem of native leadership was already emerging before emancipation, but it was not yet critical.

The present danger for the missionaries of the early thirties was in another direction. Against the background of slavery, the doctrine of Christianity had revolutionary implications. The missionaries might not have pointed this out to the slaves, but they were convinced themselves that Christianity and slavery were incompatible. Although they sincerely denied any intention of starting a slave revolt, this did little to ease the minds of the planters, who saw only that some of the "saints," whose stated aim in Britain was to end their labor system, were organizing and teaching their laborers.

*　　　　*　　　　*

The white caste in Jamaica was afraid, and increasingly afraid as the 1830's approached. There was good reason for their fear. Except for the lack of arms and training, the slaves had a vastly superior position in the island. They were held in check only by fear of reprisals and whatever beliefs they themselves may have had about the justice, or hopelessness, of their situation.

Partly, at least, their submission depended on the knowledge that there was overwhelming force in the hands of the whites, not on the island alone but backed by an all-powerful king overseas. The planters saw to it that the slaves were reminded of the king and impressed with his power on every possible occasion. Another source of submission was the obvious superiority of the whites in certain techniques, like reading. Since this superiority helped the slave to justify his own inferiority in social status, the planters tried to keep slaves from learning to read.

Akin to the importance of literacy was the Negro legend, which may not, however, have been widespread, in which the lot of the slaves is blamed on some original sin committed by the primitive blacks, the consequences of which had followed their race ever since.[41] One form, originally a Mandingo legend, tells of the origin of the human race with the creation of one white and one black man. At first the black man was God's favorite, but one day God let down from heaven two boxes, one large and one small. The black man, as favorite, was given his choice. His greed led him to choose the large box, and the smaller went to the white. "Buckra box was full up wid pen, paper, and whip, and neger's, wid hoe and bill, and hoe and bill for neger to dis day." [42]

In spite of such legends, Negro sentiments of subordination were never strong in any part of the New World and certainly not in Jamaica.[43] There had been a long tradition of servile revolt, with some sort of trouble cropping up every few years. The outbreaks of insubordination might be nothing but a flurry of runaways in some particular part of the island, the mutiny of a single estate, or the murder of an occasional overseer or book-keeper. Any of these troubles, however, might break into open war, and the government troops were not sure of winning. Though most slave revolts failed, the maroon Negroes of the Jamaican hills had fought the whites successfully in the eighteenth century and won the freedom and autonomy of their communities. The slaves were, in fact as well as in the eyes of the planting class, constantly on the borderline between acceptance of their position and blind rebellion against it.

As the date of emancipation approached, there were new solvents at work on the submissiveness of the slaves. Slavery was under attack in England, and the campaign was discussed in Jamaica. The news was spread through the overheard conversations of the whites, by rumor from slaves who had been in Britain with their masters, by occasional literate slaves or people of color who were willing to read newspapers aloud. The final form in which this information traveled around the island was none too accurate, but the idea was prevalent that "Wilberforce and the King" were trying to help the slaves, or even that freedom had already been granted. It was also generally understood that the Jamaican white caste was somehow successful in opposing the powerful overseas rulers. The growing strength of the external danger to the Jamaican social order thus tended to increase the internal danger.[44]

*   *   *

If the attitude of the slave toward his white master can be taken to be an indefinite mixture of awe and respect, the attitude of the master toward the slave was more definite, if more ambivalent. It was a combination of fear on one hand, leading to the picture of the slave as the lazy savage and murdering brute, and a desire to justify the institution on the other, leading to the picture of the happy Negro, harmless but fitted only for his life of hard work. In Matthew Lewis' *Journal* of a visit to his Jamaican estates both attitudes are found, with no attempt to square the one with the other. He discussed the way his contented slaves worked without a whip, the genuine affection he thought they felt for him, their proprietor, and their enjoyment of estate work. At the same time he talked of their resentfulness and rebellions, the poisoning of proprietors and the murder of bookkeepers.[45]

Individual writers went even further, in both directions. William Hosack, later an important political figure in Jamaica, wrote a long poem in 1833 in which the idyllic picture is drawn.

> And now the happy negro homeward goes,
> Contented as the honey-laden bee,
> Because his heart no earthly sorrow knows.
> Deluded sons of Britain! would that ye,
> The proud, the brave, the omnipotent, the free,
> Beheld him seated at his ample meal,
> With all his children smiling at his knee!
> Then would ye know the nature of his weal,
> And honestly confirm, the truth of this appeal.[46]

Only a few years before, the Rev. George Wilson Bridges, the Anglican rector at St. Ann's Bay, had written against just this bucolic vision. He said, of the Negro race:

Their simplicity has lately been praised by their interested advocates in England; yet they abstain only from what they have never known: whatever they see, they covet; their desires are insatiate, and their sole industry is the hand of violence and rapine.[47]

Bridges was willing to carry this interpretation even further. In another work he advanced the idea that the Great Chain of Being had gradations for man. The human scale goes downward from the white to the Hottentot, where the gap to the highest of the animals, the orangutan, is not great.[48]

Bridges, Hosack, and Lewis were all writing, directly or indirectly, on the controversy over emancipation. All three had spent some time in Jamaica in close contact with Negro slaves. The attitudes of white Jamaicans covered a range of opinion as wide as that in Britain, where many had never seen a Negro. If the Negro was unprepared in the 1830's to become a free member of a free society, the white Jamaican, for all his claims to special knowledge of "the Negro character," was equally unprepared for his role of leadership in that society.

And there is no doubt that the Negro was unprepared. He had a way of life, with a system of education, social ties, habits, and modes of thought, but these had all been developed out of an African heritage in a way that fitted him to be a slave in a European-dominated society. It had been a long process, but the end result as it stood in 1830 was a Negro culture no better adapted to accept rapid change to a free-labor system or assimilation of European culture than African culture had been.

Emancipation, however, implies Europeanization only in retrospect. In the 1830's the future of Jamaica was still in doubt. In any case, it would mean rapid cultural change for the majority of Jamaicans, and the new culture would not be a new creation, but a further movement and a further adjustment in the culture of the Jamaican slaves. This much was certain: the Negro would neither go back to the life of his African ancestors, as the planters feared, nor be transformed overnight into an English agricultural laborer, as the emancipationists seemed to hope.

III

European Jamaica

The White and Colored Castes

IN THE YEARS BEFORE EMANCIPATION, the white colonists of Jamaica held a position curiously analogous to that of the Negro slaves. Both were products of a culture foreign to the island. Both were members of a society transplanted to an alien environment and set up there for the sole purpose of growing tropical staples. Both had lost part of their former way of life in transit and, in a new and strange environment, had taken on new habits, attitudes, and patterns of thought. With the Negroes and whites alike, the adjustment to Jamaica produced something new that was not quite African and not quite European. Neither was it quite Jamaican — not, at least, in the sense of being common to all Jamaicans. There was one Afro-Jamaican pattern and another, quite different, that was Euro-Jamaican. In most respects they were still as far apart as the original African and European cultures had been.

The social structure of Jamaica was peculiarly West Indian, and, to an extent, it reflected in social status the economic order of the planting system. But there were also non-economic forces at work. One of the most important of these had produced, over the years, a new racial group, the people of color. At the end of the 1820's they still formed a separate legal caste, partly African in racial origin but rapidly becoming European in culture. Within a few years they were to become the most important segment of European Jamaica, and already they were numerically more important than the whites.[1]

Of the three racial divisions, the colored people were the most Jamaican of Jamaicans — the only group that was native to the island. In spite of this fact and in spite of their European cultural heritage, the brown men had long been subject to an elaborate set of disabilities designed to keep them from rising into the white ruling caste. Not the least of these was the fact that a colored man might still be a slave, though, in practice, as a relative of the ruling caste, he was usually kept a domestic servant rather than a field worker. People of mixed ancestry were white by law only after four generations of mating with whites.[2] Even the free man of color was barred both legally and socially from the white community. He was limited in the amount of inheritance he could receive, to prevent parental generosity from breaking the caste line. His legal and educational rights were circumscribed, his political and civil rights were limited, and the deficiency legislation effectively barred him from the planting economy that was the real life of the country.

In spite of these regulations, some of the brown population had grown in wealth and education in the early decades of the nineteenth century. They maintained pressure on the Assembly, on Parliament, and on the Colonial Office. Gradually the restrictions were removed in a grudging retreat under the insistence of the home government, and in 1830 all free men were declared equal in civil and political rights without regard to racial origin. Although the people of color were still not accepted socially by the white community, at least they were no longer a separate legal caste.[3]

Even after the disabilities were removed, their influence was still seen in the occupational and social habits of the colored people. The poorer colored men took great pains to avoid manual agricultural labor, since this work was the mark of slavery. Wealthier colored men might be the proprietors of estates, but until the 1830's the deficiency laws forced them to hire white managers. Thus the only outlet for the colored class in agriculture was management of a small plantation or settlement growing minor products with the help of a few slaves. Since this was a limited field, very few colored men were professional planters.

Most of the colored people, and all of the most prominent, were townsmen.[4] This fact had a number of important consequences for the future place of the class in Jamaican affairs. The people of color were not as interested as the whites in preserving the estate system — they had never been heavily involved in it. Even though they accepted a great deal of the white scale of values, it was the value judgment of the white fellow-townsman, rather than the planter. Political and economic differences between town and country in Jamaica, therefore, were likely to take on racial overtones.

The concentration of the colored class in the towns also helped the educational and political advancement of the group. First of all there was more opportunity for education there than in the countryside. In addition, the man of color who wanted to advance was forced to try for a professional or mercantile position — positions which required more education than that of an apprentice planter. Thus the more able colored people drifted into journalism, trade, and the law, where they were also in a position to enter politics easily. Even before the Act of Emancipation there were colored members in the House of Assembly. This development, again, would probably have taken much longer, given the stiff franchise requirements, if the towns had not provided pockets of well-to-do colored voters.

Although social discrimination against the people of color lasted well beyond emancipation, it was always applied unequally to the two sexes. The white Jamaican on the estate had traditionally formed alliances with female slaves, and the same pattern of sexual relations carried over into the towns, where it added to the bitterness of the colored men. In the years before emancipation the "licentiousness" of the Jamaican whites was notorious in the anti-slavery press of Great Britain — reflecting a striking difference between the standards of social behavior in Jamaica and those of the England that was just becoming "Victorian." White men were kept from open marriage with colored women by the strict code of caste separation, but it was expected that a "housekeeping" arrangement would be made with a lady of color. This was perfectly open and approved by the community. Women of color even considered this more honorable than marriage with a man of their own class. The housekeeper's children would be provided for and were often treated with as much parental pride as their white half-brothers and half-sisters. Unlike the children of similar unions in the American South, they were able to assume a place in society higher than their mothers had attained, because of their lighter complexion. Occasionally this sort of "marriage" was protected by a contract requiring the man to give bond for payment of a large sum to the lady if he should marry or leave the island. It secured the lady's tenure without involving the man in loss of caste through the ceremony of marriage. As a result of the "housekeeping" system, in 1830, of 1,338 children born free and baptized in the Church of England, 958 were illegitimate.[5] One can assume that most of the remaining 380 were the children of white women, whose racial pride made them insistent on marriage.[6]

The Jamaican custom of interracial sexual alliances was received, quite naturally, with very different feelings by white and colored men. The white Jamaicans took a strong line with their British critics on this score. Rather than justify their practice as an allowable form of immorality for a colonial society without many white women, they defended it as having a higher morality than contemporaneous Britain. They pointed out that their alliances were relatively permanent and avoided the evils of prostitution, infanticide, and unnatural neglect of illegitimate children.[7] For the colored men, however, the practice added sexual competition to other sources of racial animosity. In the town, for example, there was a colored "society" with its separate social functions. Here, where the chief entertainment was dancing, colored men gave dances for colored girls, but white men also gave dances for the same colored girls, and the colored men were rigorously excluded.[8]

In spite of this and other social barriers, the brown people were very close to the attitudes and general outlook on the world of their white neighbors, at least in the sense that some colored people were found holding every shade of opinion found among members of the white class. The people of color were very conscious of their European heritage and extremely proud of it. While fewer colored people than whites went to school in England, those who remained in Jamaica worked hard to suppress anything that might imply African origin. They discriminated socially against the darker members of their own class, they

were just as prejudiced as the whites in their relations with
Negro slaves, and finally a minority of the colored group joined
the whites in the fight against emancipation.[9]

Even though some colored men had all the usual white Jamaican's attitudes, the balance of opinion in the colored class was
different from the whites. As we have seen, the Wesleyan Methodists became the special colored sect. This brought many colored people into contact with British humanitarianism and the
British religious revival. It brought them a little closer to the
prevailing pattern of British opinion than the Jamaican white
caste. It created for the Colonial Office a group of Jamaican
politicians who could often be counted on to vote with the
Governor in support of humanitarian policies originating in
Britain.

The pro-British alignment of the colored Jamaicans is all the
more surprising, since they were also the Jamaican group with
the strongest attachment for their own island.[10] Even before
emancipation they thought of Jamaica as their country and developed a feeling of patriotism — a feeling very uncommon
among creole whites, who still thought of England as "home"
though they might never have been there. Both the greater patriotism and the leaning toward British policies were the natural
outcome of the colored man's position in Jamaican society.
Even after legal discrimination was gone, his status halfway between the two "pure" racial groups made for psychological insecurity. His attempt to emphasize the European part of his
racial heritage made him reject the African part, but at the same
time the local white caste refused to recognize him as a European
and an equal. His insecurity, however, could be partly compen-
sated by greater loyalty to Britain and greater loyalty to Jamaica.

*   *   *

Although the tensions between the colored and white members of the European society were by far the most serious, there
were many stresses and strains within the white caste itself. Some
of these originated in the plantation economy and the position
of Jamaica in the colonial system. There was a tight order of
social precedence on the sugar estate. The three grades of

planter — attorney, overseer, and bookkeeper — tended to form three separate social classes. Attorneys considered themselves vastly superior to overseers, and overseers tried to keep a similar class line between themselves and the bookkeepers. Some overseers even insisted on dining alone on the estate and banished the bookkeepers to their own quarters.

Class distinctions were maintained in the militia as well, where all whites and free colored people were forced to serve. The attorneys were officers; overseers who could supply themselves with a horse of the requisite value were in the preferred ranks of the cavalry. Bookkeepers were most often infantrymen, while the colored men and free blacks were segregated in their own units. It was a social affront for a bookkeeper to step out of his station and enroll in the socially preferred cavalry, even though the overseers had lately been bookkeepers themselves. Even within the class of bookkeepers the ownership of a horse was a mark of exaggerated importance — a symbol of respectability that kept one out of the ranks of the "walking buckras." [11]

These distinctions were not English class distinctions carried over to Jamaica, since the class origin of the Jamaican planter was most often a subject he preferred to forget. Instead, they were the creation of men who needed "position" in society as part of the reward for their self-exile. The result was a strict class order within the planting class combined with considerable social mobility, if one conformed to the standards of the planting society.[12]

All whites were not immediately connected with the planting system; but almost all were indirectly interested, and many lines of social strain can be traced to the economic relations of the planting system. One of the chief lines of social antagonism separated planters and merchants. Although the senior partners of the great mercantile houses lived in England or Scotland, there were branches in Kingston and some of the larger parish towns. The branch managers were often wealthy and ranked with the planting attorneys and resident proprietors among the social elite of the colony. There were also a number of humbler local merchants who dealt in the entrepôt trade or internal commerce. To the planting class, the mercantile interest as a whole seemed simply to be a leech on the really productive activity

of the colony, and the feeling increased as the planting economy
slid further downhill in the decades following emancipation.[13]

The rivalry between planter and merchant sometimes merged
with a broader rivalry of town and country, but townsmen were
nevertheless tied to the planting interest by many bonds of interest and sentiment. The prosperity of all depended ultimately
on the prosperity of the plantations, and for individuals the de-
pendence could be narrower still. Doctors, for example, were
needed on the estates to care for the slaves. By custom, medical
care was provided by a contract system, the doctor receiving an
annual fee for each slave in return for a weekly visit to the estate
and other visits in case of emergency. Since fees were moderately
high for the work performed, medicine was a very lucrative profession. There were some three hundred practitioners in 1833,
almost all of whom owed their position to the favor of the planting attorneys.[14] The legal profession was not quite so dependent,
but the most valuable practice on the island grew out of the complicated system of plantation credit and the confusion of land
titles. Much of this practice was controlled by planting attorneys,
and it was also monopolized by a few old legal firms and a half
dozen barristers practicing before the Supreme Court in Spanish
Town. Many solicitors had a hard struggle to make headway
against favoritism and had to fall back on the litigation of the
less prosperous members of the community.[15]

The medical and legal professions were tied to Jamaica and
the planting system in still another way. Neither the doctors nor
the lawyers were in the first rank of their professions by British
standards. Although some claim to British training was usually
necessary, many had come to Jamaica because of poor expecta-
tions at home — like Richard Mango in Freeman's *Pickwick
Jamaica*, undecided whether to take up masonry or medicine.[16]
They were, therefore, in much the same position as the young
planter who had "come out" to make his way in the world —
their prospects, their ambitions, and their ties to "home" were
akin to those of the planting class.

Perhaps the most valuable local ally of the planting class was
the clergy of the Established Church, although the planters took
little interest in religion. If they leaned in any direction, it was
toward the "high and dry" religion of the eighteenth century,

and this was what the Jamaican Church supplied. Until 1824, official control had rested with the Bishop of London, which is to say that in practice there was no episcopal control at all. During this earlier period, the Governor had the power of appointment over the rectorships of the island. The long tenure of the Duke of Manchester, the planters' governor par excellence, had resulted in a series of appointments that reflected little credit on the church, but provided the planters with a clergy friendly to their interests. With no more than one or two clergymen for each parish, and parishes the size of English counties, it was hardly to be expected that the clergy would do more than minister to the religious needs of the white population. Since these needs were few, the post of rector tended to be a well paid sinecure. The incomes from six of the twenty-one parish livings came to more than one thousand pounds currency, and the rest were all over five hundred pounds, in addition to rectories, glebe lands, and slaves, which were sometimes furnished.[17]

The appointment of the first Bishop of Jamaica, Christopher Lipscomb, brought a note of disunity into the Jamaican clerical scene from his arrival on the island in 1825. Before that date there had been some mildly evangelical clergymen, but they shared the outcaste position of the dissenting missionaries. An effective episcopal control would mean more evangelicals. Lipscomb's early attack on clerical abuses, such as absenteeism, was the beginning of a long series of controversies between the bishop and the Jamaican clergy — a struggle waged with the House of Assembly allied to the clergy and the Colonial Office to the bishop. During the years before emancipation the clergy won easily. They imposed the requirement of two years' residence in Jamaica for the ordination of a new clergyman, used the Assembly's power of the purse against the bishop, and were almost successful in transferring the power of clerical appointment from the Governor to the Vestries, where planter control was secure.[18]

Just as some religious differences in Great Britain were exacerbated as a result of their transfer to the different social situation of Jamaica, others were weakened. There were on the island two groups of whites not of British extraction. The largest and most important of these was the prosperous Jewish community.

They were mainly Sephardim who had come to Jamaica as early as the seventeenth century. By the 1830's they were well established, mainly as merchants, but occasionally in planting as well. The other non-British group was a smaller community of French Catholic creoles from Saint Domingue, who had come to Jamaica as refugees from the Negro uprising at the end of the eighteenth century. In Jamaica they were respectable and industrious, if no longer wealthy. Most of them grew provisions for the Kingston market on small plantations with only a few slaves.[19] Both these groups had been domiciled in the Caribbean long enough to have acquired the same outlook as British planters. In addition, they and the British whites were so surrounded by the colored and black majority that among themselves religious and national differences tended to be of little importance.

They had little importance, that is, so long as the religious difference implied no difference of social attitude toward the subject race. In Jamaica, dissenters and evangelicals were subjected to much the same sort of social or legal discrimination that was reserved for Jews and Catholics in Britain, while Jews, Catholics, and the Established Churches of England and Scotland were favored by the island Legislature. In the late twenties, the Assembly passed a series of acts giving complete civil and political liberty to Jews, and it made a special effort to obtain English approval. One of these measures finally received the royal sanction in 1830, long before Great Britain herself showed a similar religious tolerance.[20]

Leaving the missionaries out of the picture, since they were not admitted to real membership in the white caste, the most important source of social friction for white Jamaica was not so much within the island as in the difference between creole and Briton. There was some economic basis for this rift, even among people who belonged, in a broad sense, to the planting interest. In addition to the natural friction between the Jamaican planter and his British merchant-creditor, dissension was almost as pronounced between planters who returned to England as absentees and those who stayed to take care of the property. On the one side there was a feeling of jealousy and envy for those who had been fortunate enough to escape from their exile — a feeling that shaded off at times toward a sense of Jamaica as a community separate from Britain and thus toward the bare beginnings of Jamaican nationalism. Although this nationalism was later to slip from the hands of the white to those of the colored Jamaicans, a white Jamaican journalist of the early thirties expressed it when he wrote of the absentees:

. . . the haughty aristocrats who have property in that Island, and who may obtain seats in the House of Commons, have no community of interest, no identity of feeling with the resident inhabitants of Jamaica; to these aristocrats, what may become of the people of that country is and ever must be a matter of perfect inconsequence, so long as they can, by any other means, retain in England what they call their station in society; that is, live among *your* aristocracy, imitate their vices, and surpass their follies.[21]

On the side of the absentees there was the fear, often quite justified, that the estate was being managed in the interest of the attorney rather than the proprietor. This fear for loss of income led to the attitude of the absentee in the novel, *Marly*, who ". . . would sooner entrust his estate to a negro than an attorney." [22]

These differences, partly economic in origin, were also reinforced from another direction. During the eighteenth century the creole whites had built up a body of social habits and customs that had come to be quite different from nineteenth-century standards in Britain. While only about three white Jamaicans in every five had been born on the island, a higher proportion were creole in outlook, having been "creolized" by their years of living in Jamaica. Even though the Peace of 1815 brought safer sea transport and thus easier travel between Jamaica and Britain, rapid changes in the mother country — including the growth of humanitarian sentiment — outweighed the improvement of communication. By 1830 Jamaica and Britain were further apart in outlook than they had been before the Wars of the French Revolution. The new areas of conflict over slavery were added to the older friction between the metropolitan smugness of the new arrival and the pride, conservatism, and feeling of colonial inferiority on the part of the creole.

* * *

Absenteeism, slavery, and concentration on staple production for a distant market made the Jamaican economy unhealthy and insecure, and the social malaise and psychological insecurity of the white Jamaican arose from causes that were much the same. His attitudes and values were a mesh of contradictions between cruelty, pride, and stubbornness on one hand and a genuine friendliness, freedom from restraint, and open hospitality on the other. Furthermore, whichever quality was uppermost at the moment was likely to be emphasized in a manner that was far from halfhearted. This general lack of moderation was outstanding in the Jamaican press, and it was frequently noticed by travelers, as in Richard R. Madden's summation of Jamaican public affairs.

> In a word, where all things, both buckras and blacks
> Are in fits and by starts either rigid or lax;
> And in faith as in politics, never it seems
> Are content if their notions are not in extremes! [23]

The extremism of public life was by no means unconnected with the contradictions of the creole personality, and the personality of the white creole was in turn greatly influenced by the conditions of Jamaican life.

Even the bitter opponents of the planting class found them kind and generous to strangers and democratic within a narrow circle.[24] Hospitality was, in fact, a special point of pride with white Jamaicans. When William Hosack wrote a long poem in praise of his island, he mentioned that,

> No weary traveller here dreads hostile band —
> A welcome guest is he made everywhere;
> Since all are strange on Caribbean land,
> All meet, as strangers meet, with open house, and hand! [25]

And in making this point Hosack also suggested an explanation of one paradox in Jamaican life — the peculiar combination of tight social stratification with the ideal of hospitality. The white Jamaican was himself a stranger. He was a transient and a climber, without permanent interests or ties to the country in which he lived — only temporarily balanced there, waiting for better times. As a stranger he turned to other strangers to meet his own loneliness. But as a climber he was insecure in his social position, and more insecure still from the reflected insecurity of his society under attack. His position could be fortified, however, by raising the barriers against those below him in the social scale. Consequently, these barriers were raised against the colored man and the new bookkeeper.

Isolation also played a part in creating the West Indian code of hospitality and friendliness. The isolation of the planting class on the estate during most of the year was more real than Jamaican distances indicate. Roads were few, and there was no public transportation. Travel by horse or private carriage was expensive, and during the rainy season many districts were cut off from the outside for weeks at a time. Social contact with other planters was so difficult that the visit from one estate to another became the "visitation," a favorite social function in which the entire household would move to visit another family, staying for several weeks or even longer.[26]

More important still was the psychological isolation of the small white caste, always a tiny ruling minority among the great and unfriendly mass of the slaves. Thus the white stranger was welcome in the town as well as on the estate, if not as a rare diversion at least as a potential ally — another person who looked the same, among so many who looked different.

The openness, the free-and-easy lack of formality, and even the open disdain for some of the English code of behavior were partly an outgrowth of the impermanence and isolation, but they were also reinforced by other aspects of Jamaican life. Few white Jamaicans had wives to act as arbiters of social behavior, and many other of the bonds of sentiment, loyalty, fear of public censure or of losing caste were no longer as strong as they had been in Britain. A similar relaxation of restraints is often noticed among travelers in a foreign country, soldiers on leave in a strange town, or a primitive people "detribalized" by contact with urban life. Not all white Jamaicans felt this relaxation, but each generation of newcomers brought some of it into their attitudes. Eventually it built a code of behavior that was permanently more lax than the British code. The Jamaican Pickwick, like other English travelers, saw it as a pleasant freedom, but also as bad manners.

At all events, Sam . . . this is a country where every man throws aside the restraints of formal society and fashion, doing only that which contributes to comfort, ease, and amusement . . . But, there is a freedom of manner about many here highly familiar, not to mention intrusive and unpleasant.²⁷

Alongside the easy manners of the creole there were also the pride and stubbornness and quick temper that are so often associated with slaveholding societies. White Jamaicans tended to be bad compromisers, arrogant, and tenacious of everything in their society that was attacked by outsiders. This attitude grew partly from insecurity and isolation, but still more from the institution of slavery. The creole child had a great deal of freedom at all times, the really stern discipline being saved for slaves. In addition, he was brought up to a position of command, with authority first of all over slave playmates and later over all Negroes. If he went back to England to school, he usually left at an early age and grew up away from the responsibilities of the planter's life, often with too generous an allowance. In short, he was "spoiled." ²⁸

These various elements combined to produce the personality and behavior summed up by R. R. Madden in a way that echoes the surprisingly unanimous verdict of other travelers:

The defects of the Creole character are more than counterbalanced by its virtues. If they are easily moved to anger, they are still more easily incited to kindness and generosity; if they are "devils being offended," they are frank and honest to their enemies, and faithful beyond any people I know, to their friends. I wish they were less proud, because their noble qualities would be more appreciable, and I would be glad to find them less captious, because their personal courage has no need of such demonstrations on slight occasions.²⁹

But for all the pride, prejudice, and outward self-assurance of the white Jamaican, he was never quite at home in Jamaica. He was still the exile, the temporary resident. The more articulate expressed their feeling of exile in different ways. A note of self-pity is found in the closing stanzas of "The Exile," an anonymous poem of about 1830:

> At times when I think to return,
> Pale sickness compels me to stay;

And in languishing accents I mourn,
As the years are fast rolling away.

Since nothing is here to be found
But disease, disappointment, and grief,
Let my days run with quickness their round,
And death bring the exile relief.[30]

In comparison with this, William Hosack represents the other extreme. He finds himself an exile, but still an exile who has thrown his lot with his new country.

A stranger amidst strangers, lone and drear,
Unlink'd by flesh and blood to thee or thine,
I am the exile of a bleaker sphere;
Yet ne'ertheless, loved isle, thou art the shrine
To whom my knee is bent, my thoughts incline,
And whatsoe'er betide thee — woe or weal,
Thy thrift, or thy misfortune shall be mine.
To me thy glorious solitudes appeal,
With a most winning smile, and my affections steal.[31]

The vast majority of white Jamaicans probably felt their exile differently at different times, but these two positions can be fairly taken as the poles between which their feelings moved.

The feeling of exile is the key to one of the most important psychological characteristics of the white Jamaican. Just as the man of color was split between two racial groups, having something of both but belonging to neither, the white man was split between two societies, the one in which he lived and the one to which he hoped to return. In the years preceding emancipation these two societies were not only different, they were antagonistic. The Jamaican, and especially the creole, found himself with a character formed by the conditions of colonial life, with his home, however temporarily, established on the island, and with his economic interest founded on the social and economic institutions of the colony. At the same time he was psychologically an alien and an exile, and the final purpose for which he had exiled himself was to return to England more prosperous than he had left it. His chief emotional attachment was to Britain, and this was true even of the white creole. Yet it was precisely from Britain that Jamaican society was being attacked, and the steady economic decline was constantly in the background. Under the circumstances, it is hardly surprising that few Jamaicans met the future with the healthy self-confidence and amenability to compromise that was necessary for a successful adjustment to the nineteenth century.

*   *   *

In 1831, James Stephen, at the Colonial Office, wrote,

There is no civilized Society on earth so entirely destitute of learned leisure, of literary and scientific intercourse and even of liberal recreations. Perhaps it would be difficult to find a white man in the island of Jamaica who does not regard England as his home and the Colony as his place of Exile.[32]

This was substantially true, if comparison were to be made with Europe or North America, but it was hardly fair of Stephen to expect either learned leisure or literary intercourse from a society like Jamaica. Given the fact that the leisured class was automatically drained off by absenteeism and the free population only amounted to about 65,000 people, the quantity of Jamaican literary production is surprisingly great. There were a modest but adequate number of newspapers, libraries, improvement societies, schools, periodicals, and book publishers. Considering the size of the audience, Jamaica was probably close to the level of the English provinces in these matters. The group of literate and thoughtful people was, of course, too small to develop either original literary expression or ideas at a high level of intricacy; but the means were there for disseminating ideas received from outside, and these means were enough to create something that could be called Jamaican public opinion.

One of the principal drawbacks in Jamaican intellectual life was the lack of a decent educational system. There were three principal schools on the island — Jamaica Free School in St. Ann, Wolmer's Free School in Kingston, and Titchfield Free School in Port Antonio. These institutions, all foundations managed by trustees, gave a moderately bad education, including some study of languages. In addition there were schools in each parish and a few private schools for females, but the whole system suffered from the fact that anyone with the means sent his children to England for all but the most elementary education.

For the further education of adults there was a small circulating library in Kingston and the library of the House of Assembly in Spanish Town. A number of improvement societies had also been organized, beginning with the Cornwall Agricultural Society in 1807. Although individual societies often died, they were constantly being resurrected under new names, so that, at any moment, there was likely to be some sort of organization in about half of the parishes. These groups devoted most of their effort to the improvement of planting, but they also branched out into other fields. The Jamaica Horticultural Society of Kingston, for example, had assembled a thousand-volume library by the late thirties. The decade of the 1840's was the period when improvement societies received the most active support, but throughout the middle decades of the century they provided the chief centers of intellectual life in rural Jamaica.[33]

The libraries and improvement societies, however, could only serve a limited number of people. The rest of the population depended on the newspapers, and, in the early 1830's, Jamaica was decidedly "over-papered." Between 1830 and 1834 there were more than twenty different periodicals published in Jamaica — most of them weeklies, biweeklies, and monthlies — all with small circulation. Most editors of these journals were amateurs who started a publication and ran it a few years, eventually failing only to be replaced by another enterprising journalist.

The papers of most general circulation, the Kingston dailies and semiweeklies, were read all over the island, though the subscription price (about five pounds currency a year) was so high that only the relatively wealthy could afford them. In the early 1830's, the *Jamaica Despatch* was the largest of the dozen or so newspapers. Its five hundred subscribers put it far ahead of the others, few of which had as many as one hundred.[34] Founded in 1832, it replaced the *Jamaica Courant,* which had just collapsed, as the chief organ of the planting class — taking over the tone of violence and scurrility against the emancipators, the government, the Negroes, and the missionaries, which had been the stock in trade of the *Courant* in the 1820's.

In addition to the *Courant-Despatch* succession there were six smaller papers in Kingston in the early 1830's, but they were so small that they tended to come and go fairly rapidly. With one exception, the general editorial policy was much the same as that of the larger paper. The exception was the *Watchman*, edited by two colored men, Robert Osborn and Edward Jordon. It was the organ of the people of color — and through them, of the humanitarian interest in Britain.

The remaining newspapers were the two semiofficial *Gazettes*, one in Kingston and one in Spanish Town, and the local papers of the parish towns. Among these the most important were the northside papers in Montego Bay and Falmouth, where the *Cornwall Chronicle*, the *Cornwall Advertizer*, and especially the *Cornwall Courier* of Falmouth, echoed the *Despatch's* vituperative outbursts for the benefit of the northside planters.

Another group of Jamaican publications were the weekly or monthly journals of opinion, usually only a few sheets written by one individual. In this class were A. H. Beaumont's *Isonomist* and James Geddes' *Patriot*, both published in Kingston. In this class also were the journals representing the views of the dissenting missionaries — the *Christian Record* of Kingston, the *Colonial Reformer* of Spanish Town, and the *Struggler* of Montego Bay.

For the medical profession James Paul published the *Jamaica Physical Journal*, carrying articles on tropical medicine and also more general subjects in the natural sciences. This was short-lived, but it represented a type of journalism that was later revived under different auspices. Still another type of journal cropping up from time to time in nineteenth-century Jamaica was the literary magazine. It was represented in the 1830's by *Sheridan's Jamaica Monthly Magazine*, which was published unprofitably between 1832 and 1834.

None of these periodicals was high in quality, though Sheridan aimed for an improvement of the island's literary taste. Most of them showed the pride and quick temper that seemed to mark the Jamaican personality, and their concentration on petty quarrels and local affairs reflected the isolation of Jamaica from the larger world. While they supplied the island with some line of contact with the outside, they also passed this information through a pattern of distortion that fitted it to the Jamaican outlook. Thus, they were the chief intellectual bond with the Empire as a whole; but they were also an important instrument in the process of creolization that made Jamaicans of the new arrivals from Britain.[35]

The press was not, however, the most important instrument in this process. It reflected the attitudes of Jamaicans and gave the planters what they wanted to hear, but its influence on the newcomer was mainly negative — it merely filtered out non-colonial sentiments. The West Indian attitude was more often enforced on the newcomer through social pressure than through intellectual conversion. Isolation among a subject people, isolation on the estates, a sense of insecurity arising from the years of economic decline — these all worked to produce a desire for conformity. The planting class was on the defensive — afraid of a slave rebellion, afraid of the missionary influence, afraid of the British humanitarians. The natural reaction was to tighten their ranks by making certain that they at least had nothing to fear from their immediate associates. The process of enforcing conformity was not always conscious, but the pressure was still there. In the militia, in the Vestry, on the estates, and even in the towns, the white man who was suspected of "saintship" or too much friendliness toward the Negroes could expect no promotion, no employment, and no friends. Even if he were a proprietor, the *Courant* and similar journals could make life very disagreeable for him.[36]

*   *   *

From their surroundings in a slave society the Jamaicans had developed a way of life that had little to recommend it in any period, yet they were half-proud that it was their fashion, as one Jamaican put it,

. . . to go to law, to fight duels, to smoke cigars, to have liver complaints, and enlarged spleens, to live at your neighbour's expense, to humbug absentees, to be well paid for executorships, to make money and spend it, to swear out of jail; and, if there be truth in Holy Writ, to be d —— d for it! [37]

These gentlemanly habits were aristocratic vices acceptable enough to the eighteenth-century Englishman. They did not go down so well with the reforming humanitarianism of the nineteenth century. Insouciant good nature and openness seemed to the Briton nothing less than moral laxity. The value of the devil-may-care spirit was no longer appreciated, and the time was soon coming when the bad qualities that went with it would no longer be tolerated.

It would be hard to imagine a society worse prepared to face social revolution than European Jamaica in the 1830's. It was divided into mutually antagonistic racial groups, with each group, in turn, in a state of psychological unbalance. It was constantly menaced by a dissatisfied servile population, and from overseas an unyielding humanitarianism seemed bent on destroying the colony. It is hardly surprising that the white and colored Jamaicans failed, in the next three decades, to meet the challenge of emancipation and adjustment to a free-labor society. The unexpected is that they accepted the challenge at all — that they showed the vitality to struggle with the problem for thirty more years in the face of continuing economic disaster.

IV

Defenses Against Revolution

EUROPEAN JAMAICA HAD LONG BEEN CON-SCIOUS of the growth of humanitarian sentiment in Great Britain. Since the last years of the eighteenth century evangelicals, dissenters, and others in England had been working against slavery. At first it was only the slave trade that was seriously attacked, and it was abolished in 1807. After this beginning there was a growing threat to the institution as a whole, even though the leaders of the humanitarian party in Britain were not themselves thinking in terms of full emancipation until some years later.

For the West Indians, the crucial act — the unmistakable writing on the wall — was the passage through the British House of Commons of Canning's resolutions of 1823, stating the intention of the British government to abolish slavery in the colonies. This was not to be immediate, but gradual, and buttressed in the meantime by measures for the amelioration of the slave regime.[1] From that time forward the Jamaicans were on the defensive — opposed to the stated policy of the home government and fighting a rear-guard action against the emancipators, the dissenters, and the government itself.

The important battle, ending with the act of emancipation of 1833, was British rather than West Indian. The colonists had the powerful support of the "West India interest," but the struggle took place in the British Parliament, before the British public, and in the surroundings of British politics. In the end it

came to the Jamaicans as a finished decision. During the later
1820's and the early 1830's, however, the British struggle over
slavery forced Jamaicans to rethink their own position toward
their labor system. They had either to develop intellectual and
political defenses against the enemy, or simply wait for the revolution that was so obviously on its way.

They developed their defense, and they developed it out of
the raw material of psychological attitudes and sentimental attachments that already existed in the colony. They also developed it in a way that had a profound influence on Jamaican
thought about society and politics. In the process of defending
slavery they originated or took over sets of argument and tendencies of thought, and these were thoroughly spread by the
island press. These intellectual preconceptions and attitudes
and even institutions became so deeply entrenched that they
formed the basis for the white Jamaican's adjustment to emancipation.

Since, on the intellectual side, the Jamaican defense was
erected in the shadow of the more important struggle in Britain, Jamaican polemical writing merges imperceptibly with the
British proslavery and antislavery literature. It is usually possible to distinguish Jamaican authors from others, but the line
between mother country and colony is at times purely arbitrary.
The Jamaicans followed the main lines of the general proslavery
position, and when they differed in detail it was mainly a matter of emphasis.

*   *   *

It would be impossible to draw up a sequence of logical points
stating the case of the Jamaican planters and their allies against
emancipation. The case was not presented logically. Instead, it
appeared in a series of pamphlets appealing to the emotions of
the English public and in the reports of travelers and missionaries to the island. The only work of Jamaican origin that can
be considered a full-scale treatment is the Rev. George Wilson
Bridges' *Annals of Jamaica*, and even this volume is formally a
history of the island and only indirectly a defense of slavery.[2]
There were, however, a series of arguments repeated again and

again by Jamaicans — some representing the real conviction of the writer about the dangers of emancipation, others designed to impress the British public with the justice of the West Indian cause, but all finally believed in through constant repetition.

These arguments were all designed to meet an attack that was based on absolute moral principles. In the eyes of the humanitarians, slavery was indefensible, being contrary to the Law of God. And yet, as W. L. Burn has shown in connection with the larger British emancipation controversy, the West India interest abandoned the strongest logical defense. They failed to put forth a serious claim that slavery was a positive moral benefit to the entire community, including the slaves. Instead they took the weaker, relativist position, that the benefits deriving from the system outweighed the evils it involved.[3]

Jamaican defenders of slavery followed the same pattern. Most writers simply began by admitting that slavery was an evil. They not only admitted it, but they often did so in no uncertain terms. Augustus Beaumont, a proprietor of the *Courant,* wrote, in a pamphlet subsidized by the Assembly of Jamaica, "I am not — I never was an advocate of slavery — the system is abhorrent to every manly feeling — it is degrading to human nature. . ."[4] Yet he ended by justifying its continued applicability to Jamaica.

Even Bridges, the archdefender of slavery, wrote, "Let it not be thought, then, that I can ever become an advocate of slavery. I avowed it before, and I again repeat it, I detest the barbarous institution, as a curse. . ."[5] But he also ended by justifying slavery in Jamaica. Other colonists who claimed to share this abhorrence found it necessary to explain at the same time why the situation of Jamaica made emancipation impractical.[6]

Not all Jamaican writers were quite so open in admitting the basic injustice of slavery. One anonymous pamphleteer, for example, stated at one point the principle that there is ". . . no abstract, natural, or original right, that any one has to any thing, not even to free agency," and went on to maintain that all liberties are dependent on specific legal provisions. On the surface this appears to be a fundamental attack on the position of the emancipators, but a few pages later this author made the usual admission of sin:

The fact of slavery being in itself a wrong, does not affect the proprietor of a sugar estate more than the purchaser of sugar. We have no right for the sake of general justice to inflict partial evil, in order to cure an evil caused and continued by common consent.[7]

Nowhere in the Jamaican writing that has come to my attention is there a defense of slavery as an institution that is morally just or right *on principle.* There were, to be sure, occasional offhand statements that might be taken to imply this kind of principled defense. Among these, one of the most common was a comparison between the material well-being and happiness of the slaves and the poverty and misery of the English working class. It would have been an obvious extension of this argument to say that the slaves were better off *because* of the institution of slavery. But this was exactly the kind of argument the Jamaicans seemed unwilling to make, and the original comparison was left without elaboration.

The fact that Jamaicans were inconsistent in accepting humanitarian moral standards and defending West Indian property rights at the same time did little to mitigate the violence of their feelings. Bridges' treatment of the slave trade is especially striking. At one point he made the suggestion that perhaps the slave trade was a blessing in disguise, since it saved the poor Africans from a horrible death in Africa and brought them into contact with "civilization" and Christianity.[8] He also attacked the evangelicals who had procured the abolition of the trade as "unprincipled advocates of humanity," "enemies of Jamaica," and "self-interested and misguided men." This would seem to establish Bridges' position as a defender of the trade, if it weren't for the fact that, in almost the same breath, he called the slave trade ". . . a cruel and disgraceful trade, that could not but poison the source of national manners, obliterate the sense of virtue and religion, and almost extinguish the instincts of nature." [9]

Bridges was not only inconsistent in dealing with the slave trade, he also weakened his own case against emancipation by discarding the religious justifications of slavery then in common use. It was not that he simply omitted them. He mentioned the arguments from the Bible — slaves as descendants of the sons of Ham, slaves allowed by God to the Jewish people, Christ's failure to make an explicit statement against slavery — and he quoted from Paley and Bishop Watson of Llandaff to show recent authoritative approval of slavery by the Church of England. Yet in the end, he rejected all of them and concluded that slavery cannot be sanctioned by Christianity. In fact, one of his arguments against legislative emancipation was based on the belief that Christianity would slowly but automatically destroy slavery through the operation of "the new moral code which was to reform the earth and remodel the heart of man." [10]

The failure of Bridges and other Jamaican proslavery writers to present a consistent and well-reasoned case for their institution was not simply a piece of bad logic or literary ineptitude. It was a reflection of deeper tendencies of Jamaican thought. The key weakness was the admission that slavery was morally wrong. It might be possible to explain this as a piece of planned, general hypocrisy on their part, designed to cater to the known antislavery prejudices of the British public, but it would have been politically senseless to give up a strong argument from principle in favor of a series of weaker ones — especially if this were done merely to cater to the prejudices of the opponents. It would have been foolish, that is, unless the Jamaicans themselves were completely convinced that the stronger argument could not stand.

This seems to have been the case. The proslavery writers were Jamaican in their social and economic surroundings, but they were English in education, in intellectual environment, and in emotional attachment. They lived in one society with intellectual equipment largely formed in another. They felt called to defend slavery, because they saw no way of preserving their society without it; and they felt called to condemn it as immoral, because they were convinced of its immorality through their training and through the prestige of British opinion.

In this instance, the humanitarian movement in England not only prepared the British electorate to force a revolution on the West Indians by destroying their labor system — it also prepared the Jamaicans for the revolution by destroying their own confidence in that system. Though the white caste of Jamaica was unwilling to the last to accept the emancipation act with good grace, thirty years of humanitarian propaganda had left it unable to defend slavery with real conviction.[11]

Since the Jamaicans were unwilling to use the kind of argument that would enable them to paint their labor system as a moral blessing, they were all the more anxious to show it as an economic and social necessity. This was the ground on which they chose to argue their case, and it necessarily involved them in quantities of diffuse argument. They had to balance the amount of injustice against the amount of economic profit — a discussion necessarily inconclusive because these are incommensurate quantities.

There was an occasional maverick argument, like that advanced by a member of the House of Assembly, who tried to convince the British upper class that the emancipation of the West Indian Negro was the first step in the destruction of all social order.[12] Most Jamaican writers, however, stuck to wellworn lines of reasoning. These were picked up and used over and over again from the early 1820's onward. They fit logically into three groups.

The first of these was the set of arguments designed to demonstrate that slavery was a beneficial institution to the people of Great Britain and therefore could not be given up immediately. The specific points were as old as the "Old Colonial System." They were the same arguments used to show the value of colonization in general. They emphasized the value to England of the colonial trade as a school for seamen, to the Crown from the high sugar duties, the usefulness of Jamaica as a "vent" for British manufactures, the work created for British laborers by the expenditures of absentee proprietors, and the numbers of people engaged in trade and shipping to Jamaica. The entire case was based, sometimes tacitly, on the assumption that the end of slavery would mean the end of sugar production in the colonies.[13]

The second set of arguments tried to show how little the evils of slavery bothered the Jamaican slaves. The most common device was the comparison already mentioned, between the physical comfort of the Jamaican slave and that of the British workingman. The Jamaican writers liked this argument: it gave them a chance to counterattack their attackers. A. H. Beaumont, in stating his hatred of slavery, added that it was evil,

. . . whether in its undisguised form in Jamaica, or in its insidiously masked character in other countries, where it assumes the semblance of freedom, in order better to trample on the rights of man; centering the object of the real, tho' disguised solicitude of the rulers, in the welfare of a few haughty Aristocrats. . .[14]

Again and again the Jamaicans came back to the assertion that the slave was happy and contented and, oddly enough, without making the claim on racial grounds — without stating that the Negro was incapable of appreciating the "higher" things.[15]

The third set of arguments dealt not with the system of slavery as it existed, but with the predicted results of emancipation. This was a much more complex point, and it required more theoretical justification. It required striking a balance between the good and evil that would result from an event that was still only foreseen. Over the years this argument in its various forms led the white Jamaicans to construct a mental picture predicting the results of emancipation. It had an importance, therefore, extending beyond the struggle over emancipation. It fixed, for the whites, a preconceived view of the situation they would meet, once the slaves were free.

Their view of what emancipation would bring was not entirely theoretical. Just over the horizon were the mountains of Haiti, where the slaves had successfully rebelled against their French masters in the 1790's. Jamaicans had fought then in Haiti, and refugee French planters had made their homes in Jamaica. Now, and later in the century, the Republic of Haiti was watched very closely by the white Jamaicans — both as a warning for the present and a portent of the future. The most elementary argument predicting the future was simply to point to Haiti as a horrible example of the only previous emancipation in the Caribbean. In doing this, Jamaicans called up a picture of anarchy — the burning plantations, the destruction of the white inhabitants, and finally a new order in which the former slaves were no better off than they had been under the French.[16]

The white Jamaicans did not stop here, however; they looked for theoretical backing for their predictions, and they found it in two different directions. The first of these was a return to the teachings of Burke about revolutions in general. The pro-slavery writers stressed the complexity of human affairs and the gradualism that was necessary, if even an obvious abuse were to be reformed. The author of *Marly* summarized this position in his novel.

If good was certain to arise from an instantaneous manumission, let it at once be done. But if the intelligence of mankind has been derived from the experience of ages, and our own experience of revolutions has surely been enough, those must evidently be in error of a dangerous nature, who would interfere with any long established system, unless they proceed upon the best, and what time has proved to be an adviseable mode of procedure, preparatory to abolishing long standing laws, whether they are against or in favour of nature. Man is not a machine to be managed like a piece of clock work or a steam engine. He has too many passions and prejudices to be submitted to be treated like a piece of inert matter. His passions must be set at rest, and his prejudices must be silenced, before he can safely be made to submit to laws, even though framed for his own advantage.[17]

Argument in the second direction took a number of different forms — all of them supporting in one way or another the thesis that Jamaica could not be economically productive without forced labor. At its most naïve, this argument was simply the outright statement that the Negro congenitally disliked work and would not work unless forced. In more formal language it was claimed that the slaves did not have complex desires — that they missed being the "economic man" — and, therefore, that the economic motive at work in Britain did not apply in Jamaica.[18]

Other writers went further. To the notion that the Negro had a limited demand for goods, they added the idea of a tropical exuberance which supplied this demand without work.[19] At this point in the argument the slave was completely removed from the area of economic "law." The Negro's own nature had repealed the laws of unlimited demand, and the nature of the tropics had repealed the laws of limited supply. No system of work for wages could lure him to turn a hand.

Many writers let the case stand at this point, but most Jamaican commentators were not yet satisfied. Although planters thought the Negroes were lazy, they also knew the myth of tropical exuberance was nothing but a myth with very little foundation in fact. The more thoughtful proslavery writers, therefore, turned also to a consideration of the ratio between the available amount of land and the available amount of labor. It was argued that most of the land in Jamaica was unoccupied and could be had for nothing or practically nothing. At the same time the population was relatively small, and it had to be densely concentrated on the estates to produce "higher" products. This made for "civilization." But the concentration of labor could not be accomplished by economic pressure, since the high yield of the unoccupied land in the tropics would enable the laborer to live with little work — or at least to be better off than he would be with plantation wages. Therefore, it was argued, slavery was necessary to force by artificial means the labor that was forced elsewhere by economic pressure.[20]

This was an excellent argument from the Jamaican point of view. It gave the whites an opportunity for justifying slavery, though wrong, as a temporary measure that would no longer be needed once the population was large enough to press on the means of subsistence. It had something of the aura of prestige that economic theory was just beginning to have in England, and it was, in fact, one of the considerations behind Edward Gibbon Wakefield's plan for "systematic colonization" — a plan that was to have important results for the Empire as a whole. Finally, as we shall see, it was a line of thought that was to have a long and important future in Jamaica.

*   *   *

As the movement for emancipation gained momentum in Britain, the fears of the white Jamaicans grew stronger, and the defense of their social order tended to overflow into fields other than polemics and propaganda aimed at England. It led to a reassessment of the Jamaican constitution and an attempt to shore up the position of Jamaica against pressure from the home government. It led, especially, to a long religious controversy in which religious freedom, just then victorious in Britain, was called into question in the colony.

The religious controversy grew naturally out of a situation where the various Christian sects had come to represent racial divisions and subdivisions and the ministers spoke for the social, as well as the religious aims of their congregations. To the white Jamaicans, evangelical and dissenting missionaries represented the humanitarian party of Great Britain, and this party was the enemy itself. Since their first days in Jamaica, the missions had been able to grow only sporadically between periods of active opposition from the white colonists. Between 1802 and 1815 this opposition had been especially severe, with legislation against unlicensed preaching. There followed a period of relative freedom, until a second wave of opposition was touched off by Canning's resolutions of 1823. This wave slackened off about 1829, but the animosity was still there and would crop up again.[21]

Nor was religious animosity a monopoly of the planting class. As missionaries became more aroused emotionally in the struggle against slavery, the planters and the planting society came to represent incarnate evil. Even without the emancipation question, there was a long tradition of mutual recrimination between planters and missionaries over the religious instruction of slaves. The essential point of the planters' case was simple — the teaching of the missionaries tended to inflame the slaves with ideas of spiritual equality, and thus worldly equality. These ideas "unsettled" them and led to revolt. Therefore, planters tried to prevent their slaves from holding religious meetings or visiting missionaries.[22] In the House of Assembly they passed legislation to curb missionary activity — though these laws were eventually disallowed by the home government. To the missionaries, these activities were nothing less than religious persecution — further evidence of the sinfulness of the slaveholders and the doctrinal error of the Church of England which they supported.

The planters' case, however, was rarely based on considerations of religious doctrine — a subject in which they had little interest. Bridges tried to use a religious argument against missionary teaching, claiming that a choice of Christian sects confused the slaves and slowed down the work of Christianization; but Bridges' sincerity is questionable, since he took very little interest in Christianizing slaves.[23] The prevailing view of the planting class is found in the report of the House of Assembly Committee on Sectarians in 1828.

Your committee, appointed to inquire into the establishment and proceedings of the sectarians of this Island,

Report, That they have taken the examination of sundry persons, which examinations are annexed, and that the principal object of the sectarians in this Island, is to extort money from their congregations by every possible pretext, to obtain which recourse has been made to the most indecent expedients.

That, in order to further this object, and to gain ascendancy over the negro mind, they inculcate the doctrines of equality and the rights of man; they preach and teach sedition even from the pulpit; and by misrepresentation and falsehood, endeavour to cast odium upon all the public authorities of this Island, not even excepting the representatives of Majesty itself.

That the consequences have been abject poverty, loss of comfort, and discontent among the slaves frequenting their chapels, and deterioration of the property of their masters.[24]

It was the social implication of missionary activity that bothered the planters. As we have seen, the House of Assembly was more tolerant of different shades of merely doctrinal opinion than the House of Commons had been. The Jamaican white was proud of his lack of prejudice in religious matters. Augustus Beaumont's semiofficial pamphlet stated the case.

. . . the fact is, that in Jamaica the legislature troubles not itself with the religious opinions of any man, be his complexion or station what it may: believers and unbelievers, Christians, Jews, Mohametans and Pagans, are allowed to go to or from Heaven as they please, only it refuses to allow upon the portion of earth under its guidance, the establishment of a parsonarchy. . .[25]

The pattern of religious difference in Jamaica was superficially like that of Britain — the same doctrines were professed by the same sects, and religious quarrels were often stated in much the same language — but this pattern was superficial. Beneath the surface, there were very great differences of religious motivation.

Jamaican social and racial conflicts were expressed in religious controversy, and doctrinal questions took on new and un-English meaning. This tendency gave an astonishingly religious color to the events of the revolution and left a heritage of religious conflict for many years to come.

*   *   *

In addition to overflowing into the field of religion, the struggle over emancipation overflowed into the field of politics and constitutional theory. From the passage of Canning's resolutions, Jamaicans began to prepare their constitutional resources of opposition to the British government. This is not to say that Jamaican political leaders had been conciliatory in the past. Obstruction of central policy had always been easy under the Jamaican constitution — though the government of the island was neither responsible nor truly representative.

The key institution was the House of Assembly, which, together with the appointed Legislative Council, made up the island Legislature. In the early 1830's, the Assembly had forty-five members, two from each parish, except Kingston, which had three. Over the years the Assembly had built up its powers. It had, first of all, won out against the Council in a gradual but constant struggle over legislative initiative. By 1832 the Council could neither initiate legislation nor amend money bills, though its assent was still necessary for a bill to become law. The Assembly also had its own executive in the form of a number of permanent boards. The most important of these were the Board of Public Works, the Board of Public Accounts, and the Commissioners of Correspondence. Members of the Assembly were ex officio members of the boards. The boards continued to sit even after the prorogation of the Assembly and the Board of Accounts audited the colonial expenditure. In effect, this gave the same body the power of appropriating money and spending it, thus partially bypassing the official appointed executive.[26]

The Governor was the chief of the excutive, acting as Viceroy, Captain-General, and Chancellor. He was the organ through which the Imperial Parliament transmitted its orders to Jamaica — by way of the Cabinet and the Colonial Office. But Jamaican relations with Great Britain were further complicated by the Jamaica Agent, the official representative of the colony in London. In the 1830's the Agency was held by William Burge, who served from 1830 to 1846 after twenty years at the Jamaican bar and a period as Attorney-General of the island. His duties were, "To attend to whatever affects the interest of the colony, to endeavour to promote these interests and secure the consideration of them by Her Majesty's Government. . ." [27] In this capacity, he was appointed by the Legislature of Jamaica, paid from the revenues of the island, and took his orders directly from the Commissioners of Correspondence — which is to say, from the Assembly.[28]

But the Jamaica Agency was more than a pipeline for transmitting pressure from the Assembly of Jamaica to the Imperial Parliament; it was also a trusted source of information from Britain — and a source that sifted the news, sometimes distorting it to meet colonial prejudice. Burge's views were given great weight by the Assembly. Both before and after emancipation he tended to direct strategy in the struggle against the home government, telling the Assembly which move it might make most successfully.[29]

Although it was endowed with special power through the permanent boards and special representation in the Imperial capital, the Assembly was still far from responsible. The Governor could withhold his assent to measures, either directly or through the Legislative Council, which he controlled by his appointive power. Once signed by the Governor, a measure could still be refused royal assent by the Colonial Office in London. As a result, the Constitution of Jamaica was not suitable for efficient government unless home government and Assembly were in basic agreement. The Assembly had too little control and too little responsibility to enact its own program of legislation in the face of British opposition. At the same time, it was an admirable instrument for obstruction and opposition to any program of British origin. In the 1830's it was the chance of successful opposition that appealed to Jamaicans — at least to those represented in the Assembly.

Although representation in the House of Assembly was highly inequitable, even among the white caste, it was far from the

completely oligarchic institution it is sometimes pictured. Jewish and free colored people were allowed to vote for the first
time in 1832, and the number of registered voters in the election
of 1838 compared favorably with the relative size of the electorate for the unreformed House of Commons or that of contemporaneous France under the July Monarchy.[30] On the other
hand, the registry of only 2,199 potential voters in that election
compares very unfavorably with the thirteen thousand individuals who received compensation as owners of Jamaican slaves,
although the prevalence of absenteeism would account for much
of this lack of interest. In addition, rural areas were grossly over-
represented. In 1838, for example, the three members for Kingston represented 151 voters each, while members for three of the
country parishes represented less than ten voters each. Thus
the Assembly had a sprinkling of merchants and a few professional men but a majority of attorneys, overseers, and small
proprietors.[31]

Though the Assembly was the best political defense of the
planting class, there was a second line of defense in the institutions of the judiciary and in local government. In the judicial
establishment, a system of central courts duplicated the powers
of the English central courts. There was the Supreme Court,
sitting under a Chief Justice appointed by the Crown, and two
assistant Justices. Assize Courts had jurisdiction in the three
counties of the island, and there were courts of Chancery, Error,
Vice-Admiralty, and Common Pleas. The Governor had difficulty enough finding justices with legal training for the Assize
Courts, but in the magistracy, juries, and Vestries of the twenty-
one parishes, his control faded away and the planting class came
into its own. The Governor still had the power of appointment
to the local bench of Justices of the Peace, but the amateur
Justices were required to be residents of the parish. The Governor might revoke a Commission of the Peace for gross parti-
sanship or neglect of duty, but the dismissed Justice could be
replaced only by a man of "position." In the country districts
this necessarily meant another planter would be appointed.
Justices were often the same men as the electors to the House
of Assembly. They could, therefore, use their legislative power
to bolster their judicial power, and the Assembly kept trying,

in the face of executive opposition, to increase the jurisdictional competence of the Justices of the Peace and the administrative powers of the parish Vestry. This came to much the same thing, since the Justices were ex officio members of the Vestry in addition to their individual judicial powers and their greater joint judicial powers when meeting together in Quarter Sessions or as a Court of Common Pleas.[32]

The Vestry was also a more powerful body than its name implies. Meeting under the chairmanship of the chief magistrate, or Custos Rotulorum, of each parish, it was the organ of representative local government. It was made up of the Custos, the Justices, the Rector of the Church of England, and ten vestrymen elected annually by the freeholders of the parish. The Vestry assessed local rates and appropriated them for the upkeep of the jail, the roads, and other parish works.[33] Here was an organization made to order for planter control, and this control was relatively secure. While the Governor or the Colonial Office could block any attempt of the Assembly to grant additional powers to the Vestries, once an act was passed and approved, the sole power of initiative lay with the Assembly. Thus a governor unfriendly to the planting class faced legislative obstruction in the Assembly and administrative obstruction in the parishes.

In the last analysis, the only danger to planter control of the Assembly and the Vestries was a change in the constitution of the island or a widespread change in land ownership. The home government recognized the right of Jamaicans to legislate for themselves, always reserving the right of the Imperial Parliament to change or abolish the colonial constitution if necessary. The planters could use their political powers for a series of delaying actions, but they were always in danger of standing too firmly on an unpopular issue. If they were to do this, they might lose the right of self-government altogether.

*   *   *

This danger was recognized in Jamaica. As a result there grew up a series of claims and arguments denying the powers of the Imperial Parliament, except in matters touching the

Empire as a whole. The claims of the House of Assembly to the sole power of internal legislation for Jamaica had not been completely consistent, but there were a number of useful precedents. One of the most useful was a series of resolutions passed in 1815 and aimed at preventing an Imperial Act for the registration of slaves.

Resolved, that the inhabitants of this island have not had the liberty and privileges of electing and sending any knights and burgesses, or others, to represent them in the high court of Parliament, and explain the condition of their country, and ought not to be bounden by laws, or touched and grieved by subsidies, fees or penalties, enacted, granted and imposed without their assent, other than such external regulations in respect to commerce as are necessary for the commonweal of the empire.

Resolved, that the inhabitants of this island have always acknowledged the power and authority of Paliament to make all laws necessary for the general benefit of the empire, or affecting the whole subjects thereof; for regulating our external relations, navigation, trade and commerce, and have not been disposed captiously to raise difficulties about the exact limits between this constitutional jurisdiction and the right of internal legislation.[34]

These claims were not recognized by Great Britain, but they were repeated again and again by the supporters of the Assembly, and by the Assembly itself. They were built up by the island publicists into a rationalized argument for a measure of independenece from the mother country — the extremists coming very close to treason, the more moderate merely justifying the official position of the Assembly. The controversy has a familiar ring. Journalists, writers of resolutions, and pamphleteers went back over the ground that had been covered sixty years before by the North American colonists and would be covered again during the next twenty by the Canadians. Only the language of the Jamaicans, however, is closely parallel to the North American movements for self-government. The reality behind the language was actually much closer to the Southern states' use of states' rights as a device for protecting slavery.

As a political movement, Jamaican separatism reached a peak in the summer and early fall of 1831 — only a few months before a slave rebellion marked the beginning of the island revolution. The planting class were concerned at that particular time with the threat of Imperial legislation to force the amelioration of the slave regime, though they also sensed a heightened danger of actual emancipation by Imperial fiat. In consequence they went back for polemical ammunition to the Anglo-Saxon traditions of political liberty and the ideas of eighteenth-century liberalism.

In terms reminiscent of the American Revolution, they argued that the imperial regulation of their internal affairs infringed the "rights of Englishmen" — that it was equivalent to "taxation without representation." They claimed to be ". . . as fully entitled to make laws for their own government, by their own representatives, as the people of England by theirs," [35] and they recalled Magna Carta and the Bill of Rights in defense of their position.[36]

The legalistic argument was continued by making the regulation of slavery a question of the rights of property. It was claimed as an "axiom" of British government that the King could not deprive people of their property without indemnity. A public meeting in the parish of Manchester passed a resolution of protest, implying a contract of government.

. . . we cannot be considered contumacious if, in this our destitute situation, we pursue the most constitutional mode of requiring to be absolved from our allegiance to a government that considers us no longer worthy of its solicitude and regard, for it is inconsistent to expect that the subjects of any government can lose their property, and submit to their lives being endangered, and at the same time be bound by the duties of allegiance when the protection of their sovereign is withheld from them.[37]

This was, of course, based on the unstated assumption that imperial regulations to ameliorate slavery would bring about a slave revolt.

Another sort of argument that occurs in the Jamaican separatist literature alongside the "rights of Englishmen" and the "contract of government" is an appeal to the "law of nature." Again it was assumed that imperial policy was endangering the lives of the white Jamaicans. In self-defense they could appeal to a higher law than those binding Britain and Jamaica together.

If the present system of fraud, peculation, avarice, oppression, impolicy, injustice, is persisted in by the ministers, it is then that loyalty, which has hitherto been your hope, your guide, your heaven, must be banished from your hearts; and that you appeal to the Great God of the universe, who has taught you that self-preservation is the first law of nature.[38]

The Assembly itself never quite crossed the line between its traditional claims to autonomy in internal affairs and a claim to full sovereignty or the right to secede. In writing to Britain as Commissioners of Correspondence, however, it came very close to the latter position — basing its stand on the same higher law of self-preservation.

We profess and shall maintain the right of governing ourselves in such matters [as the amelioration of slavery], and the Ministerial project will be utterly disregarded here. . . We must however express our belief that your Government entertains a systematic design to compel us to manumize or abandon our Slaves by making their maintenance a burthen to us; and if this belief is well founded, we must look to other sources for our preservation.[39]

Statements of this sort from official sources were coupled with an undercurrent of talk about the possibility of armed rebellion against England. Both seem to contradict the attitude of respect for England and the longing to return that were also common among the planters of this period. The attitude of the white Jamaicans was indeed contradictory on this score. They disliked Jamaica and considered it their place of exile, but as the pressure for emancipation increased they were also attracted by the possibility of separation from Britain — perhaps with the aid of a foreign power, most likely the United States. The movement for political separatism, however, had no emotional basis in love of Jamaica — its only basis was fear of what might happen as the humanitarians gained power in England. When the anonymous author of "The Exile" tried to whip up patriotic enthusiasm, his failure showed the contradictions of the separatist position.

> I love thee Jamaica, reviled as thou art,
> By a faction forgetful of all that is just,
> Who seek by detraction's most cowardly dart
>   To lay all thy glories low prostrate in dust.

Their object ever
This isle to sever
From the loyalty most in this life we hold dear,
And create a flood
Of their brethren's blood.
When Britain stood lonely with victory contending,
She grateful acknowledged the succour you gave,
And she dare not deny, when your rights you're defending,
You Britons were born, and as Britons behave.[40]

The author's chief complaint is not against Britain, but against the "faction" of humanitarians who are forcing Jamaicans away from their true British loyalty by endangering the Jamaican social structure. The "Jamaica" that is loved in the poem is not the island — not, at least, as a homeland — it is the opportunity to live on the island so as to return eventually to the real "home." There is no praise in this literature of Jamaica or colonial life, or even of the colonial social order. The planting class had given up defending slavery, but they insisted on the political freedom to abolish it in their own good time.

The result was a movement with no emotional basis beyond a false nationalism that ran counter to the stronger attachment to England. It was separatism out of fear and social necessity alone. In this way the status of real nationalism in Jamaica became paradoxical. The white caste, who felt alien and had no love of the country, were the political separatists. The colored class, who were in the process of developing a more genuine national feeling, were to be among the strongest supporters of the British government.

Partly because it lacked a basis in sentiment, partly because it met opposition within Jamaica, and partly because it could never have the support of the absentee owners of the land, the Jamaican separatist movement of the early 1830's never carried words into action. Before 1833 it had been tried and discarded. It had important side effects, however, in strengthening the constitutional claims of the Assembly. It left a heritage of political ideas, even though the separatist movement did not reappear in strength after emancipation. The strongest remnant was the determination to uphold the constitutional autonomy of the island, and the idealogical basis of this determination continued

to be political liberalism. These political tendencies were only
the most unexpected of the many by-products of the prerevolutionary opposition to the British humanitarians.

*   *   *

In 1831 the Jamaicans stood on the brink of revolution, and
they knew where they stood. The white caste had considered
its position, assessed its strength, and examined its weakness.
The process of reaction to British demands and arguments led
to the development of a particular set of ideas about society,
about religion, and about politics.

The white Jamaicans had lost confidence in the moral value
of slavery as a social institution, but they had strengthened their
defense against emancipation in both political ideas and political institutions. As a by-product, religion had become a focus
of class and race conflict. Beginning with a rising of the slaves
in December 1831, the Jamaicans were faced with the necessity
of making rapid adjustments to a constantly changing situation.
These adjustments were made against the background of preconceptions built up during the last years of the slave regime.

V

The Jamaican Revolution

1831-1839

REVOLUTIONS ARE FREQUENTLY SUMMAR-
IZED in one outstanding document which proclaims the intentions of the revolutionaries. For the American Revolution there
is the Declaration of Independence; for the French, the Declaration of the Rights of Man and the Citizen. There is also a document for the Jamaican Revolution of the 1830's — "An Act for
the Abolition of Slavery throughout the British Colonies; for
promoting the Industry of the Manumitted Slaves; and for compensating the persons hitherto entitled to the Services of Such
Slaves," 3 and 4 Wm. IV, c. 73. This document, however, was
more than an epitome of the Jamaican revolution. In one very
real sense it *was* the revolution — an act of the Imperial Parliament overthrowing the old social order in the West Indian
colonies and laying the basis for a new one. It forced drastic
social change on Jamaica, and it forced this change through the
power of the imperial government rather than through a revolutionary party within the colony.

In another sense, however, the Jamaican revolution was something more than an enactment from overseas — it was also a
process within the country itself. While the emancipation act
was forced on Jamaica, it was not forced on unwilling, but un-
resisting, slaveowners, as the slaves waited meekly on the side
lines for deliverance. The official date of Jamaican emancipation, August 1, 1834, has real meaning as an epoch-making date
in Jamaican history, but its meaning is only slightly different

from that of July 4, 1776 or July 14, 1789. All three are only
the most decisive and convenient dates in a period filled with
complex and rapid change — merely symbolic time markers,
useful for fixing the end of one era and the beginning of another. In Jamaica, as in France or North America, the period
of revolution was almost a decade, and the revolutionary decade
itself was preceded by a long period of preparation and followed
by an equally long period of adjustment.

The revolution moved through a series of stages — each a
period of forward movement followed by a reaction — till at
last a new situation of relative stability was reached. There were
three such stages. The first began in December 1831 with the
revolt of the slaves in the western parishes and was followed by
a wave of repression and reaction against the blacks, the missionaries, and the people of color. The second was the British-
originated emancipation act of 1833, which abolished slavery
and established a state of half-slavery, the Negroes serving their
former masters as "apprentices." This time the reaction took
the form of obstruction in the Jamaican Assembly and on the
estates, ultimately bringing the failure of the apprenticeship
system and its premature end in 1838. The third stage was of
the utmost importance for Jamaica; but it took place almost
entirely in Britain and was political rather than social. It was
the attempt in 1838 and 1839 to alter the Jamaican constitution
and deprive the planting class of political control over the newly
liberated Negroes. This movement failed. The planters emerged
with an alterd social organization, but they kept political control
over the island.[1]

*   *   *

By 1831 a potential revolution had been growing for many
years, both in Britain and in Jamaica. The slaves' old desire for
freedom and the habit of rebellion were still strong, and the
chance of success was steadily greater as the Negroes adjusted
to the New World and were better informed about the white
society above them. During the early decades of the century,
slavery became less harsh, and, as his position improved, the
slave could see the possibility of still more improvement. His

ROBERT OSBORN　　　　　GEORGE WILLIAM GORDON

EDWARD JORDON

FALMOUTH COURTHOUSE

MORANT BAY COURTHOUSE

THE ESTATE

THE SETTLEMENT

part-time work on his own provision ground was an immediate alternative to the rigors of estate work, if only estate work could be avoided. As he became more settled in Jamaica, cadres of religious organization and resources of leadership made a concerted rising easier. During the same years, the reform movement and humanitarianism had been growing in Britain. As these movements developed, it was only a matter of time until the planters would face a severe crisis from without, as well as one from within their society.

By an odd quirk of history, it was the July Revolution of 1830, in France, that set off the chain of events leading to revolution in Jamaica. From the rising of Paris a contagion of rioting spread to England. It was reflected in a stronger reform movement in Parliament, and in November 1830 the Tory, Wellington government resigned and was replaced by a new coalition pledged to Parliamentary reform.[2] In Britain popular demand for reform was simultaneous with a renewed drive for slave emancipation. The two movements reinforced each other, and both derived support from the revolutions sweeping the Continent. Even before Parliamentary reform was accomplished, the Whig government began to work for the more drastic regulation of slavery throughout the Empire.[3]

It was the new effort at amelioration that so disturbed the white Jamaicans in the summer of 1831 and brought about the separatist movement with its series of parish meetings, protests against the infringement of Jamaican rights, and talk of breaking away from Great Britain and joining the United States. The ruling class began to worry and to talk much more openly than before of the dangers of emancipation and various possible means of avoiding it. Much of this was, to say the least, injudicious. The planters made no attempt to keep their plans secret. They even allowed slaves to attend the protest meetings, if they merely listened quietly. The island press was full of violent threats and proposals of all sorts, but if the excitement was communicated to the Negroes, the planters were not alone at fault. Missionaries also realized that emancipation was going forward in Britain, and some, at least, kept their congregations fully informed about it.[4]

Through all these channels, the slaves learned that friends in

England were working for their freedom and were strongly opposed by the local planting class. There was a change of temper
in the summer of 1831. More slaves ran away than usual, and
bookkeepers and overseers reported hearing more talk of freedom among the Negroes.[5] A few days before Christmas there
was an even more inauspicious incident. A driver at Salt Spring
estate, near Montego Bay, refused to administer punishment.
Then came the Christmas holiday, a dangerous period under
normal circumstances, with a legal holiday on Christmas and
the following two days. As usual the militia were called out and
stood by to keep order. The slaves were to be back at work on
Wednesday, December 28. On Tuesday night, December 27,
watchers in Montego Bay saw the buildings of Kensington
Estate burst into flames, followed by the firing of other estates
in the hills behind the town. This was the beginning of the
revolt — the sight that planters had dreaded for years, with an
exaggerated terror strengthened by stories of Haiti.[6]

Though militia was on hand, it was stationed in the coastal
towns where many of the planters had also come for protection
during the holiday. Only the Western Interior Regiment, about
250 white planters under Col. Grignon, an attorney, had an
inland post on the Montego Bay to Savanna-la-Mar road near
the junction of the three parishes of St. James, Westmoreland,
and Hanover. On December 28, Grignon retreated part way to
Montego Bay, reinforced in the meantime by a company of
colored militia. That night he fought a light engagement against
a Negro attack, which was completely routed. Grignon, however, continued his retreat to the Bay and left the entire interior
to the blacks.[7]

The Earl of Belmore, Governor of Jamaica, immediately declared martial law and dispatched reinforcements and regular
troops to Montego Bay. The troops arrived on January 1, 1832,
and the reoccupation of the inland areas began. Contrary to
the original fears of the planters, the revolt had not spread
beyond the four western parishes, and there was no organized
attack on the towns. An amnesty proclamation was issued for
those who surrendered without being implicated in murder or
arson. After this, there were only a few flurries of organized
resistance.[8]

Except for the burning of estates, there had been relatively little violence by the Negroes. This was not so of the reoccupation. The militia, especially, took advantage of the opportunity to release some of its pent up fear of servile war. The repression was bloody, with violations of the amnesty proclamation and many executions by courts-martial on very little evidence.[9] In the final accounting, about a dozen whites had been killed and 160 properties burned, though often only the dried cane in the trash house was fired. Even in the disturbed area, there were some estates where the Negroes had remained quiet and no damage was done. On the other side, about four hundred Negroes were killed during the military operations and another hundred executed following the courts-martial.[10]

The Negro side of the rising is much less clear than the white military operations that crushed it. The only evidence is that of Negro leaders who were induced to confess before they were hanged, and the white person recording the confession often slanted the report to support his own theory about the revolt — missionaries blaming the intemperate talk of the white planters, the planters blaming the missionary influence. In some instances there were two or more contradictory confessions from the same rebel leader.[11]

In spite of confused evidence, at least a general pattern is clear. The rebellion was not the work of one organization, but a combination of different movements under separate leadership — each group rising separately once it was clear that Negroes elsewhere were rebelling. Throughout the disturbed area Negroes believed that the King had freed the slaves and the royal troops would not fight. To secure freedom the planters' militia, but only the militia, would have to be beaten in the field.

The best reported of the individual plots, and perhaps the one that sparked the whole movement, was an organization formed in the summer or fall of 1831 by Samuel Sharp, a slave in Montego Bay and a class-leader in Rev. Thomas Burchell's congregation. Intelligent and literate, Sharp was disturbed by the fear that the planters might prevent emancipation. He either believed, or told others he believed, that the "free paper" had been issued by the King in the spring, and the whites had been keeping it back. During the fall of 1831 he made several trips to the estates in upper St. James, meeting with the drivers and Baptist class-leaders. The burden of leadership fell on these two groups, although the same individual was often both leader and driver. Working through these men, Sharp planned a strike for the day after the Christmas holiday. According to plan, a driver was to go to the "busha," or overseer, on each estate and simply tell him the slaves would not work. The bushas were to be kept on the estate till they promised to pay wages for further work. In effect, Sharp had detached the Baptist missionary organization from the white missionaries and was using it as a European trade union leader used the combined bargaining power of the workers.[12]

The firing of the estates disrupted the strike the evening before its execution. This effectively killed whatever slight chance there may have been for a nonviolent movement against slavery. From then on rebellion and repression took their course. The first fires may have been accidental or set by a slave who had had too much to drink, but more likely they were the work of a separate organization. In coastal St. James to the north and east of Montego Bay the rebel organization seemed to be under the control of Native Baptists, rather than Sharp's official Baptists; and in the further interior was the shadowy figure of "Daddy Ruler" Tharp, still another leader of rebels, from his title either a Native Baptist or a myal man.[13] In any event, all parts of the rising were so strongly under the influence of Native or official Baptist class organization that the rebellion was, in fact, what the Negroes called it — "the Baptist War."[14]

*　　　　*　　　　*

The Baptist War was important far beyond the immediate danger that the Negroes might temporarily seize part of the island. This threat was actually slight. The Negro organization was weak, firearms were few, there was no agreement about objectives, and the basic misconception that the King's troops would not fight was soon dispelled. A more important result was the reaction of the white Jamaicans, and, like the black revolt, the white counter-movement was organized on a religious basis, masking real objectives that were political and social as well.

From the first sight of the burning estates, the white inhabitants of Montego Bay and other towns near the disturbed area took the revolt to be what they had long predicted — a rising brought on by the dissenting missionaries, the allies of the blacks and the friends of the humanitarians. William Knibb and two other Baptist missionaries were arrested in Montego Bay but later released. William Burchell was also apprehended as a conspirator, when his ship arrived from England in early January. Elsewhere on the island missionaries were arrested in a flurry of panic; but only two were ever brought to trial, and both were acquitted.[15]

Even though most of the arrested missionaries were soon freed, this was only the beginning of their difficulties. The *Courant* of January 6 expressed the opinion of most white Jamaicans.

Shooting is . . . too honourable a death for men whose conduct has occasioned so much bloodshed, and the loss of so much property. There are fine hanging woods in St. James and Trelawney, and we do sincerely hope, that the bodies of all the Methodist preachers who may be convicted of sedition, may diversify the scene.[16]

While martial law lasted, there was little danger of white Jamaicans taking the law into their own hands, but after February 5 they again had the protection of Jamaican courts and Jamaican juries. Toward the end of January the anti-missionary reaction gained an organizational base through the formation of the Colonial Church Union. The movement was begun in St. Ann's Bay by Rev. George Wilson Bridges and a member of the Assembly from St. Ann. Working through the cadres of the militia, it spread into other parishes. By the summer of 1832 there were branches throughout the colony. The only important place in which the Union failed to gain a foothold was the city of Kingston.

As the name suggests, the Colonial Church Union was to operate behind a religious façade, officially dedicated to defending the doctrines of the Church of England. Actually it was a planters' organization, aimed at creating a more effective framework for the whole range of planters' objectives. The first of these was the expulsion of dissenting missionaries from the country. This was indeed a religious aim, but the Union also followed the line of the old Jamaica clergy in opposing the episcopal organization and the Church Missionary Society.[17] The first overt action to which the Union turned its hand was a program of chapel-wrecking. Especially in the months of February and March 1832, ex-militiamen and Unionists wrecked, burned, or dismantled more than seventeen chapels, mostly Wesleyan and Baptist. They also attacked private houses sheltering missionaries and intimidated dissenters by violence and threats of violence. Many missionaries were driven into Kingston for safety, and Knibb and Burchell left the island for a time — partly as a precaution, but also to arouse public sentiment in England.[18]

In the meantime, other elements of the planter reaction helped the missionaries' case against the Church Union. There was a concerted tightening of slave discipline, especially in religious matters. The planters not only tried to prevent further missionary work but also to root out evangelical Christianity among the slaves. This brought them onto especially dangerous ground, since, in British eyes, they were guilty of using their power as slaveholders for religious persecution.[19]

Still more serious opposition was aroused among the colored class, who had served loyally in the militia during the slave revolt but were unwilling to go further. The large colored population of Kingston prevented Church Union violence there, and in other towns the colored people helped to protect missionaries from the white mobs. Occasionally these conflicts took on the more serious aspect of a combined racial and religious riot. It was not simply the fact that many colored people were dissenters. The Unionist attacks included raids on Jewish and colored merchants who were not, and the religious conflict broadened into a general struggle over separatism, humanitarianism, and the old rivalry between town and country.[20]

Through the first half of 1832 the crisis deepened, while the Earl of Belmore's government remained inactive and the colored people became more alarmed than ever in the fear that the planters' separatist movement might succeed.[21] In April,

Edward Jordon, most prominent of the colored leaders, was indicted for "constructive treason" on account of an antislavery article in his newspaper, *The Watchman*. If he had been convicted it might well have touched off a white-colored racial war.[22] He was acquitted, but the tension continued to build up through the summer months, as the colored people organized to oppose the Church Union. In late summer the situation relaxed somewhat with the arrival of Lord Mulgrave, a new and stronger Governor who definitely aligned himself on the side of the colored men against the Unionists. The Chuch Union was greatly weakened in the fall, when Mulgrave began a policy of removing Unionist militia officers and magistrates from office. Some elements of the Union organization dragged on into late 1833, but its real power was broken when a royal proclamation was obtained early in the year declaring it an "illegal association."[23]

By the summer of 1833 the first phase of the Jamaican revolution had run its course — ending, apparently, in a stalemate. The slave revolt was defeated, and the planters' counterrevolution had also failed; but the stalemate was more apparent than real. The slave revolt impressed Britons and Jamaicans alike with the difficulty of keeping a people subject against its will. The failure of the Colonial Church Union ended overt Jamaican resistance to emancipation. The bitter-enders of the proslavery party had made a stand and found the combined opposition of the colored class and the British government too much for them. Their defeat was so clear that there was no longer any danger of armed opposition to a British act of emancipation. Finally, the planters in their reaction had lost any advantage the slave revolt might have given them in British opinion. So far as Jamaica was concerned, the most decisive battle for emancipation had been fought and won.

*   *   *

While the first phase of rebellion and reaction were taking place in Jamaica, Britain herself passed through a period of political crisis, emerging early in 1833 with a new Parliament, elected on a broader suffrage and thus representing more middle-class dissenters and evangelicals. At the same time, the West India interest had lost public support because prominent absentees had associated themselves with the opposition to Parliamentary reform. Conditions in Britain were more favorable to emancipation than ever before. In January 1833 the cabinet decided that the slaves should be freed. The majority of Parliament would support this action. The only question was the form emancipation should take.

This was a ticklish question. If the English had convinced the Jamaicans that slavery was morally wrong, the proslavery arguments of the West Indians had also convinced the English that outright emancipation was not only dangerous to the public peace of the islands but would spell the end of the plantation system. In the various plans for emancipation, it was generally assumed that the Negro would not work for wages without coercion. The essential problem of the planners, therefore, was to devise a plan of emancipation that would both end slavery and preserve the estates.

The first Colonial Office plan was formulated as early as 1831 by Lord Howick (afterward 3rd Earl Grey), then Under-Secretary for the Colonies. He tried to meet the Jamaican objection that free Negroes would not work for low wages because of the large amounts of unappropriated land in the colony — an objection that received special attention just then through the popularity of E. Gibbon Wakefield's work on Australian land problems. Howick's scheme would impose a high tax on all cultivated land not previously used for sugar cane. This, it was hoped, would force Negroes to work on the estates for wages, rather than on their own provision grounds. The plan was ingenious, but it was discarded by the Cabinet after Lord Mulgrave in Jamaica pointed out the utter impossibility of enforcing such a law in that colony.[24]

A second and very elaborate plan was the work of Henry Taylor of the permanent Colonial Office staff. Taylor aimed at education, rather than control, so that the free laborer would acquire habits of "self-command and voluntary industry." The Negro would thus be "saved from a life of savage sloth and the planter from ruin." [25] According to this plan, the government would buy the slave two days' freedom each week. By working

these two days for wages, the slave could gradually buy full freedom, one day at a time — the whole process taking an able-
bodied Negro about three years. This scheme was open to the
obvious objection that it penalized unfairly the old, the young,
and the weak, who might never be able to buy their freedom.
In the end it died in the Colonial Office through the opposition
of Lord Howick.[26]

Though neither of these plans was put into effect, they are
important as roads not traveled at a crucial turning. They also
indicate the direction of Colonial Office thinking about the
future role of the free Negro in the West Indies. Both Howick
and Taylor were to have an important place in formulating
West Indian policy, and they continued to see the problem of
the free West Indies in the same light as they had seen the problem of emancipation. In later years they still thought of the
deficiency of plantation labor as the chief problem barring the
way to their principal objective — the prosperity of the plantation system.

The plan of emancipation finally adopted was originally the
idea of Edward Stanley (afterward Earl of Derby), who came
to the Colonial Office in March 1833. It was similar to Taylor's
plan in its chief objective — training the slaves to plantation
work, rather than using controls to see that they did nothing
else. The slaves were to be legally free from August 1, 1834, but
to work as "apprentices" to their former masters three-quarters
of each week. In Parliament the plan was at first opposed by
both the West India interest and the abolitionists, but a modi-
fied version put into the emancipation bill by James Stephen
of the Colonial Office was more acceptable. The bill was finally
passed into law on August 28, 1833.[27]

The final version laid down general principles for emancipation, to be enforced by local legislation in each colony. Twenty
million pounds compensation was voted to the former slaveowners, to be paid only after the colony had passed an acceptable local act of emancipation. All children under six years of
age were immediately freed, unless destitute or uncared for by
their parents. Other slaves were legally free, but apprenticed
part-time to their former masters. Praedial, or field, slaves in
Jamaica were to serve forty and one-half hours each week until

August 1, 1840. Non-praedial, or household, slaves were to serve full-time, but only until August 1, 1838. The act also provided for compulsory manumission, at a judicially determined price, in case an apprentice wanted to buy his full freedom. The administration of the system was given to a corps of Special Magistrates, recruited from outside the planting class and paid by Great Britain. These men were to guarantee fair play on both sides.[28]

Whatever merit the plan may have had as a piece of social machinery, it was badly vitiated by the fact that enabling legislation was left to the Assembly of Jamaica. Neither the aims nor the methods of the Jamaican ruling class were those of the British humanitarians, yet the vast field of new and necessary legislation was left to the Jamaicans. Not only the emancipation act and two Acts-in-Aid but new police, vagrancy, and judicial legislation were needed to meet the changed condition of society. The Colonial Office kept a close watch over this legislation as it was sent to Britain for approval, but the Colonial Office was also anxious to have the coöperation of the colonists in establishing a free-labor society. The success of the emancipation act depended very largely, therefore, on the attitude of those Jamaicans with political power.

The first reaction of the white Jamaicans was apprehension for the future of the island, but it took the form of foot-dragging acceptance of the apprenticeship system rather than open opposition.[29] As the day of emancipation approached, there was bitterness and pessimism. The *Jamaica Despatch* carried a black border on its issue of July 31, and there was a great deal of muttered foreboding; but the general reaction was to keep within the letter of the law and make the best of apprenticeship as long as it might last. As a leader in the *Kingston Commercial Advertizer* put it:

The fate of the colony is now sealed, whether it be good or evil . . . Prudence, self-preservation, and expediency, loudly proclaim the necessity of employing means for rendering the changes now recognized and legalized by the Legislature of Jamaica conducive to the public good. A great duty lies before us, which is to rightly inform the negro mind, and prepare him for performing those duties to himself, his neighbour, his master and the country, so essential to the welfare of all, and to the peace and happiness of society.[30]

What the white Jamaicans took to be the proper method for "informing the negro mind" was already evident when the first set of enabling legislation was passed in December 1833. Several measures were too coercive to meet the approval of the Colonial Office; but the Jamaican version of the Emancipation Act was accepted, though many felt that it barely conformed to the letter of the Imperial act — and not at all to the spirit.[31]

It was felt that some allowance could be made, since enforcement would be in the hands of Special Magistrates, not the Jamaican overseers or the local Justices of the Peace, but it is unlikely that any group of men could have fulfilled the assignment of the special magistracy. Their job was to stand between the former masters and the former slaves and provide a basis for mutual confidence and understanding that would last beyond the period of apprenticeship. But the Special Magistrates were underpaid, overworked, and badly recruited — often having little understanding of the law or of West Indian conditions. Many accepted the facts of Jamaican life — their job was almost unbearable without the friendship of the local overseers, and the price of that friendship was to become a "planter's friend," enforcing on the apprentices the punishments planters could no longer apply directly. Others resigned and went home, giving up hope of fair enforcement in the face of local enmity. Some, however, stayed on and did their best. In the end the Special Magistrates succeeded at least in keping some sugar production without, at the same time, causing a new servile revolt, but the animosity between planter and Negro was stronger at the end of apprenticeship than it had been under slavery.[32]

In this phase of the Jamaican revolution, the planters' reaction took place in two fields of obstruction — the Assembly and the individual estate. Lord Sligo arrived in the summer of 1834 as the new Governor who was to administer the apprenticeship system. Almost immediately, he came into conflict with the Assembly, and this developed into a running fight that lasted to the end of his stay on the island. The conflict covered a whole range of issues connected with the enforcement of apprenticeship — many of them only petty questions of legislative privilege — but added together they became an issue of great importance. Sligo was determined to have a liberal enforcement of the act of emancipation. The Assembly was equally determined that enforcement should be coercive and directed from within Jamaica. The result was a constant harassment of the Special Magistrates — the Assembly continually trying to move all possible power to the hands of the regular Justices of the Peace, the Vestries, or the Assembly itself. It ended in the summer of 1836 with Sligo's resignation and a partial victory for the Assembly.[33]

On the estates the most common form of obstruction was to impose petty annoyances on the apprentices, even though the letter of the emancipation act was not violated. The law provided that the usual legal allowances of food and clothing be continued for the apprentices, but it said nothing about the "customary indulgences," like the weekly issue of salt fish, which were often stopped as soon as official slavery ended. This practice may have saved a little money for the proprietor, but it also embittered the apprentices. A similar difficulty arose over the distribution of working hours. In the first years of apprenticeship, most estates worked five eight-hour days, rather than four and a half nine-hour days. The five-day week was a little more convenient for the estate; but it was also a source of rancor for the Negroes, who needed to work in their provision grounds Friday afternoon to prepare for the Saturday market.[34]

More serious still, though not so general, were the illegal abuses that crept into the system. Many overseers tried to keep the special magistrates from visiting estates to hear the grievances of the apprentices. Others continued to punish the apprentices without going through the legal form of calling on the Special Magistrate. Even when the magistrate was called in, there was a way of avoiding the intention of the law. Whipping had been abolished as a part of labor discipline, being replaced by a period in the parish workhouse. The workhouse, however, was controlled by the Vestry, rather than the Special Magistrates. Thus the flogging that had been abolished on the estates reappeared as a regular part of workhouse discipline.[35]

These abuses became more serious and more common as time

passed. There was a mounting chorus of protest from British humanitarians as more and more information came back from the West Indies. Sir Lionel Smith, Sligo's successor, had a continually harder time protecting the apprentices and keeping the Assembly under control. Finally, toward the end of 1837, both Smith and the Colonial Office agreed that the apprenticeship system must be corrected by imperial action. They had strong backing from British public opinion — a series of especially damaging accounts of the Jamaican apprenticeship system having been published and widely read in 1837. For lack of a new policy, the ministry obtained an amended imperial act of emancipation in April 1838, designed to remedy the abuses of the old act and especially those practiced in Jamaica.[36]

This news reached Jamaica just as apprehension was again rising with the approach of August 1, the date when non-praedial workers would be completely free. With four years' experience of apprenticeship, the Jamaican planters had gained faith in the possibility of continuing estate production without slavery — if only they were left to manage their own affairs in their own way. Thus they were willing to make a sacrifice to preserve their constitutional autonomy. Rather than accept British dictation, the Assembly abolished the apprenticeship system altogether and freed praedials as well as non-praedials on August 1, 1838.[37]

This act closed the second phase of the Jamaican revolution. What had begun as a humanitarian experiment in training the former slave to work for wages, ended as a system of coercion almost as brutal as slavery itself. But, even though the relations between masters and apprentices had deteriorated, the transition to freedom was made without further bloodshed. The British humanitarians had won their victory — they had abolished slavery — but the victory was incomplete so long as the white and colored minority remained in political control of the island.

*   *   *

It was the third phase of the revolution that settled the political future of Jamaica. In a sense, it hardly deserves recognition as a separate step. The revolution had already gone as far as it would go, but the long conflict between the Assembly and the Crown officials followed by the sudden end of apprenticeship prepared the ground for the final crisis and the political victory of the planting class.

The end of apprenticeship stopped one controversy between the Assembly and the Colonial Office, but the basic issues concerned in the struggle were undecided. The Jamaican ruling class and the Colonial Office had very different ideas about the future of the Negro. He was no longer a slave, but his freedom had still to be limited and protected. He had to be educated and directed toward a new way of life. The questions remained — directed toward what? educated by whom? In the last analysis the answer rested with the British Parliament, which had to decide whether to respect the Jamaican constitutional claims or to protect the national investment in compensation money. This decision, even more than the apprenticeship system, was to set the future course for Jamaica.

The Assembly of Jamaica left no doubt of its own stand. When it abolished apprenticeship, it issued one of its strongest constitutional claims. In form the protest was merely a restatement of the old position.

. . . that this island has of right confirmed by time, usage, and law, an independent legislature; that, by its authority alone, can taxes and other burthens be imposed on the people of Jamaica, or its laws, when once sanctioned by the Sovereign, be repealed, or altered, or new laws be enacted.[38]

But this time the language was even more violent than usual. The Assembly derided the House of Commons for the poor quality of its legislation and went on to spell out a threat of further action.

We will also acknowledge that they [the House of Commons] can seize by force on the powers which they do not possess in law or reason; but there cannot be two legislatures in one state. If the Britsh Parliament is to make laws for Jamaica, it must exercise that prerogative without a partner. The freeholders of Jamaica will not send representatives to a mock assembly, nor will representatives be found to accept a service so docked and crippled. The popular branch of the legislature will cease to exist, and if any taxes are demanded, they must be levied at the point of a sword.[39]

The Assembly had only to wait till its next meeting, in October 1838, to carry out its threat. In September an Imperial act for the regulation of West Indian prisons was proclaimed in Jamaica. On October 31 the Assembly passed a series of resolutions reasserting its claims and refusing to do business unless the offending act were removed. The Governor, Sir Lionel Smith, prorogued and then dissolved the Assembly, but a new Assembly meeting in December stood by the resolutions of its predecessor.[40]

Perhaps through the political astuteness of William Burge, or perhaps only through chance, the issue was drawn on a point calculated to embarrass the Melbourne Government. The Colonial Office pointed out that the constitutional issue was merely a smokescreen hiding the duty of Britain to protect and guide the West Indian freedmen. Given a choice between yielding control to the white Jamaicans or calling their bluff, the Cabinet chose to call. A bill was brought into the Parliament suspending the constitution of Jamaica for five years. At this point British politics entered the picture. Melbourne's majority included a Radical wing, who, though supporters of emancipation, were even stronger supporters of constitutional liberty. When the Jamaica bill came to a vote in May 1839, ten Radicals voted with the opposition, reducing Melbourne's majority and forcing his resignation.[41]

British politics intervened again, however, when the young Queen refused to dismiss her Whig Ladies of the Bedchamber. Peel, the Conservative leader, refused to form a Cabinet. As a result of the "bedchamber crisis" Melbourne came back into office. This time, he could not hope to carry the full Jamaica bill. Instead he introduced a new bill, which passed in July, making temporary provision for the government of Jamaica but restoring the old powers to the Assembly. Coercion having failed, the only alternative left the Government was conciliation. In September 1839, Sir Charles Metcalfe arrived in Jamaica to carry out the new policy of conciliating the entrenched planters whose powers could not be taken from them.[42]

* * *

Between the revolt of the slaves in December 1831 and the beginning of the Metcalfe government in September 1839 there had been a genuine revolution in Jamaica, but it was an anomaly among revolutions. The victorious party within the country had been successful, mainly through outside help, in achieving a sweeping social change. The majority of Jamaicans moved from the position of slaves with few legal rights to that of full cititzenship in the community — with no legal bars on account of color, enjoying the full civil and political rights of the white planters themselves. But the political power that enforced the revolution was withdrawn. Control remained with the same small ruling class of white and colored Jamaicans who had exercised it in the last days of slavery. In effect, the British humanitarians had mustered enough political strength to put through the emancipation act, only to lose at the very end the extent of power necessary to keep a guiding hand on the new social order. The Colonial Office still sent out Governors and influenced some aspects of policy, but, partly because there was no clear idea in London of what policy to follow, the Jamaicans were left to hammer out their own future within wide limits allowed them by the home government.

PART II

THE ROAD TO MORANT BAY
1834-1865

VI

The Two Economies
and the Two Jamaicas

HAVING WON THE FINAL POLITICAL PHASE
of the Jamaican revolution, the ruling minority found itself in
control of a revolution it had not made and did not want. The
Assembly and its supporters in England had shut out the Colonial Office from the detailed management of the emancipated
society, even though the Crown's power of disallowance still
prevented open reaction. The white Jamaicans had thus assigned themselves the job they said was impossible — the management of a tropical, staple-producing economy under a system
of free labor. For twenty-seven years after final emancipation,
the ruling minority worked at making the "free system" a success, as they understood success. Year by year the failure became
more evident. Finally in 1865 there was a new Negro rising at
Morant Bay and another bloody repression like that of 1832.
In 1866 the Assembly admitted defeat and resigned its powers
to the Crown.

This surrender marked the end of the post-emancipation
epoch. It marked the failure of the European and the African
Jamaica, formed as they were by the environment of slavery,
to adjust to the new conditions created by the revolution of
the thirties and the new position of Jamaica in the world at
large. The following chapters will examine the role of ideas in
the different aspects of Jamaican history after emancipation,

especially the interplay of ideas and action that helped lead Jamaicans down the road to Morant Bay.

Obviously neither the European nor the African Jamaicans recognized their problem as an intellectual one, since neither group was given to setting its problems on a theoretical basis. What confronted the planter on the estate or his representative in the Assembly was the necessity of making a series of *ad hoc* decisions in answer to an enormous number of new questions. Furthermore, these were not questions that could be answered on the basis of habit or past experience. They grew directly from the new situation created by the revolution, and answers appropriate to the slave regime would not do — especially since the Colonial Office and British opinion held ultimate political power and stood firmly against any overt return to slavery. The former slave was in a similar position — he had to decide what to do with his freedom, now that he had it — and his decision-making was still less self-conscious than that of the planter.

For the European Jamaican, the intellectual problem in its broadest setting was to find a viable set of ideas to explain the proper working of a free-labor tropical society. It was not necessary for these ideas to be consciously held, nor was it necessary that they be a single interdependent "system" of thought. But the Jamaicans needed to act correctly in a new situation, and for correct action they needed at least a tacit understanding of their aims and a slightly more explicit understanding of how these aims were to be achieved. From emancipation onward, therefore, the European Jamaicans began to try to explain their position and to search for a solution to their problems. Some of their ideas are only implied by their actions, but more often they argued for one course of action rather than another and thus set their ideas in a rational framework. Though these ideas can hardly be glorified by the name of "theory," they were an expression of what Jamaicans wanted to do, and often of why they wanted to do it.

In the end European Jamaica failed to solve its problems, and, as we shall see, the failure was partly intellectual. But if this failure came about because the ideas of the ruling class were not adequate, in execution, to the problems they should have solved, the Jamaicans are excused in part by the difficulty

of their situation. The white Jamaicans' belief in the justice of
the old regime had been slight — so slight that the revolution
was accepted with a kind of grudging tolerance. But if the
Jamaicans had shown little confidence in the slave society, they
had none at all in the new regime of free labor. Nor had the
humanitarians, originally the authors of the revolution, any
ideas that could be borrowed. For them, emancipation was a
moral duty. They had done their duty and now they were finished. Their only continuing interest was to prevent a relapse
into slavery. The ex-slaves were ultimately to show what they
wanted with their freedom, but this was of no help to the
planting class.

Thus Jamaicans of the ruling class had only two readily available sources of ideas, neither of which really fit the situation in
which they found themselves. One source was in the ideas and
the example of contemporary Great Britain and the Empire.
The mother country was indeed a free-labor society with an
economic order that might be copied in Jamaica, but the British situation was otherwise very different. British thought in all
fields was principally oriented toward an explanation of British
society and a solution of British problems. These problems were
those of a temperate country entering a period of political democracy, economic growth, urbanization, and industrialization.
Ideas designed to solve them could hardly be helpful to a declining planting society in the tropics.

The other source was the body of Jamaican beliefs, attitudes,
sentiments, and emotional reactions that had been built up under slavery. A direct return to slavery was, of course, impossible, but the old regime was the only kind of tropical society
within the experience of most Jamaicans. One tendency, therefore, in the reconstruction of a new tropical society was to build
on the model of the old with the single omission of slavery. Another important part of the Jamaican intellectual heritage was
the group of ideas developed as a part of the defense against
revolution. These ideas included, as we have seen, certain tendencies of political and social thought, and, most important of all,
they included certain predictions of the situation that would
result from emancipation. The Jamaican ruling class was therefore partly prepared by its own intellectual background to meet

its new problems, though most of that background was com-pletely inappropriate to the new era.

Since these two sources were all that were available, it was from these that the Jamaicans borrowed in their attempt to lay the foundations for a new society. The very inappropriateness of these sources, however, made direct borrowing difficult. Sug-gestions from their source had to be transformed into theories or projects directly applicable to the new status of the island. As time passed there was also an opportunity for new solutions by trial and error, and for new thought by Jamaicans, based on their own experience. But, as the older problems were solved, the passage of time brought new ones and made big problems out of little ones. Most important, it brought major economic changes and with them new relationships between the African and the European Jamaica.

*   *   *

Both British and Jamaican influences were evident in the basic orientation of the planting class. In terms of Herskovits' "focus of culture" the planters' culture was focused on econom-ics just as strongly as Negro culture was focused on religion. This attitude was produced by many elements. The planting culture before emancipation had been strongly materialistic. The planter came to Jamaica in the first place for economic gain, and often at the sacrifice of other things in life. His answer to the humanitarian demand for emancipation had been that slavery might be morally wrong, but that it was economically sound and would be continued. In England as well, there was an increasing interest in economics. The immense growth of pro-ductivity coming with the industrial revolution, the prestige of the "classical" school of economists, and the materialistic out-look of the new class of factory owners were different aspects of a broad change in Great Britain. While the material basis for the British economic emphasis was absent in Jamaica, British ideas and British attitudes helped reinforce the materialism of the Jamaican ruling class. In any case, the planters could hardly avoid being concerned about economic matters. The plantation system had been in decline since the early century and remained in decline until long after the crisis of Morant Bay.

As a result of all these factors, Jamaicans not only emphasized economic thought, but also cast noneconomic thought in economic forms. In 1849 a Jamaican political leader said, in speaking of the sugar market:

The English prices current is the social, and political and moral barometer of this country, and it appears to be pointing downwards, and must therefore fill us with gloom and apprehension.[1]

Even the abolitionists, who had attacked slavery on moral grounds, were overtaken by the economic emphasis — they wanted moral righteousness, but they wanted it to pay financial dividends. Joseph John Gurney, a Quaker leader in the Anti-Slavery Society, said to a Jamaican audience:

It is of primary importance to the cause of freedom . . . that Jamaica should prosper. I mean, prosper pecuniarily. . . We must prove, by the example of such a region as Jamaica, that free labor is more economical and productive than slave labor, and that the just and equal liberty of all citizens of a state, has an unfailing tendency to increase its wealth.[2]

Gurney was to be disappointed. Emancipation was not an economic success. It looked, in fact, like an all-out failure and seemed to bear out the earlier forebodings of the white Jamaican. Events of the revolutionary years brought no new evidence to change the pessimistic predictions, though there was a wide range of difference, even among pessimists. William Hosack, who had more common sense than poetic ability, was almost hopeful.

> Land of palm and pine! * while thus I gaze
> Along the moon-lit shores my hopes and fears,
> Like meeting waters rise: — Oh, may thy days
> Beneath the dawn of Freedom bring no tears!
> But mildly lengthen into many years
> Of happiness — An envy of the isles. . .[3]

But the Assembly was still predicting doom, even after the first year of apprenticeship.

* Pine apple [Hosack's note].

. . . it is impossible for us, without abandoning the evidence of our senses . . . to divest ourselves of the painful conviction, that progressive and rapid deterioration of property will continue to keep pace with the apprenticeship, and that its termination must, unless strong preventive measures be applied, complete the ruin of the colony.[4]

The Assembly was, of course, talking about the export of staples and, though it overstated the case, the overstatement was not great. Sugar production dropped about half between the decade ending in 1833 and the decade of the 1840's.[5] The price of sugar in London was also tending downward, with the result that Jamaica received less money for a smaller crop. The decline in the quantity of coffee exported was even more precipitous, but the problem was not simply one of quantity produced. By the 1850's, the value of the export component of the Jamaican economy was barely one-half that of the thirties, and it never really recovered until well after 1865.[6]

Foreign trade figures have no validity as a general measure of the health of all economies, but for the Jamaican planting system, which was kept alive by exported staple products, they have a great deal of meaning, and there was no mistaking the nature of the Jamaican decline. It was not comparable to the ordinary business cycle, or even to the run of deep depressions in late nineteenth-century Britain called the "Great Depression." It was not even comparable to the slump of the other West Indian colonies after emancipation. By 1865 the total British West Indian sugar production was back to the level of the 1830's; [7] Jamaican production was lower than ever and still going down.

Decline of the plantation system changed the face of the island. In 1852 it was claimed,

. . . wherever the eye is turned, wide-spread ruin meets the view. The bustle of business is no longer perceived in our towns; shipping has almost deserted our harbours; the busy industry of the sugar-estate has given place to the stillness of desolation, and the cultivated field is lapsing fast into its primeval state of weeds and jungle.[8]

Of the sugar estates that had been the life of the island before the revolution, one-third were gone by 1847 and one-half by

1865. Three-fourths of the coffee plantations had also become "ruinate," along with a quarter of the cattle pens.[9]

If Kingston was ramshackle in the 1830's, it was to become much worse. An American visitor described it in 1860:

> Kingston looks what it is, a place where money has been made and can be made no more. It is used up and cast aside as useless. Nothing is replaced that time destroys. If a brick tumbles from a house to the street it remains there; if a spout is loosened by the wind it hangs by a thread till it falls; if furniture is accidentally broken, the idea of having it mended is not entertained. The marks of helpless poverty are upon the faces of the people whom you meet, in their dress, in their very gait.[10]

He also said,

> I know of no country in the world where prosperity, wealth, and a commanding position have been so strangely subverted and destroyed, as they have been in Jamaica, within the brief space of sixty years.[11]

It was against the background of constant economic decline that Jamaicans had to attempt to build a new social framework based on free labor. In a growing economy the problem would not have been so serious. Growth would cover many economic dislocations. Decline had the opposite effect of showing the bare bones of stress and strain, not only in the economy, but in social and political adjustment as well.

As early as 1847 Hosack's moderate hopefulness of the 1830's was answered by another Jamaican poet.

> Queen of the Emerald Isles that gem the wave,
>   Whose dark blue waters o'er the coral sand
> And rocks that girdle in the Carib's grave,
>   Rose ceaseless onward to the halcyon land
> And tombs of the Caciques! Isle of the brave
>   And the unfortunate! — once the grand
> And wealthiest of the ocean's sons — alas!
>   Jamaica! You are come to a sad pass.[12]

*   *   *

There were so many variable conditions behind the economic decline of Jamaica that neither a long list of contributing causes nor the selection of any two or three factors for special emphasis makes a very satisfactory explanation. The Jamaicans themselves spent a lot of time and effort doing both. In spite of the tautology, the simplest explanation is still the most accurate — Jamaican sugar and coffee producers were not able to grow their products at a cost below the price offered in their market. As they failed to lower costs or to change to other crops, the estates went out of cultivation.

The sugar economy had been in decline even before emancipation, but the end of slavery created new problems. Jamaicans claimed that free labor was more expensive than slave labor, and it was certainly true that most Jamaican estates could not produce sugar as cheaply as the slaveholding plantations of Cuba and Brazil. The cost of labor, however, was only about half the total cost of production, and to blame the entire picture of high costs on emancipation neglects many other factors. About half of the Jamaican sugar estates survived till 1865, and some of them made a profit. Free labor may indeed have been more expensive than slave labor, but if it was, the difference was not great enough to prevent surviving estates from competing successfully with the slaveowners overseas.

Neglecting the problem of emancipation, which fell equally on all, the difference between success and failure in Jamaica appears to lie in other conditions making for high costs. In the early century some estates had been planted on land suitable for sugar only under conditions of very high prices. These marginal producers were the first to go, while estates with better land continued to be profitable. Another group of survivors were estates with resident proprietors or lessees, who avoided the high fees of attorneys and overseers and perhaps profited from more careful management. Large estates had a better chance than small ones. After the 1830's, an estate producing less than about 150 hogsheads of sugar annually had difficulty meeting the high fixed costs for management and machinery — and many Jamaican estates produced less. Debt service was another fixed cost that could be prohibitive. This problem was severe, since many Jamaican estates had been mortgaged to the hilt in the days of higher property values, and it was legally very difficult to remove encumbrances.[13]

The planters' difficuilty was not with costs alone — even the small, heavily mortgaged, absentee-owned estate with second-rate land could have gone on producing, if the price of sugar were high enough. The price of sugar, however, had dropped steeply after the Napoleonic Wars. It rose again in the late thirties when production was hampered in all the British colonies by the end of slavery. With the forties, however, sugar production increased in the other British West Indies and the price dropped steadily. At the same time, protective duties were me-moved in a series of steps ending in 1854, when all sugar entered Britain on equal terms of free trade.[14]

After the removal of the protecting duties, most Jamaican planters blamed free trade for their continued decline — free trade and emancipation were, in fact, taken as twin blows struck at their economy by the economic and humanitarian dogmatists of Great Britain. While emancipation certainly made planting more difficult, it is not possible to credit the Jamaican claims about the suger duties. The greatest decline in Jamaican sugar production came before, not after, the equalization of the duties, and even though Jamaican production declined somewhat after 1854, the decrease was partly accountable to other causes. In the early 1850's there were a series of dry years, and an epidemic of cholera in 1850–51 swept away a large number of sugar workers. This is not to say that the British government could not have protected Jamaican high-cost producers by appropriate fiscal measures. It might have, but it would have been politically impossible. Even if British consumers had been persuaded to pay a premium for colonial sugar, there was no hope of justifying the measures needed to protect Jamaica from the competition of her sister colonies, where sugar still flourished.[15] The root of the matter, however, was not protection. By the middle of the nineteenth century large-scale production by new methods had permanently lowered the world price of sugar, and the Jamaican estates were high-cost producers in relation to that price.

*   *   *

The white Jamaicans were quite correct when they took the decay of the plantations and the export trade for the decay of

European "civilization" on the island. But, without the assumption that the welfare and the very existence of the country depended on the plantations, the colony was not yet as ruined as they supposed. This assumption was made by most Britons as well as by the white Jamaicans, but it neglected a new and growing aspect of the economy. From the beginning of the apprenticeship, Negroes began to leave the sugar and coffee estates and go into the "mountain" where they could work the land on their own account. Paralleling the gradual failure of the plantations, the small settlements increased in number and productivity, and their importance to the whole economy was far greater than their influence on export statistics.

Even in its best days the planting economy only occupied a small part of the island. Now with emancipation, the unoccupied land was open to settlement, by purchase, by rent, or simply by squatting. As the ruin of the plantations progressed, the ruinate of an absentee-owned and uncultivated estate could simply be appropriated by any person who chose to use it — often with very little chance of being discovered by the authorities. And the "back lands" of cultivated estates were so little known and badly surveyed that a squatter sometimes lived there for years without causing a stir.[16]

It was more difficult to buy a small plot with a clear title, but it could be arranged. In spite of a general unwillingness of the planting class to sell land to the Negroes and a belief that an estate of the usual size constituted a "property" that must be kept intact, there were always a few proprietors who would break up an entire estate into one-acre plots for sale or rent, rather than keep the land idle. This provided the opening for a former slave to become a small settler for a relatively small cash outlay. Good provision land was generally available at five to ten pounds per acre, and sometimes for much less.[17] After paying an additional two to six pounds for clearing and about three pounds for a survey, this land might yield crops to the value of thirty pounds per acre per year.[18] And if the necessary capital were not available, good mountain land could sometimes be rented for twenty to thirty shillings per acre annually.[19]

It was the movement of the small settlers that provided some faint basis for the Carlylean picture of "Quashee" sitting under the "pumpkin" tree and existing without work, while the estates in the valley were thrown up for lack of labor.[20] Carlyle's legend to the contrary, the economy of the small settlers was not a simple subsistence economy. Their principal products were fruit, yams, plantains, breadfruit, and even sugar for local consumption, and they also grew ginger, pimento, and coffee for the export market. By the mid-forties, the sale of provisions had developed into a widespread system of internal trade between the "mountain" and the sugar parishes where estate survival was greatest.[21]

This trade brought prosperity to some parts of the island, while the old sugar areas declined. New towns grew up in the interior. In St. Thomas-in-the-Vale, Linstead became a sizable center, where middlemen bought the produce of settlers from the surrounding hills and shipped it through the Rio Cobre gorge to Spanish Town, Kingston, and the sugar estates in the parish of Vere. On the north coast Portland became a provision parish. Its twenty-eight sugar estates had dwindled to only four in 1854, but in the same period settlement had progressed so far that by 1858 there was one freehold property for every five inhabitants. The former slaves were not only managing their own land but also shipping provisions by sea to the windward parishes of Trelawney and St. James where surviving sugar estates provided a better market. In the far northwest, the parish of Hanover became relatively prosperous with a balanced development of local and export production. In 1860 there were still twenty-nine large sugar estates, but there were also over two thousand properties of less than ten acres and some five hundred rented small settlements. Many of these small settlers worked on the estates part of the year for wages, but many also had a marketable surplus from their properties.[22]

Jamaican statistical records in the nineteenth century were inaccurate at best and designed, in any case, to measure the export economy. The number and productivity of the small settlements is uncertain. The most reliable estimates indicate about 50,000 small properties by 1865, but many of these were certainly not completely self-supporting.[23] One thing, however, is clear — while the gross national product may have dropped in the years after emancipation, the loss for the country as a whole was not nearly as serious as the drop in export figures would indicate. The white and colored classes, however, concentrated on the export figures for sugar and coffee, the ruin of the estates, the decline of Kingston and the outports. What they saw was real enough, and to them it was of vital importance; but it was not the only development in Jamaica.

*   *   *

Jamaicans of the ruling class thought the settling movement was exactly what they had predicted before emancipation — the result of too much unused land in relation to population — but this was not quite the case. The prerevolutionary planters' prediction, however, was correct in only one sense — without the large tracts of cheap and unoccupied land, settling would have been impossible. But the ratio of land to population only provided the opportunity. There were several other important factors urging the Negroes to take advantage of it. Some of these were deep-seated Negro attitudes. Others were chance developments of the transition from slavery to freedom. Still others grew out of slavery itself.

One basis for the settlement of the Negroes was created by the Jamaican planting system. A specifically Jamaican characteristic, lacking in some of the other West India islands, was the provisions ground system for feeding slaves. It developed a backlog of training and experience in the cultivation of root and tree crops, in the management of provision grounds, and in marketing, and it developed a familiar and desirable alternative to work on the estates.[24] In another sense the planting system fostered settlement because it provided such bad training for wage labor. Slavery instilled a discipline, but it was the discipline of group work and constant supervision. It was no adequate substitute for the voluntary discipline of the modern industrial worker. The inheritance was long-lived, and it helped produce the set of attitudes noted by Lord Olivier when discussing the Jamaican workingman in the early twentieth century.

. . . he has no mechanical habit of industry. He has no idea of any obligation to be industrious for industry's sake, no conception of any essential dignity in labor itself, no delight in gratuitous toil. Moreover, he has never been imbued with the vulgar and fallacious illusion which is so ingrained in competitive industrial societies, that service can be valued in money.[25]

While he might work very hard on his own property, he was less willing to sell his labor regularly for a fixed sum. Furthermore, work on the sugar estates was associated with slavery, and it was often avoided for this reason. Even before emancipation, the free black people refused to work on sugar estates, since this work was the badge of slavery.[26]

The connection between sugar work and slavery was not entirely the fault of the blacks. The white planters were no more prepared than the Negroes for the transition to free labor, and they tended to treat the free workers as they had treated their slaves. As free men, the blacks expected to be treated with dignity and respect, and even with a certain formality. They were extremely sensitive to the rough orders of English visitors, though the visitor might be using the same tone he used toward English servants. Abusive language cut deeper than it might with a European worker, since it struck at one of the real symbols of the new freedom. Formal respect often meant more to the Negro than economic gain, and this was an area where the difference of cultural focus between the white and the black community led to misunderstanding.[27]

The heritage of African attitudes played still another role in land settlement. The Negroes retained at least a part of the African view of land ownership. A private right to usefully occupied or cultivated land was clearly recognized in West Africa, but unoccupied land was quite another matter. It was often considered the property of the tribe, or of the King, but not to be kept vacant at the whim of an individual. In Jamaica this attitude appeared as early as the first year of apprenticeship and as late as 1865 in the dogged Negro belief that the Crown Lands were open for settlement to any one who would use them. It contributed to the illegal occupation of ruinate and Crown Lands; and even when the illegality of squatting was made clear, the Jamaican moral sense was outraged that perfectly good land should be left vacant. In the mid-sixties there was a series of riots and disturbances brought on by white attempts to reoccupy ruinate after years or decades of adverse possession by black settlers.[28]

In spite of unused land and the Negro desire to grow provisions rather than sugar, the settlement movement would not have grown so rapidly merely on the individual initiative of the former slaves. Organization was necessary for the joint purchase and division of a "property" into small plots. Many proprietors were willing to sell off their land, but they wanted to sell large units; while the Negroes generally wanted only a few acres. It was the missionary movement that provided the necessary organization and experience in European business methods for the rapid development of land settlement.

Emancipation had brought an enormous increase in the membership and influence of the missionary churches. The former slaves gave principal credit for their freedom to the King and to the missionaries, and they joined the chapels as much for the sake of social and political gains as from religious conversion.[29] The result was a missionary boom lasting into the mid-forties. The missionaries had gained enormous influence over the black population, but, like the humanitarians of Great Britain, they had at first no program for the social reorganization of Jamaica. If anything, they rather expected the ex-slaves to continue working the estates as free wage-laborers. Having established themselves as the defenders and advisors of the Negroes, however, they were now confronted with two serious problems. During the period of apprenticeship, some of the more prosperous Negroes began buying land in the mountains, leaving the estates and the range of missionary influence. On the estates themselves, the missionary position was difficult. It was one thing to intervene between a planter and his slave, but quite another to intervene between an employer and his free workman. This subtle distinction in the social duties of a Christian was lost on the blacks, and they continued to ask the missionaries to bargain for wages and to enter their disputes with the planters. New policies were thus demanded if the missionaries were to retain their religious gains either among those Negroes who stayed on the estates or among those who departed for the hills.

In this situation, the different dissenting sects took different courses of action. The Wesleyan Methodists, who were forbidden by their Standing Orders to meddle in social or political questions, generally urged submissiveness and moderation on their congregations. If they intervened at all in wage disputes, they tried to do so at the consent of both parties. Somehow, helping the Negroes to buy land was not considered intervention. Therefore even the Methodists occasionally bought a moderately large run of land for resale to their people.[30]

The Scottish Missionaries took a less liberal view of settling, but they also were forced into the movement. They were fearful not only because the disappearance of workers might ruin the estates but also because they found their congregations filtering off into the hills. To counteract the danger as best they could, they followed the lead of others, buying large blocks of land, establishing free villages, and then reselling the land in small plots to their old estate congregations. Their wage policy, on the other hand, was more pro-worker than the Methodist neutrality. When given the opportunity, they decided on a fair wage and recommended it to their followers.[31] When the Negroes refused to work for less, the planters complained that the missionary had formed a workers' combination and called a strike. There was some justice in the belief that this sort of thing went beyond the purely religious calling of the missionary, but the missionaries, having led their people into the Promised Land of freedom, were unwilling to leave them there unprotected.

The Baptists were the most energetic sect in the struggle for the rights of freedmen. They not only worked harder than the others at wage bargaining, but they were first in the field with organized settlement. Their first free village, called Sligoville after the Governor, was established in 1835 in the mountains behind Spanish Town. In the next six years more than three thousand individuals were settled in Baptist villages in the western part of the island alone, mainly through the efforts of Knibb and Burchell.[32] From the beginning they took the religious calling in a broader sense than simple teaching and preaching to the people. As a prominent missionary wrote to the head of the parent society,

There are times and seasons when ministers may legitimately step forward as advocates of the oppressed and as champions for the Civil and Religious Liberties of mankind. . .[33]

It was an ideal of William Knibb to make the island into a country of small settlers, where villages called Victoria, Buxton, Wilberforce, and Macaulay would replace the Hopewell, Harmony Hall, Arcadia, and Nightingale Grove of another era. He was willing cheerfully to sacrifice "a few pounds of sugar" to the ideal of bringing forth a "noble free peasantry," [34] and his ideal became one of the aims of the Jamaica Baptist Union. Only a few months before the rebellion of small settlers at Morant Bay, the Baptists submitted to the Governor "that the future prosperity of the colony depends on the encouragement and development of the industry and enterprise of the small cultivators." [35]

*   *   *

Long before 1865, Knibb's dream had become a reality for at least a part of the island. The prerevolutionary rift between the African and the European Jamaica began to be reproduced in the forties by an economic, even a geographical separation. There were more clearly than ever two different Jamaicas — the planters' Jamaica of the coastal plains and inland valleys, and the settlers' Jamaica of the mountain freeholds. The two were separated by culture and racial caste, but even more by mutual ignorance.

The predictions of the planting class had prepared it for some such movement as the growth of small settlements. The planters recognized the movement, when it appeared, as exactly what they had expected. They opposed it when they could and ignored it when they could not, but they made little effort to understand it. Their attitude was based on the tacit assumption that there were two systems of tropical cultivation — the "free system" and the "slave system" — both designed to produce staples and little else. The sugar cane was more than simply a preferred crop, or even a prestige crop that made a "planter" of the producer. A special value attached to it as the source of hoped-for wealth, or at least as a symbol of lost prosperity. Anthony Trollope wrote, on a visit to the island.

When I hear a Jamaica planter talking of sugar, I cannot but think of Burns, and his muse that made him poor and kept him so.

And the planter is just as ready to give up his canes as the poet was to abandon his song.[36]

Although the Jamaican planter realized that the settlers were economic rivals — in the labor market, if in no other way — his emotional attachment to sugar cane kept him from considering the small settlement seriously as an alternative form of tropical cultivation. He was wedded to estate production by sentiment and interest, and he was ready to go on and buttress his position with rational justification.

The planters' position was supported by two lines of argument among English commentators on West Indian affairs. One was a further development of the *mystique* of planting. The other justified the plantation system by strictly economic arguments. Carlyle was the chief British spokesman for the first of these, dwelling on the greater "nobility" of certain crops.

> The Islands are good, withal for pepper, for sugar, for sago, arrow-root, and coffee, perhaps for cinnamon and precious spices; things far nobler than pumpkins; and leading toward commerces, arts, polities, and social developments, which alone are the noble product, where men (and not pigs with pumpkins) are the parties concerned! . . .
>
> No; the Gods wish besides pumpkins, that spices and valuable products be grown in their West Indies; thus they have declared in so making the West Indies . . .[37]

Though many planters must have felt much as Carlyle did, and there was an occasional Jamaican reference to the provision trade as a perversion of nature's blessings,[38] Carlyle's argument was not repeated in Jamaica. For one thing, he was badly misinformed about Jamaican agriculture; if it was spices you were after, they were to be found in the small settlers' pimento grounds. More important, unlike Carlyle, the Jamaicans were not concerned with "nobility" — not, at least, in Carlyle's meaning of the word. Their thought was bound up in their declining prosperity. From the beginning they placed their faith in economics, the "dismal science" that Carlyle detested. In 1839 the planters of the parish of Hanover pointed with alarm at the amazing growth of small freeholds and concluded that,

> The general prosperity of colonial agriculture, it is manifest, must

rise and fall in direct proportion to the facility of cultivating sugar estates, and the quantities of their produce actually exported; as upon the returns of such produce solely rests the means of providing any internal monetary circulation.[39]

This sort of economic argument could be extended in several different directions. It was argued that monetary circulation was necessary to support churches, schools, doctors, and even government.[40] Or, in another way, it could be shown as the basis of progress.

Above all, let the people understand that without the produce of the large properties we should have scarcely any export trade, and consequently no contact with the outside world sufficient to keep us in the march of civilization and improvement: and that without the existence of an upper class giving tone to society by its manners and example, they would soon revert to a state of barbarism.[41]

Still another point was made to show that progress was possible only through the estate system. Following Adam Smith, it was sometimes argued that the key to progress was the increasing division of labor, bringing with it increasing trade and increasing productivity. A large agricultural unit obviously had a greater division of labor than the single-family unit of the small settler, therefore settlement was a retrogression in efficiency that was likely to bring a decrease of gross national product.[42]

It was only natural that the economic arguments for the plantation system should be accepted in Jamaica. The plantations were supported there by emotional ties, without the necessity of argument. These arguments, however, were also accepted in Britain, and it was a British colonial theorist who gave them their clearest exposition.[43] British support was hardly unexpected either, since British economists thought of agricultural problems in terms of their own problems in Britain. In this period, the Irish land problem received more attention than the West Indies, and the alternatives were much the same — either create larger and more efficient units, or else break up the estates for the benefit of small freeholders. In thinking of Jamaica, as in thinking of Ireland, the successful example of English agriculture was before them, and the majority of English economists favored larger and more efficient farms. And it must be admitted that they were probably right. They were right, that is, on the abstract question of economic efficiency, removed from the social setting of either Ireland or Jamaica.[44]

In any case, the bias in favor of the plantation system ran as strongly in the Colonial Office as it did in Jamaica, and it helped to further the alienation of the small settlers. Early in 1865, a group of settlers in St. Ann petitioned the Queen to open some of the Crown Lands to settlement. At the request of Governor Eyre, an official pronouncement was prepared in answer to the petition. It was read from the pulpit and placarded throughout the island as the "Queen's Advice." Over the signature of Edward Cardwell, the placard ran, in part:

I request that you will inform the Petitioners that their Petition has been laid before the Queen, and that I have received Her Majesty's command to inform them, that the prosperity of the Laboring Classes, as well as that of other Classes, depends in Jamaica, and in other Countries, upon their working for Wages, not uncertainly and capriciously, but steadily and continuously, at the times when their labor is wanted, and for so long as it is wanted; and that if they would use this industry, and thereby render the Plantations productive, they would enable the Planters to pay them higher Wages for the same hours of work than are received by the best Field Laborers in this Country; and as the cost of the necessaries of life is much less in Jamaica than it is here, they would be enabled, by adding prudence to industry, to lay by an ample provision for seasons of drought and dearth; and may be assured that it is from their own industry and prudence, in availing themselves of the means of prospering that are before them, and not from any such schemes as have been suggested to them, that they must look for an improvement in their condition; and that Her Majesty will regard with interest and satisfaction their advancement through their own merits and efforts.[45]

The "Queen's Advice" was one item in the final bankruptcy of government policy. Four months later the settlers of St. Thomas-in-the-East rose against the local authorities.

*   *   *

The Negro settlers had no answering arguments to justify

their own form of tropical economy, though a few white and
colored Jamaicans sometimes argued for them. The apologists,
however, were rarely advocates of further land settlement —
they merely said that the settlers seemed to be prosperous
enough or defended their right to do what they wanted with
their freedom.[46] The occasional Governor or planter who recognized the movement as a success from the Negro point of view
felt that, on the whole, it was to be regretted. They took the
attitude taken by Governor Darling in summing up Jamaica's
position.

> Thus it is that Jamaica at this moment presents, as I believe, at
> once the strongest proof of the complete success of the great measure
> of emancipation, as it relates to the capacity of the emancipated
> race for freedom, and the most unfortunate instance of a descent in
> the scale of agriculture and commercial importance as a colonial
> community.[47]

There were very few indeed of the planting class who thought
of the settlers' economy as a possible solution to the economic
problem and equally few who paid attention to occasional warn-
ings like that of T. Witter Jackson, a Stipendiary Magistrate
who knew the small settlers.

> . . . we cannot but forsee the rapidly approaching importance
> which must very soon attach to these small settlements and their
> yeomanry possessors. Like the little cloud resembling a man's hand,
> they will spread over the land and produce — who shall say which —
> a fertilizing rain or a destructive tempest. If ever there was a time
> when it was necessary the something be done by a government for
> a people, this is the people and now is the time.[48]

From the planters' point of view, the rise of the small settlers
could not be considered a success or an economic benefit to the
island. They never even produced the major crops by which
success was measured — not, at least, in quantity or for export.
They were a malignant growth on the body economic, and so
they were ignored, except when they seemed to interfere with
plantation productivity. In the planters' view, the economic
history of Jamaica between the revolution and the rising at
Morant Bay was one long decline.

For the former slave, settling was something more than even

the defenders of settlement thought. The Negro settler was not principally interested in economic success. Therefore the fact that his products never replaced the exports lost by the failing estates made little difference. What did make a difference was his escape from the estates — freedom became a reality, and not simply a change in legal status.

From the combination of economic failure and the small settlers' movment, the ruling class derived their two major problems in the decades following emancipation. They had, first of all, to make their own adjustment — to build a free-labor plantation system in the worst possible circumstances of long-run economic decline. It was a measure of the planters' initial failure in this task that the Negroes created, as their adjustment to emancipation, a competing economy of small settlements. This development, in turn, added an economic component to the existing cultural division between a European and an African Jamaica. The growing separation between the two Jamaicas brought with it new social and political problems. The failure to solve these was to be the final failure of the planting class.

VII

The "Free System" in Theory and Practice

THERE WAS NO PERIOD IN THE LONG DECLINE
of the planting economy when the planters could breathe easily
again with the feeling that a new prosperity might be on its
way. Even the mid-forties, which seemed to be a plateau in the
long descent, were filled with wild alarms of new disasters
and violent accusations hurled at the authors of present ruin.
During the whole period from emancipation to the crisis of
Morant Bay, the principal intellectual activity of the planting
class was inquiring, thinking, quarreling, and working to bring
back the prosperity of the island. Much of it was mere political
wrangling to push through pet schemes, but behind a façade
of pettiness was a real current of thought. People were genuinely
concerned with discovering the underlying causes of their failure, though they were also at work creating legends and finding
scapegoats.

Very little of the Jamaican writing on economic subjects
reached the realms of abstraction and generalization that might
entitle it to serious consideration as economic theory. Jamaicans
were interested, instead, in the specific analysis of their own decline or in plans for future progress. Both the projectors and
the myth-makers, however, reflected in their writings the underlying economic beliefs of the planting class, and these beliefs
were equivalent, in their level of generalization, to the more

formal economic theory of Europe. They cannot, of course, be stated with as much precision, but they were very generally held by European Jamaicans and they helped to provide a stable basis for the diverse and transitory reform projects.

In contrast to the relatively stable economic beliefs, the economic policies of the planting class were anything but constant. Both the public action of the Assembly and the private actions of the planters shifted and turned from one panacea to another in search of some remedy for decline. There was actually a twofold problem. The planters were still caught, as they had been since the early part of the century, in the economic scissors of high costs and low prices. In addition, the revolution of the 1830's called for the transition from slave to free labor, which would have been serious enough if the planting system were healthy and profitable. It was not, however, and the planters had to manage their economic problems and the social transition at the same time. Their many policy changes are explained by the many possibilities open to them. They had to experiment with new labor policies, and they could attack the economic problem in several different ways — by trying to lower costs, by trying to raise prices, or by trying to do both at the same time. There was, however, one stable element even in the practical search for a solution. All the plans and acts of the Jamaican planters aimed at achieving the success of their own special kind of tropical economy — the old plantation system, now worked by free labor.

*   *   *

Too narrow a concentration on the free-labor plantation system was a defect of Jamaican economic thought, but the planters' shift from their earlier concentration on the "slave system" was itself a sign of flexibility. Belief in the slave system, however, could not be abandoned overnight. Jamaicans had formerly argued that freedom would necessarily bring ruin to the island. This belief was gradually dissipated, but it was still strong during the first years of freedom. At the outset of emancipation, therefore, the planters were still too tied up in the defense of slavery to be ready with detailed suggestions about the kind of emancipation act they favored or the kind of free-labor system they wanted to follow it. In any event, they were not asked. The Colonial Office was anxious to satisfy the planters, if possible; but it only consulted the absentees living in Britain. As a result, the act of emancipation was written without Jamaican help and delivered to the island as a *fait accompli* with its main lines fixed.

There was one striking exception to the general Jamaican failure to plan for freedom — striking not only because it ran against the current of opinion, but also because it contained several worthwhile ideas that were not realized by others until much later. This plan was the work of Lyndon Howard Evelyn, Deputy Receiver-General and Public Treasurer at Savanna-la-Mar. First stated in 1831, it reflected a more considered knowledge of local sentiment than the Colonial Office schemes. It also tried to avoid the dangers foreseen by Jamaican proslavery writers, but, in the immediate situation, the plan was a complete failure. It was rejected in both Jamaica and England, and brought Evelyn financial ruin, ostracism from island society, and a broken career, although Evelyn himself was a slaveholder. If this was the price of opposing slavery, it is indication enough why such a plan was unique in Jamaica.

Evelyn's plan was based on the conviction that Jamaicans were sacrificing their chance to save the productive value of the colony by standing pat against the demand for emancipation. In the midst of the planters' furor of 1831–32, he denied the "nobility" of a last-ditch defense of slavery through separatism or any other means. He suggested, instead, that the Jamaican planters should join with the absentees in effecting a gradual emancipation on their own account. Through his plan he hoped to meet the demands of tropical agriculture as well as those of the British humanitarians.[1]

As the central agency for emancipating the slaves, Evelyn wanted a chartered joint-stock company, the Royal Emancipation Society, organized in England and controlled by a court of directors in London. It was hoped that wealthy humanitarians would subscribe, but the purpose was not simply humanitarian. The Society was also to make a profit. Its essential function was to buy West Indian estates and operate them through its own agents. Eventually it would emancipate the slaves, but in the meantime it would carry out sweeping changes in West Indian estate management — beginning with the abolition of the attorneys, agency fees, and the commission system of selling sugar and buying supplies in England. Evelyn also wanted to reform the production of sugar in Jamaica, working from a central belief that a larger scale of production and more division of labor were the keys to economic progress. This was in line with the dogma of classical economics, but coupled with it was a firm belief that man is a creature of habit and hard to change in his ways — that a new way of life can be created only by using the irrational sentiments built up by the old.[2]

It was the latter belief that led Evelyn to propose a gradual form of emancipation. The Society would buy estates a few at a time and begin by running them as they had always been run. The old offices of bookkeeper and overseer would be retained, but filled by new men especially trained in planting. Evelyn despaired of removing the irrational responses of the planting class — the new management would be married, resident, and barred to men who had ever served as planters under the regime of slavery. Under the renovated planting class, the slaves would begin by working in the old planting routine, but over a period of six to eight years, work for wages, diminishing punishments, and the habits of free workers would be gradually introduced. In the meantime, the slave's work would go to buy his freedom.[3]

Up to this point Evelyn's plan aimed at the same goal as the ill-fated apprenticeship system, and Evelyn recognized the possibility of stopping here. He suggested that a working free-labor estate could be sold to British capitalists as a going concern, supplying the Society with new funds to begin the process all over again with other slave estates. This, however, was not his ultimate goal. He hoped the Society would go on to establish free villages on the model of the English agricultural village.

Since this would be a new undertaking, with no basis in Negro habits, Evelyn worked out an elaborate scheme for using existing sentiments and attachments to further his project. He planned to begin with a chapel and a minister to give the whole project the sanction of religion and attract Negroes through their religious bent. The second step would be a school for the education and wholesome training of the young. He hoped this would attract the people, when they grew older, to the pleasant scenes of childhood. The next step was to provide houses and provision grounds for the old people, in order to use the Negro respect for the aged. Then houses without grounds were to be set up for merchants and skilled workers, whose lack of land would help encourage a strict division of labor. As a focus for village life, Evelyn would provide a market place to be a center of social activity as well as exchange — a place where the evenings could be spent in the old African entertainments. This was still another way of building a community spirit.

Near the village the society's manager would be installed as a local aristocrat to manage the affairs of the Society and serve as an example to the lower classes, who would be tenant farmers, working the land under leases from the Society. Evelyn wanted the villagers to grow crops for export as well as subsistence. This included sugar, which would be sent to a central sugar mill and boiling house, making a clean separation between cane farming and sugar manufacture.[4]

Evelyn's plan was naïve in detail, and there was never much chance of putting such a scheme into practice — still less of making it a financial success.[5] On the other hand, the Colonial Office and the British Cabinet did not succeed with the apprenticeship system, either. Evelyn went further than the British planners in realizing that emancipation was likely to be complicated by an elaborate complex of sentiments originating in slavery itself. He also recognized that slavery was an integral part of the old plantation system, and he was willing to suggest a new form of tropical agriculture to replace the estates themselves along with the old labor system. In the long run, the Negroes, on their own initiative or with the help of missionaries, set up free villages very much like those Evelyn proposed. In the long run also, the proprietors were forced into many of Evelyn's proposals for the reform of sugar planting, and, in the twentieth century, government land settlement projects have made his voice more prophetic than anyone realized in the decades before 1865.

*   *   *

In practice as well as theory, the planters were unprepared

for emancipation. Instead of making the best of the new order, some fought the apprenticeship system and succeeded in making it merely another form of slavery. Others honored their own predictions of doom by planting less cane in the season of 1834–35 and again in 1838–39.[6] A non-planting Jamaican was quoted as saying, "The planters have set their hearts upon ruin, and they will be sorely disappointed if it should not come." [7] Until the end of apprenticeship, few planters gave much thought to the situation they would meet with full emancipation.

The planters' acceptance of inevitable ruin had its place in causing the failure of the apprenticeship system, but this attitude hardly lasted beyond the first years of transition. Most planters settled down quickly after 1838 to the business of salvaging what they could under the free system. One of the first steps was to find a technique for controlling the free labor force. The simple innovation of wage payments was itself a problem, but a more serious problem was the lack of "continuous labor." Many planters believed that wages would cause no trouble, if only labor could be made "continuous." [8] The demand for "continuous labor" comes up constantly in their discussions and has to be understood in its full meaning. It was not a question of the Negroes' refusing to work on plantations all year round. They no doubt would have refused, if asked, but full-time work was not being offered all year round. Sugar and coffee being seasonal crops, the problem was to meet the special labor demands of the planting and "crop" seasons. On the sugar estates, these periods tended to coincide with the planting and harvest seasons on the Negro provision grounds. Arrowroot, for example, was a favorite settlers' crop, and, like sugar and coffee, it had to be processed as well as harvested. To do this the settler had to work full time at his grounds exactly when the estates needed extra labor for the crop season. The planters' demand for continuous labor, therefore, was the desire for control, other than wage payments, that would assure a full working force in seasons of special need.[9] Taken in the Jamaican context, it was a soft word for peonage.

The obvious way to provide "continuous" free labor was to institute a system of long-term contracts, and the House of Assembly attempted this in a series of acts beginning in 1834. The early acts favored the employer so much that missionaries warned their congregations against signing any contract at all. In effect, the Assembly blocked the way to a contract system by making the early laws too stringent, though the Negro's desire to protect his new status was so strong that more favorable legislation might not have succeeded any better. Anything that smacked of apprenticeship or forced labor continued to be anathema to the Negroes long after emancipation. After the cholera epidemic of 1851, for example, Negroes would not apply for government aid to orphans on this account.[10]

Another possibility open to the planters was to use an employers' combination to prevent land sales for small settlements, to lower wages, and to refuse employment except on a continuous basis. This failed too, and the chief reason was the general decline of planting. There were always a few desperate proprietors or agents who would break the planters' agreement because they had to save a crop or salvage a little money from a ruined estate by selling off land to the Negroes. There were a number of agreements to lower wages, or prevent land sales, or increase land rents, but they all ended, except temporarily and locally, by alienating the working class and encouraging them to become independent settlers.[11]

A more general, as well as more subtle, device for securing continuous labor was an intricate labor-for-rent scheme attempted in the early years of freedom. The planters had no monopoly on land or water or any other necessity that could be used to force labor whenever it was needed, but they did control the estates and with them the Negro village and burial ground. The Negroes set great importance on the burial place of their ancestors, and this sentiment gave the planters an initial bargaining advantage. As early as 1836 they realized that this advantage might be used to create a form of labor control.[12]

Three months after the final emancipation, the freedmen lost their traditional right to the house, lot, and provision ground they had occupied under slavery. In order to make the tenure still more insecure, the planters throughout the island served notices of eviction. The Negroes thus became tenants-at-will, who might be dispossessed without notice. Rents were set for the houses and grounds, but the amount of rent was made dependent on the number of able-bodied workers living in each house, rather than the value of the property. A typical policy was to charge a rent equal to one day's pay for each inhabitant each week. If the workers failed to turn out for work, they could be evicted for non-payment of rent, their house pulled down, and their provision grounds destroyed. There were a number of variations on the basic scheme. One common plan was to charge a very low rent if the workers worked regularly on the estate and a very high rent if they worked elsewhere. Another was simply to charge a very high rent at all times, forcing the Negroes to work in order to meet the rent bill.[13]

Where the rent-for-wages device was employed moderately, it was sometimes very successful. Seville Estate, in St. Ann, for example, gave the workers a six-months' tenure combined with a high rental of 2s. 6d. a week. At the same time, tenants received higher wages than other workers. In effect, the high rent represented a sort of investment for the worker, which could be realized only by working with some regularity.[14] On most estates the plan was not successful. Rents were generally so high that a year's rent would be enough to buy the house and grounds.[15] Excessive rents angered the Negroes and so did the fact that they were being charged for what they had always considered their own property — and with some reason, since they had usually built the houses and planted the grounds in their spare time. The Negro desire to stay in the village and near the burial grounds was a valuable lever, but it could not be pushed too far. Once the worker was evicted, the hold was broken and the planter's labor problem was worse than ever. In some areas, like the northwest coast in St. James and Trelawney, the estates were deserted altogether by resident workers.[16] In other sections the scheme merely made bad feeling among the Negros. It was not a general success anywhere, and it had to be abandoned — but only after it had played its part in encouraging Negro settlement.

Alongside the private attempts to approach a system of peonage, there was also a demand following emancipation for a "rural code" that would force the Negroes to work for wages. Here the Assembly had to be careful — the Colonial Office was on guard against any direct attempt to reëstablish slavery in another guise. Various coercive or anti-settler laws were passed, but they were hidden as much as possible in innocent-looking enactments. The annual Police Act, for example, provided, between 1835 and 1838, for the arrest of any person found carrying agricultural produce without a note of permission from the owner of the land where it was grown. This provision was ostensibly designed to prevent "praedial larceny," or the theft of growing crops, but it could be used equally well to prevent the illiterate small settler or the landowning apprentice from marketing his produce. Other "class legislation," as it was called in Jamaica, was discovered and disallowed by the home government. In this group were the Vagrancy Acts of 1834 and 1839, which were rejected because they extended unduly the legal definition of the offense.[17]

The attempt at class legislation was most prevalent in the first years of freedom, but, after a quiet period in the mid-forties, it appeared again in a variety of laws that vexed the small settlers. The offense of praedial larceny came to embrace not only the theft of cultivated crops, but also the gathering of wild products from any land at all. It became very difficult to collect damages for trespass by cattle, the principal plantation animal, while at the same time the goats and pigs of the small settlers could be killed by the police whenever they were found at large.[18] Such laws were hardly stringent enough to check the growth of small settlements, and the dissatisfaction they produced far outweighed any slight advantage the planters may have gained.

Even though the Colonial Office would have opposed a rural code to force continuous labor, there was no objection in principle to the indirect method of forcing people to work by careful taxation. Many tropical colonies in the late nineteenth century imposed a hut tax or a poll tax that could be paid only in cash, which, it was presumed, could be earned only by plantation labor.[19] Lord Howick's plan of emancipation had been similar — he had called for a heavy tax on non-plantation land and he continued to believe that the failure to force labor was the underlying cause of Jamaican decline. When, as Earl Grey, he became Secretary of State for the Colonies, he returned to his tax scheme. In 1851, after a similar plan was accepted for Ceylon and Trinidad, Grey proposed a detailed scheme for Jamaica. A tax was to be placed on houses according to the number of inmates, and the tax had either to be paid in cash or commuted to labor. In addition, Jamaican import duties on provisions were to be reduced to make the settlers' economy less profitable. Everything possible was to be done to encourage "the great staple branches of colonial production." [20]

In this case the Colonial Office not only failed to oppose the Jamaican desire for continuous labor but had even brought in definite suggestions of its own, which seemed to be exactly what the planting class had been working for so unsuccessfully. Nevertheless, an Assembly controlled by planters rejected Grey's proposal. Many factors helped defeat Grey's plan — the difficulty of enforcement, humanitarian opposition within Jamaica, and fear of provoking a rebellion — but the immediate cause of failure was the circumstance of its presentation. In 1851 the House of Assembly was in the midst of a particularly vicious struggle with the Legislative Council and the Governor. This fight, in turn, was merely a phase of a broader attack on the imperial measures for free trade — an attack in which Jamaica worked in concert with British protectionists and the other sugar colonies. At that moment the Jamaican planters were concentrating with single-minded stubbornness on the hope of getting back their monopoly over the British market.[21] They were not to be bought off by an alternative, especially if it came, as this plan did, from a freetrader — their archenemy and one of the authors of their distress.

When the free trade crisis had passed, there were occasional demands for something similar to Grey's proposal, but the Assembly did nothing more than it had done before. It imposed high taxes on boats and canoes and on the "horse-kind" of the small settler, while the planters' cattle and other animals were taxed much more lightly.[22] These taxes, however much they might anger the fisherman or the small settler, were not heavy enough to force him back into the cane fields. It is doubtful if they were ever anything more than a thoughtless way of raising revenue without being too hard on the declining estates.

The Jamaican measures, both private and public, for contract labor, rent manipulation, class legislation, and direct taxation to bear heavily on the small settler had the common aim of making

labor cheaper and easier to control. In retrospect they fit together as a complete and coördinated plan, but in the immediate
situation each device arose to meet a special problem. Only
Grey's house-tax scheme was systematic and thorough enough to
produce effective continuous labor for the estates. The others not
only failed to produce continuous labor, they also alienated the
working class, increased the split between the two Jamaicas, and
deepened the Negro belief that the ruling class were "advantage-
takers."

An important cause of this failure was the background of Jamaican economic belief. The Jamaicans had explicitly rejected
slavery, and with it they rejected the conscious attempt to intro-
duce a system of forced labor. Both their theoretical analysis of
the decline and their calls for new action pointed in other directions. The coercive measures were immediate and practical,
without theoretical justification or concerted planning. In this
instance, the planting class was acting on the unconscious resi-
dues of the slave system — trying to make labor relations what
they had always been. They were not trying to set up a new and
systematically coercive system of "free" labor. As a result, their
measures were halfhearted and incomplete, annoying to the
working class, but ineffective in coercing it.

Another contributing factor was the frustration of the planter
class — a frustration made worse by the quick West Indian temper but produced essentially by the years of failure. Both the extremism that ruined the potential value of the rent-for-wages
device and the irascibility of the Assembly in defeating Grey's
house-tax scheme were the work of the planters described by
Governor Sir Charles Grey:

> Several of these [the planting interest in the Assembly] are san-
> guine, adventurous, energetic men, some far advanced in life, or past
> the prime of it; and when these, after seeing their schemes of fortune
> break down and their hopes fade away, with the blank prospect
> of almost hopeless ruin before them for themselves and for their
> families, have given way to passion or indulged in invectives, which
> themselves in calmer moments regret and condemn, I have observed
> such outbreaks with other feelings quite as strong as those of repro-
> bation or surprise.[23]

*   *   *

Since the extemporaneous measures for controlling labor and lowering the rate of wages failed largely because they were not applied consistently and thoroughly, other measures that were not extemporaneous, but based on careful planning and justified in theory, might be expected to fare better. In respect to theory, the planters were better prepared than they had been in the matter of practical plans for emancipation. They had long since predicted that freedom would bring the failure of the estates, and they based their reasoning on the large tracts of unused land in contrast to the relatively small number of workers concentrated on the estates. The settling movement, "high" wages, and the difficulties with continuous labor all seemed to confirm the belief that the country was underpopulated. Some Jamaican writers seemed almost pleased to be proven correct in their dire predictions. A journalist wrote in 1844:

We can remember the assurances we received from the Government, from the Saints, the Anti-Slavery party, and indeed from all parties except our own . . . that the abolition of slavery would make us rich, enhance the value of our estates, and enable us to make sugar at half its former cost. We could not believe these assurances Time has proved them all fallacious, and founded in ignorance. We ourselves anticipated exactly what has occurred — the indolence of the labourer, his extortion, the increases in our expenses, and the decrease of our returns.[24]

One result of failure was to deepen the Jamaicans' faith in their own analysis. Belief in the essential disequilibrium between Jamaican land and labor became the central point in the economic creed of the planting class: it was used to explain their failure in much the same way as it was used to predict that failure.

Discussion of the relations between land and labor was not peculiar to Jamaica. Waste or unused land had been a key element in British discussions of the economics of colonization since the days of Adam Smith. Smith had, in fact, laid down the dictum that:

The colony of a civilized nation which takes possession either of a waste country, or of one so thinly inhabited, that the natives easily give place to new settlers, advances more rapidly in wealth and greatness than any other human society.[25]

In support of this position he had argued that empty land makes for low rents, high wages, and easy class relations, since the dissatisfied laborer can always leave his employer and take up land for his own use on easy terms.

The Jamaican position was exactly the opposite of Smith's view. They believed that the abundance of land was precisely the quality of their island that prevented economic advancement, and they soon had support from Great Britain. Edward Gibbon Wakefield developed a theory, first appearing in print during the summer of 1829, that the advance of new countries depends not simply on plenty of land, but on a proper balance between land, labor, and capital. Without sufficient labor, land and capital were powerless. He pointed to the United States as a horrible example of a country where "civilization" was not advancing and could not advance until population growth had filled out the continent and restored the balance. Wakefield considered American Negro slavery, on both the continent and the islands, an unsystematic and cruel way of establishing a proper land-labor balance. His own chief interest was in obtaining the correct equilibrium for the Australian colonies — artificially still, but through more humanitarian means. He proposed two measures, land restriction and induced immigration. By his plan, the government would sell unoccupied land only at a "sufficient price" — sufficient, that is, to slow down the spread of population to an optimum rate. This would create rents on the land already occupied. It would keep wages low and assure a proper distribution of labor on the older land. Since the rents thus created would be the result of government action, the government could legitimately impose taxes on them and use the proceeds to bring immigrants from Britain. The landlords would lose nothing, Britain would lose only redundant population, the laborers would have higher wages than they received at home, and the country would develop efficiently and smoothly.[26]

Wakefield's scheme for "systematic colonization" had nothing to do directly with the West Indies, but it had a considerable indirect influence on Jamaican plans for induced immigration. Induced immigration was hardly a new suggestion to the Jamaicans — the slave trade had been essentially that — but Wakefield's ideas helped make immigration acceptable to the home government. Even before emancipation, his theory gained wide popularity and acceptance at the Colonial Office, at least in principle. As a result, the Jamaican plea for more workers to fill out the colony and create an equilibrium between land and labor was also well received. British humanitarians who would shy away from the disguised renewal of the slave trade, were just as willing as the Jamaicans to transfer Wakefield's analysis from Australia to the West Indies.

Before the end of apprenticeship, the Assembly brought forth its first proposal for importing workers to depress the rate of wages.[27] Not only the planting class but most Governors fell in with the belief that prosperity could be restored by correcting the ratio of land to labor.[28] As a theoretical proposition it came to be universally accepted both in the colony and in Britain — even by the missionaries and the Anti-Slavery Society, who opposed induced immigration on grounds that wages were already quite low enough.[29]

Though the Jamaicans were aided and influenced by the popularity of Wakefield's plan of "systematic colonization," Jamaican and Australian conditions were not the same and the Wakefieldian analysis could not be applied to Jamaica. The parting of the ways came when the Jamaicans began to estimate the number of workers they would need. In 1842 prominent planters thought that 30,000 to 50,000 immigrants would depress wages to a "profitable" level.[30] The question of a "profitable" level of wages had no place in Wakefield's theory. He accepted the wage theory of Malthus and Ricardo, according to which, wages tend to equal the cost of subsistence — that is, they will equal the cost of producing the laborer and keeping him alive. If wages should rise above this rate, population would increase and drive them down again. If they fall below this rate, hunger, destitution, and disease — the "positive checks" on population — would diminish the number of workers and cause wages to rise. For a good Ricardian, therefore, wages tend to move about an equilibrium rate that cannot be altered. Wakefield recognized this and limited his analysis to new countries — countries in a state of temporary disequilibrium. His artificial restrictions aimed at achieving the Ricardian state of equilibrium as fast as possible. When he said that land should be sold only at a "sufficient price," he had in mind a price that would be just sufficient to keep wages in the settled areas high enough to produce a maximum growth of population.[31]

Jamaica stood in sharp contrast both to Wakefield's theory and Australian conditions. The island was not a new country, in Wakefield's sense. Population had not increased under slavery, and it increased very little between 1834 and 1865. There was obviously plenty of empty land, but a Malthusian would have to admit that the population was near a state of equilibrium. This made little difference to Jamaican theorists. Like Wakefield, they wanted a "sufficient price," but it was not a "sufficient price" for land. They talked mainly of manipulating the number of workers in order to achieve a "sufficient price" for labor — that is, to bring wages to a "profitable" level. There would be enough workers in Jamaica, when the wage rate was depressed enough for Jamaican planters to compete successfully in the world market.[32] Some planters estimated that the rate of Jamaican wages would have to drop 60 per cent or more to a level between 4d. and 6d. a day, if they were to meet the competition of the Cuban slave owners.[33] Few, however, were as frank as George Solomon, a Kingston merchant, who admitted that immigration might never raise the total population of Jamaica but would have to be continuous because of the high death rate among immigrants.[34] Translated into the framework of Malthusian population theory, Solomon was willing to use immigration, if necessary, to maintain a permanent disequilibrium as a means of depressing wages to a rate lower than subsistence. Taken this far, the Jamaican proposals for induced immigration were not only a harsh road to prosperity, they had also come a very long way from British immigration theory.

✳　　　　✳　　　　✳

In spite of discrepancies between Jamaican conditions, Jamaican theory, and Wakefieldian systematic colonization, the belief came to be fixed in Jamaica that the island's difficulties came from an unnatural disequilibrium between land and labor. This situation clearly called for government action. There were three things that might be done: the government might restrict the occupation of waste land; public health measures might lower the death rate and increase population; or, more people might be imported from the outside. All three of these were suggested in Jamaica, and the first and last, which were also part of Wakefield's plan, were attempted.

Even before 1838, the home government, occupied, as it was, with systematic colonization in Australia, became interested in restricting the sale of West Indian land according to Wakefieldian principles. The official policy was stated in Lord Glenelg's Circular Despatch of 30 January 1836 to the Governors of the West Indian Colonies. This document accepted the views of both Wakefield and the West Indians that too much land was dangerous to the production of staples. Governors were, therefore, ordered to stop the sale of Crown Lands to those without capital.[35]

This was an excellent measure, on theoretical principles. In the case of Jamaica it was meaningless — for one thing, the Crown had already given away more land than it owned. No one realized this, of course, because there was no land survey. On investigation it was found that, in any case, the Crown had lost control of its Jamaican lands to the Assembly, which collected the quitrents as a royal settlement on the island treasury. To make matters worse, the quitrent on much of the land was in arrears. The Assembly had failed to take any action, and legal proceedings for condemnation by a private citizen were very complex and difficult.[36] In this state of confusion the Colonial Office could do nothing, though the Assembly took the only restrictive action open to it. It refused to condemn land for arrears in quitrent, and after 1862 it stopped the sale of land for tax delinquency.[37] These measures may have prevented settlers from buying land with a good legal title, but they could not prevent squatting on unused land; and they thus added still another to the settlers' list of grievances without helping the planters.

The failure of land control left immigration the chief method of correcting the land-labor ratio. Induced immigration of free workers had been suggested as early as the 1810's — with immigration from India to Mauritius actually beginning in 1819.

It began for Jamaica during the apprenticeship, with a measure to pay bounties on each immigrant brought to the island. A few thousand immigrants, mainly from North Germany, were imported just before full emancipation, but they were not even accustomed to temperate agricultural work and the plan failed miserably.[38]

The first failure, however, was so obviously the fault of bad management, that immigration schemes were soon revived. The coast of Africa was one source. Contraband Negroes captured from slavers by the Royal Navy were another. India was a third.[39] By 1864 some 24,000 people had been brought to Jamaica; but through death or departure only 5,279 remained, and the expense was a considerable drain on the island's finances. Through 1844 alone, Jamaica had spent 150,000 pounds in public funds, or about 25 pounds for every immigrant landed.[40] Yet immigrants continued to be brought in at a similar cost in the fifties and sixties.

There can be little doubt that the few thousand immigrants had no sensible effect on the ratio of land to labor. In practice, induced immigration failed to produce the results called for by theory. Yet many Jamaicans were still pleading in the fifties and sixties, as they had pleaded in the thirties and forties, for more people to fill out the land. This poses two questions. Why did the Jamaicans fail, in the first place, to find enough immigrants? And, after having lost so much money for so little result, why did they continue efforts to find immigrants in the later decades?

The first question might be answered, as it was occasionally answered at the time, by blaming the home government for obstructing the free flow of population within the Empire. There were limitations on the departure of emigrants from Africa and India, placed by the Colonial Office and the Indian Government in the interests of the emigrants themselves. Such regulations were troublesome, but they did not stop immigration to Trinidad and British Guiana, and they need not have stopped immigration to a colony willing to cooperate with other authorities.[41]

The real answer had to be found in Jamaica and especially with the Assembly. Generally the Assembly was divided into three parties on the immigration question. All three agreed on the principle that more population would enable the planters to lower wages. The smallest of the three represented the small settlers and missionaries and therefore opposed lower wages. Another, larger group, consisting mainly of colored men, officials, merchants, and planters who did not want immigrants assigned to themselves, was perfectly willing to allow immigration, but only at the cost of the planters who received immigrant labor. The third group, mainly large sugar planters, wanted immigration at the cost of the general revenue. Even though the first group was small, the other two were constantly shifting and it was hard to maintain a majority in the Assembly.[42] This made it difficult to write an immigration act that would met the simultaneous approval of the Assembly, the Governor, and the Colonial Office.

The Members of Assembly, moreover, were no more willing to compromise on immigration than any other issue. They cried incessantly for immigrants, but often refused to take them except on their own terms, preferring to go without rather than meet the conditions set by the Colonial Office. During the crisis following the Sugar Act of 1846, they subordinated the need for labor to tactical advantage in the political struggle over protection. In a fit of pique the Assembly tried to cancel orders for immigrants already on the way from India, claiming that Jamaica would be so impoverished by free trade in sugar, she could no longer afford to pay for them.[43] At first the Jamaicans hoped for a British immigration subsidy in return for the loss of protection, but in 1848, when Jamaica was actually offered a loan for immigration and development, the Assembly became still more intransigent. Under the control of the planters' party, it refused the loan and turned instead to legislative obstruction as a way of forcing protection from the British Parliament.[44] Temporarily, at least, immigration was sacrificed along with Grey's house-tax scheme, and both were subordinated to the fight against free trade. The resulting break in the continuity of induced immigration was not the only interruption, but it was the longest and most serious, lasting a full decade.

This leaves the second question: why were Jamaicans willing to pay the high cost of importing workers, even after it was obvious that the population increase was not enough to change the ratio of land to labor? The answer can be found in a change in the practice of induced immigration after the mid-forties. Up to that time the immigration schemes had simply been a matter of paying bounties or direct subsidies to import workers. Once in Jamaica, the immigrant was allowed to contract freely for his own livelihood, though he was expected to repay his passage money. With the Immigration Act of 1845, large-scale importation of Indians began, and the form of the immigration acts changed. The Indians were brought in at the cost of the government, but they were forced to sign three-year indentures and were assigned to planters. The planter, in return, paid the government two pounds a year toward the cost of importation, his total six-pound payment amounting to about half the estimated transportation cost. In addition the planter had to supply pay and housing to the immigrant and submit to periodic government inspection.[45]

There may not have been enough immigrants under these later acts to change the general rate of wages, but here at last was a form of continuous labor. From 1845 onward, immigration acts emphasized the continuity of labor rather than the rate of pay. In 1852 the length of indenture was still only three years, but an Indian could not leave the island before five years had passed without buying himself off at the rate of three pounds each year. In 1858 the indenture time itself was extended to five years and the required residence to ten. At the same time a severe code of labor regulations grew up, applying only to immigrants and administered by the local justices.[46]

The older system of simple subsidy had been a failure, but the new system of immigration-with-indenture divided the planting class. Planters who took immigrants as a means of labor-control found they needed the support of general taxation to pay the heavy cost of importation, but the very element of control helped turn some members of the Assembly against them. In earlier years, planters who were unwilling to employ immigrants themselves were quite willing to buy prosperity by importing workers. They were not willing, however, to buy labor-control for other planters.[47]

What had begun, and continued to be justified in practice, as a scheme for correcting the ratio of labor to land ended in practice as a new and more effective means of controlling the labor force. The theoretical proposition that Jamaican decline depended at bottom on the land-labor disequilibrium may or may not have been sound. The experiment of filling up the land with imported people was simply too expensive, and it was abandoned. Even so, it continued in name, and its place was taken in fact by the system of indentured labor. The changed immigration system was not backed by theoretical arguments: it simply grew up through successive small changes in Jamaican practice, till it became the economic equivalent of slavery.

*		*		*

The land-labor ratio in theory and the system of induced immigration in practice were the chief planters' response to the problem of "high" wages, but the Jamaicans' concern with the wage problem took them in other directions as well. In fact, a preoccupation with the price of wages was a broad tendency running through most Jamaican economic writing. In discussing the land-labor ratio the Jamaicans emphasized the labor rather than the land aspect of the question, and when it came to practical measures they neglected land restriction in favor of importing more labor. It was a tendency growing naturally out of the planters' transition from the slave to the free system. They watched the wage rate as the crucial cost item simply because it was a new and variable factor in their calculations. At first it seemed a frightful imposition to have to pay any wages at all. Even after the first years of transition, they continued to distrust wage payments, although, as a matter of fact, the wage bill of a free-labor estate was usually only about half of the total cost of production.[48]

Any planter who dabbled at all in economic theory knew, as every educated Englishman knew, that there was a "natural" rate of wages. He also knew how this rate was determined.

The natural price of labour is that price which is necessary to enable labourers, one with another, to subsist and to perpetuate their race, without either increase or decrease.[49]

But the planters were also in general agreement that there was something "unnatural" about the rate of wages in Jamaica. Lord Sligo, who was a proprietor as well as Governor, believed that wages were unnaturally high because the workers, on the advice of the missionaries and stipendiary Magistrates, had combined to raise them. As evidence for this view, he showed that most Negroes in 1839 were working only four days each week and yet were able to live on their wages.[50] Others who thought wages were too high believed the disequilibrium came from the provision grounds, which gave the Negroes too strong a bargaining position.[51] Both views are examples of a general tendency to believe the economists' theory of wage determination, while at the same time introducing extraneous factors if any specific wage is discussed. Nor was this practice limited to the planters. The following exchange took place before a Parliamentary committee between Pakington, speaking for the absentees, and John Candler, speaking for the humanitarians.

Pakington: When you speak of the amount of wages being fair, at what average price do you put sugar in England?
Candler: When I speak of the fairness of the wages I am looking at the quantity of labour in the market, the demand for labour and the supply; . . . and is 1s.6d. a day too much for a man working under the tropical sun?[52]

Those who considered wages in the early years of emancipation thought the disequilibrium would disappear as the "unseen hand" of automatic economic adjustment took effect. There was, indeed, a slight drop in wage rates, but it was not enough to satisfy the planters' hopes. As a result, a new theory of disequilibrium became popular. The old pre-emancipation claim that the Jamaican worker would not follow his own economic interest — would not behave like the "economic man" — was brought out again. It was held that the Jamaican had such limited desires, that he would work only for a bare subsistence. When he had earned it he would stop.[53] If this were generally true, it would reverse the traditional supply curve for labor — the higher the wages, the less labor would be offered. Though the planters were undoubtedly mistaken in claiming a negative wage-elasticity for the supply of labor, there were irregularities in the supply of Jamaican labor that could not be explained by contemporaneous wage theory. Economic gain meant less to the black, than to the white, Jamaican, and the Negro was drawn away from estate work by many factors having nothing to do with the wages offered. The planters, however, were concerned only with the estates. Therefore, they were puzzled.

Jamaicans explained the perverse working habits of the Negro in a number of different ways, one of the most popular of which was the theory of "artificial wants." It was commonly stated that man works only because of poverty, hope for reward, or direct force. Even before emancipation, many Jamaicans had predicted that the Negro would not work because tropical exuberance removed the "pressure of necessity" found in colder climates. This belief continued after the revolution, and it left two ways of making the Jamaicans work harder: fear of punishment and hope of reward. The first of these was forbidden by the home government, leaving only hope of reward. Thus, the necessity of teaching the working class to have "artificial wants" was suggested by a number of writers and finally developed by the Rev. Samuel Oughton, a renegade Baptist minister, into a panacea to save Jamaica.[54]

Oughton pointed out, as others had done before him, that the Negro would work harder if only he wanted more luxuries. Jamaica, therefore, could be saved by encouraging a desire for material goods. This, however, was only a beginning. He went on to develop his theory and prove the intrinsic value of "artificial wants" and their connection with human progress. According to Oughton, the curse of Adam was a blessing in disguise — it was God's way of starting man on the path to progress, since it was only through the necessity to work that man learned useful crafts and advanced in skill and knowledge. Since luxuries require more skill in production than necessities, they are more important in leading man toward civilization. Not only that, luxuries also tend to raise the living standard of the working class. In combining land, labor, and capital to produce goods, luxury goods require more labor than necessities. Thus, according to Oughton, the working class receives a higher proportion of the total cost. He neglected to say who receive the luxury goods. In any case:

The cynic may snarl, as he surveys the spacious mansions and splendid equipages of the wealthy, and murmur at the unequal distribution of the gifts of Providence, but the thoughtful and benevolent mind will rejoice in an arrangement so conducive to the general welfare; he knows that the surroundings of wealth and luxury are not limted to the narrow circle of immediate observation; — that their production has employed many hands — that they have fed the hungry, clothed the naked, ministered to the relief of the sick and suffering, and caused the widow's heart to sing for joy.[55]

Oughton offered no practical suggestion beyond the hope that people would learn from him the real causes of Jamaican distress, since this alone would "suggest such measures as may tend to remedy it" and "exalt Jamaica to a higher state of prosperity than it has ever before attained." [56] In warming over the economic homilies of Victorian England for the benefit of a tropical society, Oughton reached a point in the bankruptcy of economic thought attained shortly afterward in economic policy by the "Queen's Advice."

*   *   *

In considering the problem of high costs, Jamaicans looked first at the cost of labor, but they occasionally gave some thought to other cost items as well. And, indeed, the techniques and organization of the plantation system were badly in need of reform. This was no new probem following in the wake of emancipation; older criticisms were still valid because older faults were still uncorrected. The agency system of plantation management by attorneys was denounced in the 1860's as it had been in the twenties. The commission system of selling sugar and the web of credit leading back to the British merchant needed a thorough reform. The prevalent absenteeism of the proprietors was, of course, one of the chief reasons for the abuses of attorneys and merchants, and the complaint was often heard that absenteeism was ruining the island. The diverse demands of the reformers, taken together, amounted to a call for the complete renovation of plantation management and control.[57]

The reform of planting, however, was not simply a question of organization. On the technical side there were several attempts to remedy the disadvantages of small-scale manufacture by setting up central factories to take the canes from several different estates, but none was successful.[58] Other Jamaicans wanted the government to offer prizes for the invention of labor-saving agricultural machinery; but even the vacuum-pan, which was invented near the beginning of the century, was not used in Jamaica till well after 1850.[59] In the techniques of agriculture there were other suggestions, varying from the management of plantation cattle to the use of the plow, and, since these reforms required little capital, they were sometimes put into effect.[60] But such measures were already far behind the improvements being made elsewhere, and such reforms in detail were not likely, by themselves, to save the island. The Jamaicans needed salvation on a more grandiose scale, and some of them looked for it in the renewal of trade. They dreamed of making Kingston a free port and thus an entrepôt for the traffic to the Pacific across the Isthmus of Panama.[61]

Few of these schemes were acted upon. There were still attorneys and absentees in 1865 as there always had been. The entrepôt trade failed to revive, and the technological backwardness of Jamaican planting was only slightly remedied. While the decline led planters to an active search for improvements, the improvements were often expensive and the decline itself made capital hard to find. Even where a change was not expensive, it was easier to show the need for reform than to carry it out. The planting system was old and it was firmly imbedded, not only in the habits of the planting class but also in a complex and tenacious net of financial and legal institutions.

*   *   *

There was another, more important, reason why the planting system was not reformed: only a minority of the ruling class regarded their own inefficiency as the main cause of their ruin. The economic decline was psychologically unsettling and had to be explained, but neither the reform proposals nor the theoretical analysis of wages, labor, and land could serve as a successful piece of popular mythology. To be successful, a myth also needed a villain, and it had to be a more adequate villain than either the reformers or the theorists could provide.

A "devil theory" was not long in coming, and the "devil" was already provided in the island consciousness by the old animosity against evangelicals, humanitarians, and missionaries. A direct attack on emancipation would have made a bad impression in England, but special scapegoats could be blamed for all the difficulties flowing from it without denying the morality of the act itself. In the first years after 1838, the Baptist missionaries and stipendiary Magistrates were singled out in the first organized attempt to place the blame for Jamaican distress, and this devil theory had specific political purposes and political control. William Burge, from the Jamaica Agency in London, organized a new series of public meetings, like those of 1831. The custodes in each parish called meetings and presented petitions to the Assembly or Parliament, denouncing the Baptists and stipendiaries. At the same time, Burge organized the Association of Jamaica Proprietors in London, which did the same. Eventually the whole body of memorials and petitions was printed for Parliament through the usual device of having a friend in the House call for it.[62]

All these papers had the same refrain. The island was ruined, mainly through the laziness of the Negroes. This, in turn, was caused by the Baptist missionaries and the stipendiary Magistrates, who had misled the working class and destroyed the Negro's normal love and respect for his master. The stipendiaries had given advice unfriendly to the planting class, and the Baptists had actually called strikes. There was, of course, some justice in the complaint — certainly the planters could have taken a firm hand with the Negroes more easily without the interference of either group. The campaign failed, however, to curb the Baptists or remove the stipendiaries, and it was dropped — though the two groups were still occasionally attacked in the ensuing decades.

Their place as chief scapegoats was taken by the humanitarians in general and the Anti-Slavery Society in particular. Years after the rising at Morant Bay, a planter could still say:

It was the Saints that ruined us — St. Wilberforce, St. Macaulay, and their following. Well, I bear them no malice but would they could only see now the desolation they have produced.[63]

MORANT BAY

RIO BUENO

RETREAT PENN

KINGSTON

PORT ANTONIO

SPANISH RIVER

THE PLANTING ECONOMY

It was not the emancipation act itself but the later interference in Jamaican affairs that figured as the chief complaint against the Anti-Slavery Society. The Society was blamed for the disaffection of the working class and the small settlers — and even for Negro "laziness." An anonymous poem of 1866, "The Planter's Lament," centered the attack on L. A. Chamerovzow, the Society's current chairman, blaming him for the revolt at Morant Bay as well.

> The sounds of the crunching and pressing of cane
> We almost despair of e'er hearing again;
> The boilers are empty; the still-house is dry;
> There's little to sell, and there's no one to buy.
> We offer good wages, and heartily pray
> For the poor chance of getting some nigger to pay;
> But they wont listen to us, for they've listened and bow
> To the words and the wisdom of Chamerovzow!
>
> . . . . . .
>
> The negro is lord of himself and his toil,
> The run of the land and the fat of the soil.
> He makes his own bargains for labour, and works
> Whenever he pleases, and, when he likes, shirks.
> He's a very good fellow, if but let alone,
> But you've meddled and muddled, and mischief you've sown,
> And 'tis you who have kicked up this troublesome row —
> Yes, you, my philanthropist, Chamerovzow! [64]

But on the question of slavery itself, the planting class kept the ambivalent attitude of prerevolutionary years. They had always protested their opposition to slavery on principle. They stood by this position. When they attacked emancipation, it was always in terms of the act, or the apprenticeship system, or the compensation payments. In retrospect, as in prospect, they accepted emancipation in principle and opposed it in practice. The view was summed up by the *Jamaica Magazine* in 1844:

Opposed, as we admit ourselves to be upon principle, to Slavery in the abstract, we should under no circumstances feel inclined to question the justice of the act of aboliton, so far as the effect of it was to strike from off the hands of the slave the visionary bonds which restrained them, and which canting hypocrites had magnified into the iron manicles of the days of barbarism. We would not ar-

raign the British people for the declaration of universal freedom
throughout the dominions of Great Britain, but we would nevertheless challenge the justice of that act, which forcibly, and without
adequate remuneration . . . took from the West Indian proprietor
the means whereby alone he was enabled to render available the
capital so invested. It is upon this principle, and upon this principle
only, that, speaking the voice of the injured Colonists, we arraign
the British people with the commission of an act of unparalleled
spoliation.[65]

After a few years' experience with freedom, the planters were
anxious enough to suppress the Negroes' "insolent insubordination to authority," but they preferred to work for their economic salvation without slavery.[66] Even in the days of crisis
following the economic panic of 1847 or the revolt of 1865, the
pendulum never swung as far toward negrophobia in Jamaica
as it did in Britain. Colonial writers stopped short of Carlyle's
threat to reimpose slavery or Pim's claim that Negro slavery
was a "natural" institution that had "materially aided the progress and advancement of mankind." [67]

*   *   *

In the mid-forties a new factor helped take some of the burden of blame from the shoulders of the humanitarians. Another
enemy appeared, and one so obviously dangerous to Jamaica
that even the missionaries could take comfort in having a new
scapegoat. The end of slavery had hardly come, before British
theorists were pointing out the disadvantages of allowing the
West Indians to have a monopoly over the British sugar market.
While they regretted the unfavorable effect on free-labor products, they trusted in the ultimately beneficent influence of the
"unseen hand."

As matters stand now, however, it is plain, that about two-fifths
of the price of every pound of sugar which we consume are the natural costs of the article, two-fifths are paid to the government, and
one-fifth as a tribute to the planters of Jamaica and Demerara.

*   *   *

The monopoly, therefore, approaches its termination, for this
country will not long endure the increasing price and diminishing

quantity of an article so essential to the habits of the present day. Even those who see many and serious reasons for regretting the change, which may have so unfavourable an effect on the prospects of the African race, cannot but forsee its approach; while those who contemplate it with a view only to the economical progress of the country, regard it with unmixed satisfaction.[68]

On the Jamaican side, the Assembly had been demanding still more protection — a request for it was included in the dispatch of 1833 announcing the Jamaican emancipation act.[69] From then on, they demanded, at the very least, continued protection as a *quid pro quo* for giving up slavery. As a serious controversy, however, the free-trade argument did not begin until the early forties, and it ended only after all hope of protection was given up in the late fifties. The most common Jamaican argument was a repetition of all the old mercantilist discussion on the value of colonies. It was assumed that free-trade would ruin the island and thus destroy the West Indian market for British manufactures, the West Indian shipping as a school for seamen, and the security of the sugar supply in time of war.[70]

New arguments came in as well — borrowed in part from the British landed gentry. A few planters in the late 1840's looked back over recent years and traced their misfortunes to the reformed Parliament and the rise of democracy in Britain. They saw that it was impossible to withstand the popular demand for cheap sugar, because "the Minister of the day is not the Minister of the Crown, but the Minister of the *People*. The corner stone of the British Constitution has been cast down. . ." [71] Thomas Jelly, a planter and doctor in the parish of Westmoreland, went even further. He believed England had ruined herself and her colonies alike by lowering the political barriers against merchants and fund-holders. Once these groups were represented in Parliament, their avarice led them to free trade, but in competing overseas they lowered prices, and also wages, driving the workingman downward in a spiral of increasing misery, till at last England would either "share the fate of Portugal and Holland" or be swallowed up by the gigantic rivals her free trade policy had produced.[72]

A more popular new line of argument in Jamaica attempted to show the necessity of protection to foster the free-labor economy. The planters rarely failed to mention that their sacrifice in destroying slavery deserved some recompense, and they often added the notion that their own ruin would mean a "return to barbarism" for the ex-slave. They thus tried to show the duty of the humanitarians to protect their noble experiment.[73] As one planter put it,

> Surely ½ d. or 1 d. per pound on sugar and coffee is no object to the consumers, compared with the conscientious gratification that they would have in completing the great work of freedom which they have begun.[74]

Another argument was the most popular of all. If the British public had no sympathy for the free sugar worker of Jamaica, at least it might show some feeling for the Negroes who were still slaves in Cuba and Brazil. By lowering the protective duties and admitting slave-grown products, it was argued, "The fetters of the bondsman in foreign countries will also be thus more firmly riveted by that very nation from which he had been taught to look for succor and delivrance." [75]

The freetraders could answer, on the basis of classical economics, that the operations of the "unseen hand" were ultimately just. They claimed that the Jamaican sugar producers were inefficient and the fresh breezes of competition would bring automatic adjustments and lower costs. They had long believed that, "Slave labour, it has almost passed into an axiom, is dearer than free; that is, whenever the demand for labourers is abundantly supplied." [76] The qualification to this belief was the escape clause for the Jamaican planters. It allowed them to side-step the accusation of inefficiency by returning to their old belief in the disequilibrium of land and labor.

When fully developed, the Jamaican arguments for protection were very important in Jamaican thought. They demonstrated the innocence of the Jamaicans as inefficient producers of sugar. They exposed the heinous crime of the freetraders, and made the ruin of the island through free trade into an effective myth. The land-labor disequilibrium had always been present, but it was evident only with the passage of the emancipation act. Jamaicans had known this fact, but they had accepted the free-labor system because it was morally just. Now the British were penalizing them for their morality.[77] So long as the island's prosperity was being destroyed, it was a satisfying thing to believe that the superior morality of the planting class was at fault.

* * *

Backed by a full array of justification, the Jamaican ruling class entered, in the late 1840's, into a prolonged struggle with the British government over the question of protective duties for sugar. As an attempt to change the price aspect of their predicament, it paralleled their other efforts to lower costs; and, when the choice was clear, the cost side was sacrificed to pursue the will-o'-the-wisp of protective duties. Eventually the pursuit of higher prices failed too, and the planters found themselves, in the late fifties, at a dead end from which they had to retrace their steps and begin again.

In retrospect, no other mistake of the planting class was quite so disastrous as the single-minded concentration on protective duties during the years after 1846; but, mistaken as it was, the decision followed in many ways from the position in which the planters found themselves. A planter's costs were made up of many items, and a genuine innovation, a change in the organization of planting, was both difficult and risky. In the planter's view, moreover, a higher price could be given them by a simple legislative act. It seemed safer and easier to try for the higher price. Again, the Jamaicans in the 1840's had foreseen in free trade the same dire consequences they had predicted of emancipation in the 1820's. They were, therefore, all the more ready to attribute their continued decline to the loss of protective duties.

Against this background there were also a series of chance events, some of them completely accidental, pointing to protection as the panacea of the moment. The crisis began with the Sugar Act of 1846, setting out the annual reductions of protective duties that would admit all sugar to Great Britain on equal terms by 1851. This was followed a year later by a commercial crisis in Great Britain. By this time only the first stages of duty reduction had taken place, but the crisis was serious for the West Indies. A number of West India merchant houses failed, the Planters' Bank in Kingston went under, and the price of sugar in London dropped a third. Even the West Indian aspect of the crisis had very little to do with the Sugar Act, but it was inevitable, and even logical, for Jamaicans to blame free trade for the entire panic.[78]

Another chance occurrence was the appearance of humanitarian allies. The missionaries and the planters could unite in opposing free trade, even though their motives for doing so were not quite identical. Where the planters opposed it for economic reasons, the missionaries also opposed it for admitting slave-grown sugar and coffee into Great Britain. They, as well as the planters, had always wanted a successful free system to prove the economic inferiority of slavery, but they gained an additional motive after the middle forties. The missionary churches stopped growing and began to decline. The missionaries tended to associate this decline with that of the estate system, and they looked for a return of prosperity to produce a return to religion.[79]

Jamaican humanitarians and Jamaican planters thus joined forces in 1849 for an antislavery agitation. From May to July a series of public meetings was organized on the pattern of Burge's campaign of 1839. This time the principal organizer was David Turnbull, an antislavery Scot temporarily in Jamaica. And for once all the antagonistic groups in Jamaica were united in a single endeavor. Baptist missionaries, planters, churchmen, and small settlers joined in demanding rigid enforcement of the anti-slave-trade treaties and exclusion of slave-grown products from Great Britain. A visiting Scottish clergyman remarked that it "would have done honor to Exeter Hall, in the best days of the anti-slavery agitation." [80]

The effort failed to move Britain, but its very success in uniting Jamaica misled the planting class. With the support of the Jamaican humanitarians, they expected the support of British humanitarians in the fight against free trade. They were to be disappointed. Having underestimated the strength of the humanitarian movement in the 1830's, they now overestimated it. In the end it appeared that the enemies of slavery were even more the friends of free trade.

A third chance factor also helped to make Jamaicans choose

the sugar-duty issue for their principal stand. The other sugar colonies would support them, and they also had support in Parliament from the defeated but die-hard protectionist minority, who made the Sugar Act the first target of a concerted drive against free trade. In the session of 1847–48, protectionists in the Assembly of Jamaica, the Combined Court of British Guiana, and the Parliament of Great Britain worked together toward the repeal of the Sugar Act of 1846. The Assembly investigated the causes of Jamaican distress and came to the foregone conclusion that Jamaica was ruined and only protection could save the colony.[81] The Combined Court passed a resolution to reduce official salaries 25 per cent on account of the colony's new-found poverty. In Britain the House of Commons Select Committee on Sugar and Coffee Planting found that sugar growers needed the relief of protective duties. The outcome of all this was the Sugar Act of 1848, which merely put off the final date of equal duties till 1854 instead of 1851.[82]

This relief was not enough for the Assembly of Jamaica. Some Jamaicans had tried to act more forcefully while the new sugar bill was being debated in Britain, but the Governor, Sir Charles Grey, would not call the Legislature back into session. When the Assembly met next, in August 1848, however, it called for retrenchment of expenditure, beginning with official salaries in imitation of the Combined Court. The Governor and the Council stood firm against this demand, and the result was a prolonged legislative crisis. The Assembly rejected the British immigration loan and refused to vote supply "until a measure of retrenchment consonant with the impoverished condition of the island be passed into law." [83]

This was the first of two legislative crises during the administration of Sir Charles Grey — both of them officially concerned with the retrenchment of salaries, both actually part of the fight for protective duties. The first followed an erratic course till the fall of 1849, when protectionist support in the British Parliament failed them and the Jamaicans were forced to give in. The lull ended in December 1852, when the Imperial Parliament again refused to grant protective duties and the Assembly again refused to do business. By this time, protection for sugar was a lost cause in Britain. The Assembly surrendered in October

1853 — bought off by a low-interest loan to replace the colonial debt, on condition that the Jamaicans reform the House of Assembly.[84]

The most serious consequence of the planters' concentrated drive for protection was the very effectiveness of the arguments they used to show that free trade had ruined them. They believed their own arguments, and their belief in an effective "devil theory" gave them a chance to sit back in the comfortable realization that their ruin was not their fault. This result, however, was not the only price the Jamaicans paid for their fight against free trade. The constitutional position of Jamaica as a dependent of Great Britain forced the Assembly to try devious means of influencing trade policy, in this case the means was a legislative strike. It was a gamble, but a gamble the ruling class was willing to make. If they won, it might have been worth the price — as it surely was when they won a similar fight for self-government in 1838–39. This time, however, the Assembly lost, and in losing it paid heavily with five years of near-paralysis in government, the neglect of other remedies, and loss of revenue when money was badly needed for every sort of development.

*   *   *

In spite of the great variety of discussion and argument that the Jamaican ruling class used to explain, justify, and correct the process that was taking them constantly downhill, there was still a main pattern of economic thought. The principles of classical economics were accepted: the Jamaican contribution was to apply these to the analysis of their own economy. It made little difference that the principles developed by British thinkers were designed for the analysis of their own nascent industrial society. They could be pushed and shoved and creolized in many different ways and finally made to apply to Jamaica. The applications, however, were not made in quite the same way as a British economist might make them — they were made against the background of tropical experience. Thus they were made to fit first into Jamaican conditions and then into the Jamaican way of looking at economic matters — for example, in the concentration on wages and labor.

Such changes did not alter the Jamaicans' essential respect for British economic thought. Even men like Oughton, who had very little real understanding of British economic theory, had an enormous respect for it. On some questions where the tendencies of British thought ran counter to Jamaican interest, as in the case of free trade, the Jamaican answer was copied from British protectionists or constructed out of British economic principles. There was no attempt to argue from Jamaican experience that British economists were mistaken. Even where a controversial British idea, like the Malthusian population theory, seemed to be contradicted by Jamaican conditions, it was simply ignored. The Jamaican economic writers were not interested in economic controversy for the sake of truth. They wanted solutions to serious problems, or they wanted to convince the British public that a given policy should be followed. The success of the British economic system and the prestige of British thought provided a body of ideas whose truth could be taken for granted, and the Jamaicans went to this body of ideas for solutions.

Evelyn's plan for emancipation is something of an exception to this, since it clearly grew out of a knowledge of Jamaican conditions; but here again English prestige shines through in the use of the English farming village as a model, or the division of labor as the key to progress. The scope and form of the work also bring it within the framework of British thought — it was the utopian community of the European socialists, translated into a tropical setting.

In spite of the fund of British ideas and in spite of their generally accepted economic convictions, the Jamaicans often acted as though they had no notion of where they wanted to go or how to get there. They were stubborn in one moment and weak in the next — stubborn in hoping for protective duties and weak in completing neither immigration policies nor measures to force labor from creole Jamaican workers. Both their acts and their public statements were marked by a sense of desperation.

This desperation grew partly out of their psychological insecurity of long standing and partly from the recognition of what seemed inexorable economic decline. Insecurity from both these sources made consistent action difficult, and, to make matters worse, the old division within the planter's mind between Britain and Jamaica was still active. The European Jamaicans borrowed British economic ideas and used them to explain the free system and its decline. At the same time, they continued to have other ideas about the planting system and its right operation, and these grew out of their own experience on the island. The result for Jamaican ideology was a basic contradiction, at times, between ideas originating in the two different societies.

This contradiction might take the form of two inconsistent ideas held by the same person at the same time, but just as often it made for inconsistency between an economic plan and the action that followed — in the broadest sense, between the free system in theory and the free system in practice. It was one cause for the failure of the wage system in Jamaica. Work for wages as an institution was borrowed from the capitalist economy of Great Britain, but the Jamaicans did not emerge from slavery as complete capitalist workers, trained to the system by long habit. The planting class tried two different solutions for this. They followed their theoretical ideas and tried to fill up the island with imported workers, and they applied the coercion they had learned to use under slavery. The two solutions were not compatible, especially when they tended to approach each other in practice, immigration became coercive, and coercion was softened by the influence of humanitarianism.

Ideas from Jamaican and British sources were not always incompatible, though the results were sometimes just as unfortunate when they agreed as when they did not. Failure to reform the planting system was partly the result of such an agreement. British and Jamaican experience dictated the same solution — the estate system must be preserved. Both believed it was the most efficient scale of farming.[85] English backing allowed the Jamaicans to set their economic problem in too narrow a framework. The estate system as a whole was no longer efficient, and, by concentrating on its preservation, the Jamaicans neglected two alternatives well worth consideration — the smaller scale of their own settlers and the much larger scale of the newly founded Cuban plantations. As it was, the Jamaican estate system was not even thoroughly reformed on its old basis.

Finally, still another product of the reinforcement of creole by British ideas helped ruin the planting class. This was the concentration on economic problems as the special focus of European Jamaica. While the planters were struggling with the estates, the Negroes were building a second Jamaica in the hills and building it in their own way with little European guidance. Although the economic decline was always in the background, neither the rising at Morant Bay nor the planters' surrender that followed was primarily an economic failure. It was, instead, a social and political failure, and its form was the full grown "native problem" posed by the second Jamaica of the small settlers.

VIII

Race, Religion,
and Social Adjustment

JAMAICANS OF THE PLANTING CLASS overemphasized their economic problem, but they could not ignore the increasing multitude of other problems that crowded in on them as the years passed. The governor of another West Indian colony reported in 1848, "As the question at present stands, a race has been freed, but a society has not been formed." [1] In the broadest sense, this was the crisis problem of Morant Bay, and it was a growing problem all through the years since emancipation. Instead of growing closer together in the era of freedom, the two Jamaicas had grown further apart. They were not only separate in caste and race, but to varying degrees had separate economies, separate religions, and separate cultures.

Jamaicans of all shades shared the responsibility for the division in the island society, but the ruling class and ultimately the Colonial Office held a position of special control. It was up to them either to allow the black Jamaicans to make the island a second Haiti, or to take steps themselves to orient the whole of Jamaican society toward Europe. The failure of Jamaica to move toward the second alternative was a failure of the ruling class, the missionaries, and the British government to achieve what they wanted of the emancipated population. It was a failure that can be traced in the government policy toward the ex-slaves, in the missionary movement, and in the changing racial attitudes of all classes.

*   *   *

The decision to Europeanize the island was mainly a tacit assumption of the white and colored ruling class, supported by the Colonial Office and British public opinion. The very stress they placed on the planting economy implied a social structure of Negro agricultural workers and white landlords. As William Burge stated explicitly, ". . . that country flourishes where a good feeling is perpetuated between landlord and tenant, where the ordinances of society render them virtually dependent, the employed looking to the employer for support and protection." [2]

Thoughtful Jamaicans realized that education would be necessary to transform the ex-slaves into a hard-working and grateful peasantry. All too many were "ignorant of their duty to their employers, to themselves, to society." [3] It was the plainly utilitarian value of education that appealed to the planting class, some of whom believed "that if religion would only protect agriculture and education not unfit the peasantry for labour, no more estates would be thrown up in this island." [4] At the same time, the bad state of public finances kept the Assembly from trusting too much to such indirect aid to planting.

The real burden of educational work was left to the missionaries. This was not completely futile. In the first years of emancipation the British government came to the aid of Negro education with an annual grant of £30,000 divided among charitable foundations and missionary societies in the former slave colonies. The results reported were so impressive that the grant was reduced in 1842 and disappeared from the budget in 1845.[5] With the end of the imperial grant, the Assembly did little to fill in where the Parliament had left off, but this failure was not entirely the fault of the planters. Education bills were held up in 1854 and 1856 by the opposition of dissenting missionaries, who feared grants to the Church and preferred no education to competing education.[6] In 1864 there were about one quarter fewer students enrolled than in 1837, and the quality of education had probably deteriorated as well.[7]

Another field where government social action was demanded by some planters was public health. Medical attention of a sort had formerly been supplied the slaves on each estate, because it was in the planter's interest to keep them alive. Now the slaves were free, the majority of planters were all too willing to be saved the expense of a doctor. Several Jamaicans, as well as visitors, pointed out the false economy of importing coolies, while the creole Jamaicans died from lack of sanitation and medical care. Thomas Jelly, a doctor as well as a planter, suggested a system of government stipends for rural doctors, and Earl Grey's house-tax scheme would have used part of the tax income for a medical service. A good deal more was spent on public health than on education, but the number of doctors in Jamaica in the early 1860's had fallen to about one quarter the number employed at the time of emancipation.[8]

The price of neglect was the loss of twenty-five to thirty thousand of the working class in the cholera epidemic of 1850–51. Many of these deaths could not have been prevented, but the loss could have been cut by sanitary precautions that were already known. The losses from a smallpox epidemic following the cholera were even more inexcusable, but neither epidemic was so important a drain on efficiency as the high rate of chronic tropical disease. Dr. Gavin Milroy, who conducted a medical survey of Jamaica following the epidemics, called attention to the frightful sanitation in Kingston and the other principal towns — and rural areas were not much better. He found the working class generally suffering from hookworm and malnutrition.[9] These conditions alone would explain most of the planters' complaints about Negro laziness.

In spite of the recognition by some planters that their own interest demanded higher public expenditure for health and education, the Assembly refused to spend more, and the refusal was partly a corollary of the decision to spend money on other schemes, such as immigration. But also, from the planters' point of view, illiteracy and disease had been common enough in the great days of the island's past: they were obviously not the cause of decline. Again, there was a tendency, common enough in Great Britain as well, to blame the lower orders for their own misery. Governor Sir Charles Grey answered Dr.

Milroy's report on Jamaican health conditions with the usual platitudes.

> There is no part of the world in which destitution or misery are for the most part more easily avoided by the laboring class than in the rural districts of Jamaica. . . That with all these advantages there is so much laziness, slovenliness, dirt, obstinacy and disease, cannot be denied; but I am afraid that here, as elsewhere, improvement in these respects must be a plant of slow growth.[10]

There was another, more basic, reason why public health and public education were neglected in Jamaica: they were neglected in England. Under the impetus of Benthamite radicalism and evangelical humanitarianism, the British had carried out a number of badly needed reforms, but they had not yet come to the point of free compulsory education, and the English public water supply and sewage systems were not a great deal better than those in Jamaica. Britain's reforms were those demanded by British conditions. Jamaican conditions were very different. Having few factories, she could get on without factory regulation, just as Britain, without the need for mass acculturation of a partly African population, could get on without good public education. Nor was the British population growth held up by bad diet and the endemic diseases of a tropical climate.

The Jamaican ruling class, however, found it convenient to neglect what the home government neglected and reform what the home government reformed. Thus, in making a new legal code for a free society, the Jamaican legal reform followed the British legal reform. Under slavery many offenses were punished on the estate as part of estate discipline. With freedom, the old slave code had to be scrapped and replaced by new criminal legislation. This was accomplished between 1839 and 1842, in the administration of Sir Charles Metcalfe, himself something of a Benthamite radical. The death penalty was abolished for many offenses, and the punishment of whipping was abolished completely. Other punishments were greatly mitigated, and the criminal law of the island was assimilated as much as possible to that of England.[11]

This reform was laudable, on general principles, but Jamaican criminal law, once reformed, did not stay reformed. Jamaicans were mainly a law-abiding people, but there was no strong popular sentiment against certain offenses, especially petty theft and praedial larceny. As the division between the two Jamaicas widened, convictions for theft increased, and as the problem became more serious it was met by gradually increasing the legal penalties.[12] Whipping was reintroduced for certain offenses in 1849–50, and in 1864 Governor Eyre asked the Legislature for the return of whipping and the treadmill as a general punishment for theft.[13]

*   *   *

Since the Jamaican government could not keep to the legal reforms suggested from England, would not provide for Negro education, and failed even to maintain the social services of the slave system, it could be counted as useless in the task of bringing the ex-slave within the framework of European Jamaica. Instead, the job of speeding acculturation fell to the missionaries, the only group of Europeans in close and friendly contact with the Negroes. They helped in the social struggles of the working class, and they followed the settlers into the hills and helped found the free villages. Partly as a result of this interest, the growth of membership in the mission churches was immediate and overwhelming. The Baptists jumped from about 10,000 in 1831 to 34,000 in 1845. Methodist membership in the same period almost doubled, and other missions had similar increases.

The missionaries were overjoyed. It looked like the coming of a new day for Jamaica under the beneficent influence of Christianity. Some thought a complete moral revolution had taken place.

The revelries attending births and deaths have given place to the decencies and proprieties of Christian life. Licentiousness and discord have been displaced by the sanctity of matrimony, and the harmony and comforts of the domestic circle. Revolting and degrading superstition has vanished before the light and influence of truth, as "mists before the rising sun." [14]

For others it was not simply a revolution in religion and morality, but in every aspect of the Negro character.

That cunning, craft, and suspicion — those dark passions and sav-age dispositions before described as characteristic of the negro . . . are now giving place to a noble, manly, and independent, yet patient and submissive spirit.[15]

The immense missionary success, however, brought out prob-lems that were latent in the missionary movement before eman-cipation. The missionaries, though they failed to realize it, were trying to force acculturation in the field of the Negroes' greatest interest and greatest conservatism. Religion was an area where African survivals were very strong, and they had already begun to appear in the beliefs and practices of the Christian sects. By accelerating the growth of the missionary churches, emancipa-tion also increased the number of incomplete converts, and posed a serious doctrinal and institutional problem for the mis-sionaries. Missionary ministers enjoyed a special status and financial support from overseas as agents for the conversion of the heathen. Once the heathen were converted, it was hard to justify continued support for a full grown colonial church; but, at the same time, orthodoxy had to be maintained. The problem was — when and to what extent were the Jamaicans to be al-lowed to control their own churches?

During the revolutionary years, the problem was subordinate to the missionary-Negro alliance against the planting class; but in the 1840's the alliance began to wear thin, and the cultural difference between the white missionaries and their black fol-lowers became more evident. Different sects approached the question differently, and each minister tried for a solution in his own way; but the divergent courses of the three major churches, Baptist, Wesleyan Methodist, and Anglican, show three divergent forms of missionary failure.

Each church followed a route toward creolization that was roughly parallel to its social program. In both respects, the Bap-tists were the most radical sect in the period of revolution and its immediate aftermath. They entered into a full plan of social action through advice on wages, help with free villages, and even one serious attempt at political action.[16] The good will created by social intervention, the extension of congregations made pos-sible through the ticket-and-leader system, and the preparatory work of the Native Baptists all helped the Baptists increase in numbers faster than any other church. So long as they continued to believe that compromise with the planters was only a "false and heartless truce, which is called Peace by the slaveholding spirit, but fundamentally is outrageous War against God and human happiness," they enjoyed a special position among the Negroes.[17]

This course of action exacted its price in the continued distrust of the planting class, who still doubted the religious sincerity of the Baptist ministers. As a Jamaican poem expressed it:

> Such rogues, such pleasant knaves the hope of gain
>   Allures from Albion's less generous earth;
> With greedy eyes they gaze beyond the main,
>   And plough its briny billows for a berth
> In some Atlantic Eden. . .[18]

By taking the side of their congregations, the Baptists were automatically in a position to be accused of bringing about the ruin of the island.

The fabled box of Pandora, never sent forth more evils upon an unhappy land, than those which issued from a class of men, who, assuming to themselves the character of Ministers of the Gospel, promoted dissensions, and advised, excited, and encouraged the peasantry, to look upon the members of the assembly, the merchants, and the owners of the soil as their inveterate enemies.[19]

Nor was it the planting class alone who objected to the Baptists. Other missionaries were disturbed by the quick Baptist growth and the infiltration of African religious practices. Their protests brought on a prolonged controversy beginning in the thirties and reaching a crisis in 1841, when three Baptist ministers abolished the ticket-and-leader system for their own congregations and withdrew from the Jamaica Baptist Association. About the same time, public charges of laxness were made by the Presbyterian and Congregational missions. The charges centered on the ticket-and-leader system as the chief cause of corruption, but the real difficulty was Baptist toleration of religious Africanisms. In a long list of charges, the Baptists were accused of letting congregations grow beyond the personal supervision of the minister, giving too much power to the leaders, and selling tickets for veneration as a charm. The leaders, in turn, had been requiring special dreams and seizure by "the spirit," as a qualification for baptism, and had made baptism by immersion into a superstitious rite. In short, the official Baptists were charged with having taken on the characteristics of the Native Baptists.[20]

William Knibb, as principal leader of the Jamaican Baptists, was committed to his program. He refused to accept criticism without a fight and wrote, in the summer of 1841:

> . . . I would much rather receive into my house the vilest slave-owner Jamaica ever produced, than some of the agents of the London Missionary Society. I feel no enmity to them, but such mean, snake-like, crawling conduct inspires my unqualified disgust. Under anonymous signatures, and through the vilest papers they have attacked us. But do not fear that we shall reply.[21]

The reply came soon enough. Knibb went to England, and there, in April 1842, he made a public defense of his policies and received the public exoneration of the Baptist Missionary Society. But the Jamaican Baptists, under the leadership of Knibb and Burchell, also decided that, from 1843 onward, they would sever their connection with the British missionary society and become a Jamaican church, rather than a missionary outpost. At the same time they founded Calabar College, near Rio Bueno, in order to train a native ministry.[22]

The policy might have succeeded better, but for Knibb's death in 1845 and Burchell's shortly afterward. The Baptists had extended their congregations and their finances too far in the hopeful years of the early forties. Like the other sects, they lost members after 1845, but, unlike the others, they had no regular support from overseas. In spite of this they remained an important sect and kept their place as the special enemy of the planting class.

While the Baptists were trying to build a Jamaican church, the Methodists took the more conservative position of trying to convert Jamaica while keeping church control in European hands. From the very beginning, the Methodists had appealed to a different social and racial group. Therefore, they met a different sort of problem. They had attracted large numbers of colored townsmen, and when, in the early 1830's, the colored class won their struggle for political rights, they began to resent their status as second-class church members. Racial and national feelings entered into a number of church questions. The colored Methodists especially resented the slow promotion of colored ministers and church opposition to the marriage of white ministers to colored ladies from the island. These issues combined with a doctrinal conflict between an "aristocratic" and a "liberal" faction to bring a schism within the church. Two separate secessions of the thirties led respectively by Edward Jordon, the colored political leader, and Rev. Thomas Pennock, a former chairman of the District, combined to form the Jamaica Wesleyan Methodist Association. The movement paralleled the later Baptist attempt to form a separate church for black Jamaicans — it trained colored Jamaicans for the ministry of their own church. The movement held its own but failed to grow, because it lacked outside financial aid.[23]

The Wesleyan-Methodists thus maintained European control and a European connection, but this policy also had its price. While they lost colored nationalist members to the Pennockite movement, they lost just as many socially ambitious colored members to the Establishment. After emancipation the Methodists were no longer the special church of the colored group, but rather another missionary church appealing to the black population. Since they were less identified with the Negroes' interests, they fell behind the Baptists in membership. As time passed, they also lost the confidence of the home missionary society, which had expected them to establish a self-supporting church in Jamaica. British missionary funds were diverted, in the fifties and sixties, to India and the East — a new mission field with brighter prospects than the declining Jamaican congregations. As a single compensation, the Jamaican Methodists became respectable, lost the taint of negrophilia, and even received an occasional grant from the Assembly.[24]

The action, or more accurately, the inaction of the Church of England in dealing with converts represents the opposite extreme from the Baptist solution. In spite of an annual contribution of thirty to forty thousand pounds from the island treasury, only about one-third of all Jamaican church members in 1866 were affiliated with the Establishment. The Church as a whole remained what it had been — a branch of the Church of England whose main function was to provide religious services for the colonial ruling class. Since this class was only slowly feeling the effects of nineteenth-century piety, the services tended to be much as one Trollope described in the late fifties.

> Very little excitement is to be found in the Church-of-England Kingston parish church. The church itself with its rickety pews, and creaking doors, and wretched seats made purposely so as to render genuflection impossible, and the sleepy, droning, somnolent service are exactly what was so common in England twenty years since. . .[25]

The Church Missionary Society, it is true, had been active for a few years, but it began a gradual withdrawal in 1840 and left the island altogether in 1848. There were also a few hard-working evangelicals among the regular clergy, and even an occasional curate who spoke out for the black population, but the Bishop was usually not in residence and, when he was, had no effective control over the clergy. He had no power to discipline any but the most flagrant cases of abuse, no way to get rid of ineffectives or even to move redundant clergymen from one part of the island to another.[26]

Like the policies of the Baptists and Methodists, the course taken by the Church of England also had its price — most Jamaicans simply stayed away. In the short run, this made little difference. The Church could meet the complaints of its critics by ignoring them, though they were plentiful enough. There was always a handsome majority in the Assembly against disestablishment.[27] It was only after the Morant Bay rebellion that the Church was actually threatened by serious opposition, and by then it was too set in its ways to recover. When the Society for the Propagation of the Gospel withdrew its support and cited the Jamaican clergy for failure to meet its responsibilities, the answer typified the attitude of the Jamaican Church. A self-righteous pamphlet counterattacking the S.P.G. ended with this passage:

> Oh! Friends and Brothers! Friends and Brothers; Exeter Hall philanthropy has *indeed* its own registered thermometer, which stands at "fever heat" for the black man, at "temperate" for the coloured man, and at "freezing point" for the white! [28]

Although the same attitude was common enough in some English circles, it was hardly justifiable in the state-supported
Church of a Negro country. In 1870 the Church paid the final
price for its years of inactivity. It was disendowed and disestab-
lished by the British government.[29]

*   *   *

In spite of the great difference in religious and social outlook
represented by the policies of the Baptist, Methodist, and Anglican churches, all three had a place in the broader movement
of missionary success followed by missionary failure. Perhaps
this is no more than to say that each gained something and lost
something by the course it took — certainly none had yet found
a way of gaining the confidence of African Jamaica. All the
missionary churches gained members till about 1845 and then
lost from a quarter to a half of those members between 1845 and
1865, and the movement of loss and gain had secular as well as
religious causes.

The missionary movement was associated in the Negro mind
with freedom from slavery. The missionaries were the first
whites to show an interest in the Negro's problems, and they
profited from this interest for a few years; but to keep their
members they had to provide religious satisfaction as well as
social gains. In this field they faced the serious competition of
the Afro-Christian cults, which were offering a reinterpretation
of Christianity closer to the religious beliefs of the community.
Far from disappearing after emancipation, there is every evidence that the growth of the cults paralleled the growth of the
missionary churches, and this movement was not confined to
the Negro settlements in the hills. In 1846, the Native Baptist
congregations in the sugar parish of Vere were stronger than all
the European churches together. Even in Kingston, Native Baptists in 1860 made up half the churchgoing population.[30] Official
returns are incomplete, but it would be safe to assume that,
throughout the island, the native form of Christianity had a
firmer hold than European orthodoxy.

In their competition with native Christianity, the missionary
churches profited from their support of emancipation but lost

ground on account of other social attitudes. They set themselves up as the moral instructors, as well as the religious leaders, of the Negro community, and they used this position to conduct a crusade against important aspects of Negro life. The dissenters attacked concubinage, drumming, dancing, the Christmas festival, and Sabbath-breaking. This practically covered the field of Negro amusements, and immoral behavior in one of these respects was grounds for expulsion from the church.[31] The Establishment was especially strict in respect to marriage and discouraged the baptism of illegitimate children. This meant, in practice, that at least 70 per cent of the population was barred from the Church. In spite of decades of missionary training, Jamaicans would not get married. Young women still felt that marriage was a form of slavery, and there was no public opinion condemning concubinage.[32]

The missionary campaign against marriage customs and Negro festivals was especially damaging, since this area was one of general conflict between the European and the African Jamaican. Drumming and shell-blowing became illegal in Jamaica soon after emancipation; though it was a difficult law to enforce and aroused widespread Negro resentment. In 1841 two men were killed and several wounded in a riot growing out of the secular attempt to suppress the Christmas festival in Kingston. The disorder was so serious that the local police were defeated, and the military were called to restore order.[33] The missionaries thus came into a share of the general Negro distrust of the whites. As time passed, the Negroes tended to prefer ministers of their own color. There was a continuous loss through class-leaders who took their following away from the missionary churches to form new cults, and the Baptist attempt to train a native ministry was a failure partly because the ministers themselves left the official church and set up their own organizations.[34]

To make matters worse, the semi-Christian cults were not the only rivals of the missionaries. At the far end of the religious spectrum, the more African myal religion revived after the disappearance of the strict control of the slave system, and the practice of obeah increased. Both myalism and obeah were illegal, and the punishments were increasingly severe; but both continued to flourish.[35] Obeah was still essentially private and secret, but myalism took the form of open outbreaks of local hysteria that were bound to attract attention. One disruption, "the great myal procession," moved through the northwestern parishes from December 1841 through most of 1842. Another major outbreak came to the southeast in 1846, and there were still other occurrences in the countryside during 1848, 1852, and 1860 — and in Kingston itself in 1857.[36]

With local variations, the elements of myal practice at the beginning of the period were the usual survivals and mutations of African religion.

As soon as the darkness of evening set in, they assembled in crowds in open pastures, most frequently under large cotton trees, which they worshipped, and counted holy; after sacrificing some fowls, the leader began an extempore song, in a wild strain, which was answered in chorus; the dance followed, grew wilder and wilder, until they were in a state of excitement bordering on madness.

Some would perform incredible evolutions while in this state, until, nearly exhausted, they fell senseless to the ground, when every word they uttered was received as a divine revelation. At other times, Obeah was to be discovered, or a "shadow" was to be caught; a little coffin being prepared in which it was to be inclosed and buried.[37]

Beginning in the forties, however, the elements of Christianity became stronger in myal practice — preaching, Christian hymns, Christian phraseology, "prophesying" in the name of the Christian God — but the basic African elements were also retained. The mixture of the African and the European religions even invaded the orthodox churches, where an occasional member would be seized by the spirit during a service — a development that was sometimes disconcerting to the minister in charge.[38]

The incursions of Africanism reached a climax in the Great Revival of 1860–61, a movement that brought the final surge of missionary hope and the final depths of missionary despair. Except for a brief improvement during the cholera epidemic, the missionaries' efforts were steadily failing. Now, in 1860, they were encouraged by a revival of evangelical religion, beginning first in the United States in 1858 and then moving to Ireland and Great Britain. From the middle of 1859, missionaries tried to bring the same movement to Jamaica. Special days were set aside for fasting and prayer. The tempo of prayer meetings was increased — usually with two each day, morning and evening. Finally the Baptists set the last Sunday of April 1860 as the day for God to reach Jamaica. They were disappointed, but in mid-October religious excitement increased among the Moravian congregations in St. Elizabeth. It spread through the western part of the island and then eastward along the north and south coasts. By the middle of 1861 the new fervor had reached the whole island, and it lasted well into 1862.[39]

The missionaries who had promoted the revival were delighted. Even the Anglican Bishop pronounced it a genuine work of God,[40] but the delight did not last. As a Congregational missionary wrote a decade later:

> Like a mountain stream, clear and transparent as it springs from the rock, but which becomes foul and repulsive as impurities are mingled with it in its onward course, so with this extraordinary movement. In many central districts of the island the hearts of thoughtful and good men were gladdened by what they witnessed in the changed lives and characters of people for whom they long seemed to have laboured in vain; but in too many districts there was much wild extravagance and almost blasphemous fanaticism.[41]

In the early days, the new convert was usually struck prostrate on the church floor; but as the movement progressed other manifestations were introduced, and these bothered the missionaries. There were oral confessions, trances and dreams, "prophesying," spirit-seizure, wild dancing, flagellation, and mysterious sexual doings that were only hinted at in the missionary reports.[42] One missionary accepted the explanation of a follower that two different spirits were taking possession of the converts — the Spirit of Christ and another, diabolical spirit trying to undo the Divine Work.[43] But there was no getting around it: the Great Revival had turned African. It became more and more a mixture of myalism and Christianity, ending as a permanent addition to the Afro-Christian cults.[44] The revivalists were disowned by those who initiated the movement. The immense congregations of 1861 dwindled away, leaving the missionary churches at the lowest ebb since their decline began.

This was the final blow in a series of missionary disappoint-

ments, and it brought them a realization of failure not far removed from that of the planting class. The missionaries had
accepted the decline of the planting economy, especially in its
early years, as God's judgment on the planters and part of the
ultimate operation of Providence.[45] There was compensation,
after all, in the enormous growth of religion. When "religion"
and "morality" began to decline as well, they had misgivings.
In 1849, a missionary warned:

> . . . let the people of Jamaica be admonished if ever they should
> forget the God who broke the oppressive yoke of slavery: if ever
> they should forget their obligations to the men who for so many
> years endured so much of reproach and suffering for their best
> interests; — then indolence and wretchedness will be the result; the
> Island will be the grave of its own prosperity, and will exhibit, for
> a warning to others, the melancholy spectacle of the degradation of
> an ungrateful people, and the sin of such as apostatize from God.[46]

By 1865 it was easy for the missionaries to see this prophecy fulfilled. Especially because they were dedicated men — sincere,
hard-working, and badly paid — many missionaries developed
a sense of frustration and resentment toward the blacks who had
failed them.

The old missionary-Negro alliance was not completely sev-
ered by the events of the revival; but it was further weakened,
as it had been weakened since the revolution by increasing cultural friction. In the 1830's the missionaries were outside white
society, definitely aligned with the Negroes against the planting
class. In the 1860's, they were a part of white society, though
they were still the European Jamaicans most interested in the
majority of the country. Put in terms of the division between
the two Jamaicas, the earlier friendship and coöperation that
might once have been expected to unite the two, was itself coming apart.

*   *   *

Hiding behind every aspect of the failure to attain the cultural and social assimilation of the two Jamaicas was the background of racial distinctions and racial consciousness. The question of race was beneath the surface of every Jamaican problem,

intermingling with other issues and making all solutions more difficult. As time passed, it became increasingly serious, since many conflicts and unsolved problems could be translated into racial terms and so arise again at the next stage as a bar to mutual understanding. The threefold racial division helped to ease tensions somewhat — racial, as opposed to class, lines were never as tightly drawn in Jamaica as in the southern United States. In Jamaica the race question was often hidden behind other issues, while in the American South other issues tended to hide behind racial conflict. Many Jamaicans took a certain pride in their lack of overt racial distinctions, and the racial equality of Jamaica was frequently stressed in immigration appeals, such as the following poetic address to North American Negroes.

> The Yankee will not let you touch
> The cap of Freedom, nor so much
> As look on't; can ye hope to bear it?
> Come to Jamaica, then, and wear it!
> Here shall ye meet the kind embrace
> Of Afric's sons of kindred race . . .[47]

The white attitude toward the black Jamaican before emancipation had been one of ambivalence, and so it continued. The Negroes were still considered both "the finest, happiest, and most contented peasantry to be found anywhere" and "a set of idle, lazy, discontented vagabonds." [48] The whites also continued to show rather less discrimination against Negro women than against Negro men. A poem making fun of the black man and his missionary leaders, took quite a different view of the black woman:

> Let not the blue-ey'd Saxon think that praise
>   Of sable charms demands apology;
> Black lustrous skins beneath the torrid rays
>   Of Phoebus e'en can charm the Saxon eye.
> Thousands are beautiful in youthful days;
>   The black, the jet black, as the midnight sky,
> Polished like basalt statues, may compare
>   In grace and dignity with what's more fair.[49]

But for all the liberality of these views, there was still a linger-

ing racial fear in the white community, compounded of ignorance and their minority position in Jamaica. Planters had not
known much about Negro culture under slavery, and they never
came to understand the free working class. In addition, the
whites were steadily becoming a smaller minority, not only in
relation to the rest of the population but in absolute numbers.
The planters who stayed on were more isolated than ever among
abandoned plantations and an alien majority.[50] Until the 1860's
the planters' racial fear was only a latent uneasiness, but then,
partly through the known discontent of the Negroes and partly
through the strange doings of the revivalists, it grew into something close to a real feeling of terror. White planters began to
carry firearms. Whenever the Negroes had a noisy prayer meeting or the revival drums sounded from a Negro village, the
word was passed around, "The blacks are drilling." Such reports
were especially common just before the Morant Bay rising and
just afterward, but none of them, except the preparation for the
rising itself, were ever substantiated. The movements of the
black population, however, came to be surrounded by such an
aura of mystery, that an Anglican minister, separated by the
length of the island from the actual rebellion, reported to the
government early in 1866 that there was "a strange spirit of
mutinous evil" abroad, "the supernatural workings of Satanic
temptation." [51]

The white attitude toward the browns also deteriorated after
the mid-century, but only after an amazing improvement in the
1830's and 1840's. The colored class overcame the prejudice of
their illegitimate relatives, the old aristocracy of creole whites,
enough to be accepted as political and official equals. They were
able to hold their legal position and political power, but the
prejudice of the whites became a solid barrier in private social
functions. This tendency kept pace with the change in British
racial thinking, as the negrophile sentiments of the emancipation period passed away; but it also depended on social change
in Jamaica. One crucial element was a decrease in absenteeism.
It was not enough to break the earlier pattern of plantation
ownership, but it was enough to bring a substantial number of
resident proprietors or lessees. These men introduced a more
permanent sort of social life to the estates, and, what was much

worse, they brought their wives.[52] It was the white women who imposed the new standard of color prejudice — a prejudice that spread all through the ruling class, sometimes going to fantastic lengths in discriminating between different shades to meet an intricate social etiquette.[53]

The racial feelings of the black Jamaicans were only reported secondhand by the whites and browns, but at least the general tendencies can be set down. There was little trust or affection for the ruling class — little tendency to go to the whites for help or advice. At the same time there was no evidence of racial hatred, nor of a general desire to expel the whites from the island. The dislike of the whites was, rather, an almost universal distrust of white fairness and impartiality in dealing with the black population, a suspicion that advantage would be taken whenever possible. The suspicion applied most strongly to the planting class, less strongly to the missionaries or to British officials temporarily on the island. At the same time, there was a genuine affection for the Queen, who stood as a protective symbol and the source of their liberation from slavery.[54]

Relations between the brown and the black Jamaicans were less friendly than those between black and white. In response to white prejudice, the colored people tried to slough off all connection with their Negro heritage, and one way of doing this was to discriminate against the blacks. The blacks saw this and resented it. As a result the racial line between brown and black was already beginning to emerge as the most serious area of racial friction.[55]

The colored class was of two minds toward the white. One possibility was for brown men to earn assimilation and respect by working with the whites and taking white attitudes as their own. A newspaper editorial written by a brown man in 1862 expressed this point of view.

Let the colored men of Jamaica be true to themselves, and their progress will be certain; their best policy is to form a bond of union with their white brethren, and if this is done, no Governor will presume to keep from them the rights to which they are entitled as loyal subjects of the Sovereign of Great Britain.[56]

This was probably the majority position of the colored class throughout the period, as it certainly was in the first years after emancipation. Another view, however, became stronger in the fifties and sixties. This was the development of Jamaican nationalism, which had been growing slowly among the colored people. They were Europeanized, self-conscious, real natives of Jamaica, and visibly different from the creole whites.

The new attitude of brown Jamaicans can be seen in the changing views of Robert Osborn, who became a leader of the colored nationalists in the Assembly. In the forties he had regarded the salvation of the planting economy as necessary to the salvation of Jamaica, but later he answered claims that the country was ruined by appealing to the success of the small settlers.

We pay our debts as they become due; we meet the public exigencies by our yearly income; and there is now more substantial wealth in the colony than twenty years ago, for whatever a man possesses is his own. If it is said that the condition of the white inhabitants is, generally speaking, worse now than it was forty years ago, I admit it, and the abandonment of so many estates proves this fact; but this very circumstance has been productive of the prosperity of the other classes.[57]

He also attacked the "bastard brown men" who were the "mere mouthpieces of others," and he saw in the future a special destiny for Jamaica.[58]

. . . I have often reflected upon the real state of these colonies, and what they are likely to be in years to come. In this island the whites are disappearing by death, and by departure from it. It seems to me intended by Divine Providence that the wrongs of Africa are eventually to be vindicated in this hemisphere. . . We may make whatever laws we like, but I think they will ultimately be unavailing. The elements of our community, in whose favor you are making these exclusive laws, are wasting away, and none are returning to take their places. It seems to me that in years to come, which none of us can live to see, the government of the Colonies will fall into the hands of the blacks.[59]

The emergence of Osborn and other colored Jamaicans who agreed with him added a new problem to the existing social division and the decline of the planting economy. For the first time there was a basic difference of outlook within the ruling class — and the colored nationalists were decidedly members of the ruling class. Whether they spoke only for their fellow brown men, or for the black Jamaicans as well, they were a threat to the continued political control of the planting class.

*　　　*　　　*

Racial nationalism, as a serious political problem, developed in the latter part of this period, but it was part of a potential problem recognized many years earlier. A farsighted Jamaican saw it clearly in 1839.

I have said, in the commencement of these observations, that the African race must ultimately become dominant in the West Indies, and this may appear to some a startling doctrine . . . the case we are now considering is altogether an unprecented conjuncture, and it cannot be said that there is any actual impossibility, in the European landholder continuing to cultivate his estates, and enjoy the profits of it in security, though the great majority of those filling superior situations in Jamaica, should be descendents of the African race. This, to be sure, is the grand problem to be solved; this is the revolution, which to bring about gradually and beneficially, will require the exercise of great wisdom and policy; and here is the high and honorable task which is thrown upon the nation! [60]

This was the problem that came with Jamaica's autonomous constitution, but after their other failures it was likely to require more "wisdom and policy" than the ruling class could be expected to supply.

IX

The Failure
of Self-Government

IN OCTOBER 1865 A FEW HUNDRED SMALL SETTLERS of St. Thomas-in-the-East came down from the hills behind Morant Bay for a demonstration against the parish vestry. The demonstration turned into a riot and the riot became a rebellion — though one that was easily put down. This seems a slight occurrence to mark the end of an epoch in Jamaican history, and it was, in fact, of slight importance in itself. The Morant Bay rising became important, however, because it released tensions that had been building up during all the years since emancipation. It underlined the failure of the planting class to manage the country successfully and brought them, at the end of 1865, to a political crisis which was epoch-making in the true sense of the term. The lines of Jamaican development were broken, and the island turned in a new direction, under new rule, and with new objectives.

The revolt at Morant Bay and its aftermath were thus a second Jamaican revolution. In sweeping away the old constitution, and along with it the political control of the planting class, it completed the revolution of the 1830's. The decision of 1839 had left Jamaica with a completed social revolution but no political revolution. During the following decades, the old ruling class retained their power on sufferance. They hoped to use representative self-government and local autonomy to build the kind of free-labor society they wanted. They failed to accomplish this task, and paralleling the failure to achieve their ends was a growing disappointment with the means they had chosen. The revolt at Morant Bay was the culminating failure, and it was followed by the surrender of Jamaican self-government.

*   *   *

The Jamaican constitution was untouched by the revolution of the 1830's, but the post-revolutionary political problems were almost as pressing as those of social and economic adjustment. The political ideas of the ruling class came into sharp contradiction with the political realities for which they had been striving. In order to defend the autonomy of Jamaica, the planters had talked the language of constitutional autonomy and political liberalism. These political ideas, like the economic and social ideas of pre-revolutionary Jamaica, were of little use after emancipation — they served their purpose only so long as the majority of the population were not counted as citizens.

During the 1830's the Assembly had continued and even strengthened its liberal-sounding claims, while its legislative acts prepared for the coming emancipation. In 1834 and 1836 new franchise acts were passed, designed to prevent the Negroes from voting, once they were free. The second and more stringent of these attempted to raise the former requirement of a ten-pound freehold to fifty pounds, and it was approved by Governor Sir Lionel Smith with the specific intention that it would disenfranchise the Negroes without doing so on purely racial grounds. But these acts were passed and approved without taking into account the views of the Colonial Office. James Stephen, who had drafted the emancipation act, had no intention of allowing limitations on the ex-slaves' political liberty. He believed that, "When the people of this Country paid the price of Negro Emancipation it was never stated or suggested that the enfranchised population would obtain personal only, as contra-distinguished from Political Freedom." Through Stephen's influence, consequently, both acts were disallowed in England.[1]

In spite of its earlier attempts to restrict the suffrage, the Assembly continued to defend itself on grounds that might be called overt hypocrisy — or more charitably, perhaps, only a very short memory. In 1838 it announced:

The legislative independence of Jamaica has ever been the pride of her English conquerors. They have received with joy their coloured fellow colonists into an equal participation of their valued liberty, and they were prepared to rejoice at the extension of the Constitution to the emancipated blacks; but the British Government, by a great fault, if not a crime, has, at the moment when all should have been free, torn from the lately-ascendant class the privileges which were their birth-right; from another class, now the equals of the former, the rights they had long and fortunately struggled for, and from the emancipated blacks the rights which they fondly expected to enjoy with their personal freedom.[2]

This statement has every mark of a political trick to attract radical votes in the imperial Parliament. If such were the case, it was successful; and the Jamaican constitution was saved. But the Assembly went through with its promise, surprisingly enough, and admitted the ex-slaves to the electorate. It also set a moderately low financial requirement for the franchise — though it was probably lower in practice than the Assembly intended. By an Act of 1840, a voter could qualify in any one of four ways — by having six pounds annual income from a freehold, by paying or receiving a rent-charge of thirty pounds annually on real estate, or by paying three pounds in direct taxes. These qualifications were so low that they very quickly admitted a majority of black and colored voters, but the aristocracy still had some protection in the requirements for membership in the Assembly — an income of 180 pounds from land, or real property worth 1,800 pounds, or both real and personal property worth 3,000 pounds.[3] No small settler or Baptist demagogue was going to meet that very easily, and there were, as we shall see, other ways of restricting the suffrage without changing the explicit provisions of the franchise act.

The Assembly of Jamaica might speak the language of political liberty and even pass a relatively liberal franchise act, but this was not enough to make the British government completely happy with the Jamaican constitution. While James Stephen and other humanitarians insisted on political liberty for the ex-slaves, Lord Sligo, the able former Governor, and some of the

Colonial Office personnel warned that representative institutions were a grave danger for Jamaica under any circumstances. If the Assembly intended a fully representative government, then democracy in the hands of the uneducated blacks would result. If, instead, the white and colored classes were able to make the constitution exclusive, there would be an equal danger from an oppressive oligarchy.[4] In 1839 their warning went unheeded, and Jamaica emerged from slavery with a highly restricted Assembly but a moderate suffrage. Some of those who had opposed self-government in 1839, however, remained in the Colonial Office, and from there they kept a critical eye on the political development of the island. Thus the problem for the Jamaican ruling class was made very difficult. They had to preserve a tenuous balance — not enough democracy to endanger their own political control, nor enough oligarchy to alarm the British government.

*   *   *

It would appear at first glance that the political settlement after emancipation was quite oligarchic enough to withstand any democratic attack. Although the suffrage was broader than the planting class first wanted, hardly more than two thousand voters actually appeared on the rolls at any time. Furthermore, membership in the House of Assembly was reserved to wealthy men, and the provisions of the Franchise Act of 1840 could not be altered except by the Assembly itself. In the ensuing years, however, there were occasions when the ruling class felt its power to be threatened, and this threat, potential or real, gradually whittled away at their confidence in representative self-government.

The Jamaican franchise was restricted, but it was not restricted enough to prevent the representation of different interests in the Assembly. Nor was it broad enough to extend far beyond what may be broadly called the "planting interest."[5] Within the planting interest, however, there was room for opposed views and for the development of political parties. There had always been political factions in the Assembly, since its seventeenth-century foundation, and, as Jamaica emerged from the apprenticeship, there were two clear political parties. Their ideological differences were not great, but they represented two different ways of looking for the true interest of the plantation system. One was called the Planters' Party or the Country Party, because it was more narrowly interested in agriculture. It was the party of the wealthy planting attorneys, most of whom were white and lived away from Kingston and Spanish Town. The second party was called, at various times, the King's House Party, City Party, or Colored Party. Many of its members were also planters, but it included more of the colored class, more merchants, and more officials. While it also favored the planting interest, the City Party often supported the Governor, and the leadership of Edward Jordon helped give it the stamp of mild and conservative humanitarianism.[6] Since party discipline was difficult, the two groups functioned as shifting coalitions under individual leaders, who formed alliances and broke them according to personal interest or the old rivalries between merchant and planter, city and country, white and colored, northside and southside.

The threat to the constitutional balance came from neither of the two major parties, but from a small group, rarely more than six members, who represented the interests of the small settlers. Normally this group was too small to be dangerous, but twice during the period between emancipation and the Morant Bay rising it seemed to threaten the control of the planting class in a more serious way — once during the forties and once again during the early sixties.

The first attack was led by the Baptist missionaries, who, in 1839, began to organize their congregations for political action.[7] This threat, however, was not immediate, since the election of 1838 had already passed and another was not expected until 1845. As the date of the election approached, the Baptists under the leadership of William Knibb tried to broaden the base of their political movement by organizing a general dissenters' attack on the Establishment. In 1844 they set up the Anti-State-Church Convention to provide a central electioneering agency, but Lord Elgin, the Governor, threw their preparations off balance by dissolving the Assembly six months before its expected end. The Anti-Church-State Convention was only able to put forward candidates in five parishes. When the returns were in, only three members were clearly against the Establishment, and only six could be considered representatives of the small settlers. This was the last chance the Baptists were to have. By the time of the next election in 1849, Knibb was dead, Baptist membership was declining, and the crisis over protection had brought with it a new political situation.

This incident provides a curious example of the transfer of an English political movement to Jamaica. The Jamaican Anti-Church-State Convention was an obvious reflection of the British Anti-Church-State Convention, which met within a few months of its Jamaican counterpart. The name of the movement and the idea of opposing the Established Church in this way was picked up immediately in Jamaica, but the social and political differences between Jamaica and England made the two movements, in reality, entirely different from each other. The English dissenters led by Edward Miall were opposed to the influence of the Church on government, especially in education, and they were interested in organizing political action to end the Establishment. In a general way this was also true of Knibb's movement, but in Jamaica it was not the middle class who were being organized. It was the previously unrepresented group of Negro small settlers, and their victory at the polls would have meant a social and political revolution as well as a religious change.[8]

The interjection of the religious issue copied from Britain was, in fact, one reason for the failure of the similar movement in Jamaica. The defeat of 1844 was not a real test of the strength of the settlers' vote. The alignment in that election was not so much for or against the settlers as for or against the Baptists — and Knibb had many enemies. The most striking illustration of this fact is the position taken by various political leaders. The Rev. Samuel Oughton, most conservative of the Baptist ministers, helped to muster the black vote in Kingston, while others, who later represented the small settlers in the Assembly, helped to defeat Baptist candidates in the parishes. It was in this election that George W. Gordon, who was later hanged for alleged complicity in the Morant Bay rising, first entered the Assembly by defeating one of the Convention candidates. Oughton was no

real friend of democracy — only an enemy of the Church — while
Gordon was finally killed for taking the side of the settlers.[9]

   Gordon and others like him constituted the second threat to
the position of the ruling class in the Assembly. From the
middle-fifties onward, a stronger group was discernible to the
left of the City Party, but merging with it. For lack of a better
name, they can be called what their enemies called them — "the
demagogues." They were all men with enough wealth to sit
in the Assembly and enough sympathy with the majority of
Jamaicans to attract their votes, but they were not all of the
same political shade. Robert Osborn and the racial nationalists
belonged to this group, but they were decidedly within the
City Party on most questions of party politics. Gordon, however,
was on the far left, outside the City Party. He was colored, the
son of a great attorney of the slave era, a man of wealth in his
own right, and a landowner in many different parts of the island;
but he was also an evangelical religious fanatic, an opponent
of the Established Church and of Governor Eyre, an extreme
nationalist, and the elected representative of the small settlers
of St. Thomas-in-the-East. These qualities made him a dangerous man to all the planting interest.[10]

   Neither the Baptists nor the settlers alone posed quite so serious a political problem as the appearance of wealthy men who
would lead Jamaica away from planter control — whether, like
Osborn, because of race and nationalism, or, like Gordon,
through religiously motivated sympathy for the underdog. As
the planting order was more and more unsuccessful, the political
drift of Jamaica was toward these men. The Assembly was therefore driven to search for expedients that would preserve the
reality of political control, without losing the balance of democracy and oligarchy that was the essential condition for Jamaican self-government.

                    *   *   *

   To say that the ruling-class Jamaicans were forced to search
for constitutional expedients and to make careful adjustments
to preserve their right of self-government is not to imply that
they worked continuously or explicitly on this problem. Like

their economic problem, the constitutional problem occurred piecemeal, and it was handled piecemeal. It was also complicated by the fact that Jamaica had inherited a defective system of government and by the example of other colonies which were taking decisive steps toward their eventual dominion status.

The Jamaican constitution in the early nineteenth century was a survival from an earlier period, when the British system of ministerial government was only in the first stages of development. It retained the faults that had made for governmental inefficiency in the North American colonies before the American Revolution and continued to cause political difficulties in Canada well into the nineteenth century. The principal difficulty was the constant conflict between a British-appointed executive and the locally elected Assembly. The Assembly could refuse to pass laws and appropriate money, if it disliked the Governor's actions. At the same time the Governor could refuse his assent to legislation passed by the Assembly or could have it killed by his appointees in the upper house. Effective government was only possible when the Governor and the Assembly were in agreement.

This situation had, of course, been equally true of Great Britain in an earlier period, when the King acted as an hereditary executive and the Parliament was an elected legislature. It had been gradually settled there by the establishment during the eighteenth century of the precedent that the King could act in his official capacity only on the advice of his ministers, who were required, in turn, to have the confidence of the majority of the House of Commons. Beginning in the 1830's, Canadians began to demand the extension of this precedent to their own colonial governments. That is, they wanted the principal officials formed into a ministry, which should be chosen from the House of Assembly and responsible to it, and they wanted the Governor bound to act on the advice of this group. Under the name of "responsible government" this suggestion was incorporated in 1839 in Lord Durham's report on Canadian affairs, and it received a wide publicity in Britain. Finally, by 1848, it had become a reality in Canadian practice, and this example formed the basis for relations between the executive and the legislature in the other self-governing colonies.

In the sense that responsible government recognized the supremacy of the legislature, this was the direction in which Jamaica had been moving for some decades before emancipation. But the Assembly had not tried so much to control the Governor as to set up its own independent executive and to reduce the powers of the appointed council. Rather than making the government of the island more efficient and more responsive to popular opinion, these moves had merely made it more unwieldy and improved the opportunities for corruption within the Assembly. Shortly after emancipation, the Colonial Office suggested that the Jamaican constitution should be reformed — but this reform would have reduced the powers of the Assembly, rather than increasing them. Sir Charles Metcalfe, who was then Governor of Jamaica, answered that there was no need of pressing the planters for reform. He believed they would voluntarily surrender their powers of self-government as soon as they saw the political control of the island slipping into the hands of the Negroes.[11] In a sense this is what happened — but it came in the sixties, rather than the forties.

In the meantime, the Assembly itself made a series of adjustments in the constitution of Jamaica, although, between the twin dangers of the Colonial Office and the small settlers, there was not much room for constitutional maneuver. The first of these changes was not in the relation of the Assembly to the Governor, but in that of the Assembly to the people. After the defeat of the Baptist-led small-holders in 1844, the relatively wide franchise was allowed to stand for one more election — that of 1849 — and then the suffrage was reduced. An act of 1841 had made it necessary for any voter to present evidence of having paid all taxes before his name could be added to the rolls. This measure was made an effective bar to voting in the early 1850's by the passage of an hereditaments tax, which had the effect of levying twelve shillings a year on any six-pound freeholder. Since few marginal voters were willing to be taxed 10 per cent of their annual income, even if the payment of this tax carried the voting privilege, they simply stopped registering, and the number of voters in contested elections dropped from 1,819 in 1849 to 753 in 1854.[12]

The effective measure in this instance was a tax, and not a

franchise bill, and it was therefore allowed to stand without opposition from Britain. The change, in any event, was simultaneous with the legislative crisis over free trade, and it made very little noise in either England or Jamaica. Interest was concentrated instead on the newest flare-up of the old struggle between the Governor and the Assembly. Once again the Assembly attempted to pass unacceptable legislation as a means of coercing the Governor, and once again the Governor used his appointed Council to block the maneuvers of the Assembly. Once again there was a deadlock, but this time the example of Canada was recent and vivid. The Assembly demanded, in the name of democracy, an elected rather than an appointed Council — and some Jamaicans went further still and demanded fully responsible government on the Canadian model.[13] When the restriction of the franchise and the movement for responsible government are taken together, the tendency of the Jamaican constitution is clear. In the early 1850's an Assembly representing fewer Jamaicans than ever before claimed greater powers than it had previously exercised.

Movement in the early fifties was in the direction of oligarchy, but it was soon reversed; and the reversal was the work of the Assembly itself, not the guiding hand of the Colonial Office. Like the movement toward oligarchy, the movement away from it came in two steps, one in the relation of the Assembly to the people and one in the relation of the Assembly to the Governor. As the final settlement of the free-trade crisis, the Jamaicans undertook, in 1854, to reform their constitution in return for a low-interest loan from Great Britain. The Assembly abolished the permanent boards, which represented its earlier incursion into executive powers. In their place, it created an Executive Committee of three members, two from the Assembly and one from the Council. Here was a form of ministry that might have been made responsible to the majority of the Assembly, but the Assembly stopped short. The Executive Committee was made responsible for its policies not to the Assembly, but to the Governor.[14]

The decision not to establish responsible government, however, was a close one, and several different influences had to be taken into account. The Colonial Office remained suspicious of

Jamaican self-government, and was willing to allow the Assembly to continue in existence only because it held the promise of later improvement.[15] This meant that there would be little chance of securing English approval for a further restriction of the franchise. At the same time, economic changes were gradually diminishing the number of white residents, increasing the number of wealthy colored men, and increasing the number of black small-holders who could qualify for the franchise. In the past the Assembly would have been all too willing to settle its old quarrel with the Governor in its own favor, but this was now dangerous. Powers the planters established for themselves might fall into the hands of some future Negro majority. In the last analysis they trusted the Colonial Office more than their own fellow-countrymen.[16] Thus the reforms of 1854 were barely enough to meet the requirements of the Colonial Office, and friction between the Assembly and the Governor was as likely as ever.

The second step away from oligarchy was made four years after the new constitution, and a halfhearted step it was. The hereditaments tax had been repealed, and the Assembly again had to face the problem of the small freeholder. The only solution was a new franchise act, and the Assembly entered into a full-scale debate on the question of democracy. The Country Party favored a small electorate, but even they continued in the Jamaican tradition of paying lip service to the principle of democracy and the *mystique* of land ownership as a qualification for voting. Edward Jordon and the City Party, on the other hand, argued for a more extended suffrage, appealing to English precedent, the natural right of taxpayers to vote, and the value of representation as a safety valve. The result was the Franchise Act of 1858, which was a compromise between the two parties and probably close to the limit of restriction acceptable to the English government. The vote of the six-pound freeholder was preserved, but only at a price. The requirements for the suffrage were lowered for all other groups in order to increase the balance of votes against the small settler, and a ten-shilling tax-stamp was required on all claims to vote. At the same time, the requirements for membership in the Assembly were lowered for landowners while they remained constant or were increased slightly for other classes. In spite of the new tax on voters, the effective suffrage under this act was broader than it had been since 1849, and 1,457 voters came to the polls in 1863.[17]

Although these two steps may have saved the constitution of Jamaica from cancellation by higher authorities, they did next to nothing to make it more satisfactory as a workable instrument of government. As the sixties approached, the decay of European Jamaica became more and more evident and the possibility of maintaining the balance between oligarchy and democracy seemed to fade. Under the leadership of Wellesley Bourke, a Country-Party planter, there was a growing movement in the Assembly to make the constitution frankly oligarchic. In 1854, 1858, and 1863, bills for this purpose were introduced — all aimed, with minor variations, at raising the financial requirements for membership in the Assembly, reducing the number of elected members, and uniting the Assembly with the appointed Legislative Council in a unicameral legislature.[18] Bourke's constitution bill was defeated each time, but each time the majority against it was smaller.

The debates over these bills made it clear that most of the white planters of the Country Party agreed with H. A. Whitelocke, who said in the Assembly:

. . . at times despotism is better than representation. Some countries do require despotism — countries in which education does not prevail; and I ask if this is not the position of Jamaica? [19]

One hindrance kept this sentiment from becoming more active — a real despotism in Jamaica would not be a despotism of the planting class, but of the Colonial Office. To yield to this would be to give up a long tradition of self-government and a long fight for colonial autonomy.

Another, and a somewhat curious, objection to Bourke's plan came from a few planters, who stood by the example of England and the Jamaican claims to political liberalism and argued that the plan was "against the spirit of the age, — against the spirit of English legislation, — and against everything that is politic and right." [20] On that account they were willing to relinquish their power with something that combined good grace with an attempt to hold what influence they could in a changing country. In the words of one white planter,

There is no doubt that the class to which I belong is gradually diminishing, and it is best for us to live on friendly terms with those who are rapidly rising into power and importance. It is useless for us to lament over, and to desire to prevent, that march of civilization that is making such rapid strides in the country. I believe the influence of the class to which I belong would diminish immensely, were it known that we desire to do away with the popular rights and the House of Assembly.[21]

The ruling class had not quite yet lost all its former trust in representative self-government.

In the early 1860's, however, that faith was being dissipated, and the problem of executive responsibility remained to be solved. Experience since 1854 made it perfectly evident that an Executive Committee responsible to the Governor was no solution, since the Assembly continued to harass the Governor as it had always done. In 1860 Governor Darling created a new responsible-government crisis. In order to avoid the constant bickering with the Assembly, he attempted a constitutional maneuver that would have settled the problem by making the Executive Committee responsible to the Assembly. The political storm this move created is evidence of the distance the planting class had come from their old claims to self-government, or even from their discussions of 1854. The Assembly refused outright to accept the proffered gift of power. The City-Party Executive Committee resigned in protest on the grounds that Jamaica was not yet ready for responsible government, and the Assembly, the Council, the Colonial Office, and the absentee proprietors all supported this view. Darling was forced to let the matter drop, but efficient government was still impossible, since the Assembly both opposed the Governor and refused to take responsibility for the actions of the Executive Committee.[22]

The situation, moreover, was now more unstable than ever. Darling had shown the possibility of instituting responsible government under the Constitution of 1854 without the necessity of new legislation. The fear of future demagogic government was all the more heightened. In 1863 the crucial move was made

— and made by the same City-Party leaders who had opposed Darling in 1860. An Assembly majority of the City Party voted "no confidence" in Governor Eyre and the Country-Party Executive Committee. This move forced a general election. The City Party returned to power and their leaders to the Executive Committee, in spite of Eyre's preference for their opponents.[23]

In practice Jamaica now had responsible government, and the new popular control over the executive increased the danger of British interference. It alarmed those who feared oligarchy as well as those who feared Negro democracy. It shook the Jamaican Country Party even more, since it was they who had lost office through the change. As the mid-sixties approached Jamaica was moving toward some new constitutional crisis, but the settlers' revolt cut the process short and superimposed a crisis of another kind. It is difficult to avoid the conclusion that Jamaican fear of the demagogues, combined with the growing British conviction that Jamaicans could no longer be trusted with the control of their own government, would have ended self-government within a few years, even without the rising at Morant Bay.

*   *   *

The Morant Bay crisis was itself the result of political failure, but it was failure at another level. It had little to do with the constitutional problems of the ruling class. Instead, the immediate cause was a failure of local institutions — the judiciary and the Vestries.

The work of the Justices of the Peace had been important in Jamaica since the eighteenth century, and they had been strengthened in the early nineteenth century as a defense against emancipation. During the revolutionary years they had served as an important instrument for combating the executive and the stipendiary Magistrates, and they emerged with emancipation as the logical institution for handling the new judicial and police problems of the freed society. Certainly the only alternative was the professional summary justice of the Stipendiaries, which was thoroughly unpopular with the planting class.

The Jamaicans not only had their own tradition of rural justice through amateur magistrates, when they began to plan for a free society, there was also the analogy of the English squire. As William Burge said, in explaining the planters' point of view:

They believe that no part of the English jurisprudence has commanded more admiration than that the administration of the laws; in their most minute operation on the interests of society, is entrusted to the landed proprietors. . . They state that they do not see how it is possible to expect that confidence can be restored, as long as the labourer is continually placed in hostile collision with his employer, and is taught by the magistrate to look at him as his natural enemy, and the administration of justice is entrusted to persons possessing no immediate interest in the welfare of the country.[24]

Thus, the Jamaica magistracy profited from a general belief in what Lord Elgin called "the harmonising influence of British connexion, and the power of self-adaptation inherent in our institutions." [25]

The Jamaican magistrates were strengthened, accidentally, by another current of British ideas. The institution of stipendiary Magistrates had been a product of Benthamite demands for administrative centralization and the uniform application of law. In the interest of efficiency, the Colonial Office was willing to give to the Stipendiary Magistrates powers that would have been withheld from amateur planter-justices. With full emancipation, however, the legislative colonies were allowed to give their local magistracy the same range of powers the Colonial Office had designed for the professional justices of the Crown Colonies.[26] Some of the Stipendiaries did indeed stay on after 1838, but they were a small minority. The group of sixty-three Special Justices originally assigned to Jamaica decreased after 1838 as justices died or resigned. By 1854, there were only nineteen left, and in 1858 the Assembly refused to appropriate funds to keep the number at fourteen. With the number of ordinary Justices of the Peace at about 270 in 1865, the remaining Stipendiaries provided no more than the smallest professional leaven. The Jamaican planters were neither professional judges nor English country gentlemen. This fact alone would be sufficient to explain the failure of the local judiciary in Jamaica, where powers designed for a very different group of men were given to the attorneys and overseers.

The Justice of the Peace was the chief agent for enforcing labor legislation — both the ordinary laws for creole Jamaicans and the special regulations for immigrant laborers. He also had special powers over the police. His position on the Vestry included control of the local constabulary, and he had the extraordinary right of issuing orders to the central police, which was otherwise organized and controlled by the Governor.[27] These special powers had grown out of the still more extraordinary provisions of the Police Act of 1833, passed in preparation for emancipation. In the period of slavery one of the safeguards against slave rebellion was the system of treaties with the semi-independent maroon Negroes in the mountains. They had come to the aid of the whites in the Baptist War, and they were to do so for one last time in 1865. The Police Act of 1833 planned to create six new police colonies in the mountains, artificially reproducing the older safeguard of the maroon settlements. These colonies were to be self-sufficient agricultural communities, and they were to be separate from all intercourse with the lowland Negro population. The remarkable feature of the whole plan was that these colonies could be called into action not only by the Governor but by any single magistrate holding a general Commission of the Peace.[28]

The plan was later abandoned because it could not be prepared in time for emancipation, but it stands, nevertheless, as an institutional project of almost purely Jamaican origin. And as such, it indicates the kind of position a magistrate held in Jamaica. He represented imposed order in an alien and potentially rebellious country. In spite of the analogy to the English squire, he was very far indeed from the "natural" superior who received the deference and respectful obedience of the English villager. But the outward appearance of his office was close enough to the similar English institution to be accepted without question in Britain as the proper means of providing summary jurisdiction in Jamaica.

Later increases in the magistrates' power indicate that the most common Jamaican attitude toward the local judiciary continued to be in the spirit of the Police Act of 1833. This attitude is more obvious in the bills that were refused assent than in those that actually became law. The Summary Jurisdiction Bill of 1858, for example, provided among other things that two magistrates acting together could hear any case in which the accused would waive his right to a jury trial, except for a few reserved capital offenses. It would also have given any two magistrates the right to pass sentence in any case where the plea was "guilty." [29] The governor killed this particular bill after it had passed the Assembly, but other acts gradually increased the jurisdiction of the magistrates in a less drastic fashion.

The most important change was the increased difficulty of appeal. After 1855 a summary decison could be appealed only to the central courts, which, in practice, raised the cost so much that the peasantry were almost deprived of the right. The direct fee for an appeal was only eighteen shillings in 1865, but travel expenses, solicitor's fees, barrister's fees, and legal papers added so much to the cost that a settler might lose six months' income, even if he won his case.[30]

The failure of the local judiciary, however, was not simply the result of increased magisterial powers, or even the increased difficulty of appeal. Not the existence of authority, but its abuse, caused the trouble. The great majority of planter-magistrates intended to be just in dealing with the people, but their decisions could not avoid the influence of economic decline, the tendency to blame much of the decline on the Negroes, and the increasing division between the two Jamaicas. This was especially unfortunate, since the principal contact between the Negro and the government was through the magistrate and the tax collector. By the 1860's, the workers and settlers no longer had faith in the justice of magisterial courts. In some areas they simply stopped bringing cases before the magistrates, and the courts became little more than a means of enforcing the rule of the planters. In St. Thomas-in-the-East, for example, 256 cases were handled by the magistrates in 1864. Of these, the defendant was a Negro worker or settler in 250 cases and a planter in only two. Of the same total, 139 cases were brought on the complaint of a planter and only 78 by a member of the working class.[31] This result is all the more striking, since black Jamaicans were traditionally fond of litigation.

The local judiciary of St. Thomas was perhaps the worst on the island, but the same general situation was common. Rather than restoring confidence between the worker and the planter, amateur local magistrates were a principal influence in destroying it. During the decades after emancipation they helped produce a Negro attitude toward law and government that was unfriendly, even though it was not always rebellious. This attitude lasted long beyond 1865. In the early twentieth century a Jamaican still characterized the Negro view in these terms:

He regards them as something outside and apart from himself. They are something imposed upon him which he is sometimes inclined to think of as oppressive. The laws are "buckra laws," laws made by white men; and though he knows that white as well as black men are supposed to obey them, he is never quite sure that the white men will not be specially favored in some way. He doubts the absolute impartiality of the law. He is quite satisfied that the policeman will readily arrest him, while leaving his master to go free, though their offenses may be the same. . . Though peaceful by nature, he would like to see less of the policeman; although liberal, he has a strong objection to the paying of taxes.[32]

*　　*　　*

For some thirty years the Jamaican planting class and its allies had struggled with a complex of economic, social, and political problems. As each attempted remedy was frustrated, political tension, racial fear, and economic distress grew to new heights. By 1865, any incident might touch off a major crisis. The incident was supplied on October 11, when a group of about four hundred black settlers, vaguely organized by a Native Baptist parson named Paul Bogle, came down from the hills to the square in front of Morant Bay courthouse in St. Thomas-in-the-East. Their original aim was to protest a decision by magistrates, but the magistrates were ready for them. The Vestry met as usual, and a group of the militia were drawn up in front of the courthouse. The riot act was read, some stones were thrown from the crowd, and the volunteers fired — it was another in the succession of riots that had taken place since emancipation. This time Bogle's followers were angrier, better prepared, and more determined than earlier mobs. They drove the volunteers into the courthouse and laid siege to it. Finally, they managed to set the building on fire, driving the besieged Vestry into the open. Some escaped, but fifteen of the magistrates and volunteers were killed and thirty-one wounded. That evening Bogle and his followers retired to their village of Stoney Gut. On the following days mobs of settlers moved through the parish, attacking and looting an occasional great house and killing three more white men who were especially unpopular. The estate buildings and the crops were not burned, however, nor were white and colored people systematically attacked.[33]

Whatever Bogle's intentions may have been before the riot at the courthouse, after October 12 he tried to protect himself and his followers by raising a full rebellion against white rule. This was futile, since his men had no weapons beyond their agricultural cutlasses and the few firearms they captured at Morant Bay. In the end they never fought a single engagement against the troops sent to oppose them. The suppression was immediate and effective, and it had behind it the pent-up emotion of all the years of failure. Under the orders of Governor Eyre, troops blocked off the land approaches to St. Thomas-in-the-East. The maroons came down from the higher mountains, and other troops were landed from the sea. The rioting was stopped. Bogle himself was captured on October 23 and hanged from the yardarm of H.M.S. *Wolverine*. In other parishes, the demagogues who were considered most dangerous were arrested on Eyre's orders. Some of them were taken to Morant Bay for a military trial. Among these was George W. Gordon, who was given a quick trial and hanged in front of the burned-out courthouse. In all, 439 people were killed in the suppression, about one thousand Negro houses were burned, and six hundred people flogged by the military authorities.[34]

The exact nature and the causes of the rising are still a matter of disagreement among historians, although a Royal Commission came to Jamaica in 1866 and collected immense quantities of evidence.[35] There was some unrest throughout the island in 1865, following the failure of many provision grounds in a series of dry years and the high price of imported products on account of the American Civil War. There is no evidence, however, that discontent had risen to the point of rebellion outside the single parish of St. Thomas-in-the-East. Certainly Bogle's organization hardly spread beyond the Native Baptist congregations of the mountain settlements near Stoney Gut. It seems not to have reached the estate laborers, who generally were quiet during the period of disturbance.[36] As to the immediate grievances of Bogle and his congregation, there is no reason to doubt the statement they sent to Governor Eyre the night before they demonstrated at the Bay.

We, the petitioners of St. Thomas-in-the-East, send to inform your Excellency of the mean advantages that has been taken of us from time to time, and more especially this present time, when on Saturday, 7th of this month, an outrageous assault was committed upon us by the policemen of this parish, by order of the Justices, which occasion an outbreaking for which warrants have been issued against innocent person, of which we were compelled to resist. We therefore, call upon your Excellency for protection, seeing we are Her Majesty's loyal subjects, which protection if refused to will be compelled to put our shoulders to the wheel, as we have been imposed upon for a period of 27 years with due obeisance to the laws of our Queen and country, and we can no longer endure the same, therefore is our object of calling upon your Excellency as Governor-in-Chief and Captain of our Island, and your petitioners as in duty bound will ever pray.[37]

Whatever else the Morant Bay affair may have been, it was first of all a local rising against the intrenched magistracy and only later, if ever, a rebellion against British rule.

This was not what the ruling class made of it. Governor Eyre called the Assembly for November 7, and his opening address expressed the dominant interpretation of the planting class — an interpretation containing so much of the planters' reaction that it deserves quotation at length.

The present is, indeed, a most critical period in the history of Jamaica; and the session now being inaugurated, will, in all probability, be one of the most important and momentous ever held in this colony.

The occurrence of a most wicked and unprovoked rebellion, in the eastern division of the island, has brought sorrow and suffering upon the whole community. The valuable lives of many noble and gallant men, who were ornaments to the land, have been sacrificed (whilst peaceably meeting in the discharge of their duties to the state) by a most savage and cruel butchery, only paralleled by the atrocities of the Indian mutiny.

· · · · ·

To the prompt and decisive action I firmly believe we owe it, under God's providence, that we are able to meet here this day. One moment's hesitation, one single reverse, might have lit the torch, which would have blazed in rebellion from one end of the island to the other; and who can say how many of us would have lived to see it extinguished?

It is my duty to point out to you that satisfactory as it is to know that the rebellion in the eastern districts has been crushed out, the entire colony has long been, still is, on the brink of a volcano, which may any moment burst into fury.

There is scarcely a district in the island where disloyalty, sedition, and murderous intentions are not widely disseminated, and in many instances openly expressed. The misapprehensions and misrepresentations of pseudo philanthropists in England and in this country, the inflammatory harangues or seditious writings of political demagogues, of evil minded men of higher position and of better education, and of worthless persons without either character or property to lose. [sic]

The personal scurrilous, vindictive, and disloyal writings of a licentious and unscrupulous press, and the misdirected efforts and misguided counsel of certain Ministers of Religion, sadly so miscalled, if the Saviour's example and teaching is to be the standard, have led to their natural, their necessary, their inevitable result (amongst an ignorant, excitable, and uncivilized population) — rebellion, arson, murder.

These are hard words, gentlemen, but they are true; and this is no time to indulge in selected sentences, or polished phraseology.

A mighty danger threatens the land; and, in order to concert measures to avert it, and prevent, so far as human wisdom can, any future recurrence of a similar state of things, we must examine boldly, deeply, and unflinchingly, into the causes which have led to this danger. I know of no general grievance or wrong, under which the negroes of this colony labour. Individual cases of hardship or injustice must arise in every community; but as a whole the peasantry of Jamaica have nothing to complain of. They are less taxed, can live more easily and cheaply, and are less under an obligation to work for subsistence, than any peasantry in the world. The same laws as to the imposition of taxes, the administration of justice, and the enjoyment of political rights, apply to them and to the white and colored inhabitants alike. They ought to be better off, more comfortable, and more independent than the labourers of any other country. If it is not so, it is due to their own indolence, improvidence, and vice, acted upon by the absence of good example, of civilising influences in many districts, and by the evil teaching, and evil agencies, to which I have already referred, in all.

It is a remarkable fact too, that many of the principal rebels in the late outbreak, have been persons well off, and well to do in the world, possessing lands, cottages, furniture, horses, or mules, or other property, and with an education above the average of the peasantry.

It is necessary to bring these facts before you, in order to convince you how widely spread, and how deeply rooted, the spirit of disaffection is; how daring and determined the intention has been, and still is, to make Jamaica a second Haiti, and how imperative it is upon you, gentlemen, to take such measures, as, under God's blessing, may avert such a calamity.

These measures may be summed up in a few words — create a strong government, and then under a firm hand to guide and direct, much may be accomplished.

In order to obtain a strong government, there is but one course open to you, that of abolishing the existing form of Constitution (compensating the officers whose offices are abolished), and establishing one better adapted to the present state and requirements of the colony — one in which union, cooperation, consistency, and promptness of action, may, as far as practicable, be secured.

I invite you, then, gentlemen, to make a great and generous sacrifice for the sake of your country, and in immolating on the altar of patriotism the two branches of the Legislature, of which you yourselves are the constituent parts, to hand down to posterity a noble example of self-denial and heroism.[38]

In response to the Governor's moving address, both the Assembly and the Legislative Council came forward with statements of thanks for the quick repression of the rebellion and complete agreement with the Governor's analysis as to causes.[39] One by one the other elements of the ruling class subscribed to Eyre's theory and joined him in condemning the blacks, the demagogues, and the Baptists for the ruin of the island. The clergy of the Church of England, the Wesleyan Methodist Church, and the Church of Scotland, part of the London Missionary Society, and even one Baptist parson, Rev. Samuel

Oughton, joined in the general support of the Governor. The
custodes, magistrates, and police officers also demanded a strong
government and decried the general spirit of rebellion that had
seized the island.[40]

There were only occasional voices of protest. Eleven evangelical ministers of the parish of St. James sent in a petition stating
that most Jamaicans were still loyal subjects, but Eyre merely
forwarded this to the Colonial Office with a note saying that
these were precisely the demagogues who were dangerous.[41]
Very few indeed were willing to take the stand of Henry Clarke,
a Church of England curate, who wrote,

> The only consolation I feel under the heart-sickening circum-
> stances of this insurrection, is the knowledge that it has overthrown
> that detestable tyranny which for 200 years has so cruelly oppressed
> the poor black people of this island. Considering the wrongs done
> to the negroes by the governing class, my astonishment is not that
> the rebellion has now occurred, but that it has been so long
> delayed.[42]

Even the Baptists had lost their old fire and hastened to cover
themselves against any possible blame for the rising. In the early
months of 1866, the Baptist congregations flooded the government with memorials protesting their loyalty and declaring
their thanks for the Royal Commission that had just arrived to
make an investigation.[43]

*   *   *

In the session of the Legislature opened by Eyre's address, the
Assembly first set to work providing him with the strong government he wanted. Measures were passed extending the powers
of the Governor to deal summarily with the prisoners who were
still untried, to prohibit the importation and sale of agricultural
cutlasses, to form the maroon Negroes into military clans, and
to stamp out once and for all any religious activities not controlled by the European churches. These bills were all eventually disallowed, withdrawn, or deflated, but they show the
direction in which the Assembly thought it had failed. The
political conflict over these measures was clear. Those that passed
did so with clear support from the Country Party and opposition

from the demagogues. The City Party supported most of them, and thus they passed without difficulty.[44]

The important item in Eyre's request was the amendment of the constitution, and this was a more complex problem. In Great Britain, the prevailing opinion after the rising was strongly against representative government for Jamaica, but, short of an act by the imperial Parliament, the question of a new government was in the hands of the Jamaica Legislature.[45] No matter how much they might fear democracy, the planting class had a long tradition of opposition to the Colonial Office. The British were still blamed in part for Jamaica's ruin and for not helping in her distress. Most planters, in the spring of 1865, would have agreed with Charles Royes, Custos of St. Ann, who wrote,

. . . no people have ever suffered more than the people of Jamaica from Imperial Legislation, from the injurious Sugar Duty Bill of 1846, — to the measure of last session. It has only brought me, and other West Indian proprietors, years of toil, painful anxiety, and ruin; and to the emancipated population . . . starvation.[46]

But alongside this attitude, there still remained in the minds of most white Jamaicans, the old conception of England as their real home and Jamaica as their place of exile.[47] This sentiment could be transformed into the belief that somehow or other England could solve Jamaica's troubles, if only she were given a chance. During the constitutional debates one member said, ". . . if the Executive Committee are not able to discharge the duties of the country, we should obtain a master-mind from England, and I will live to see it." [48]

At the beginning of the fall session of 1865, there were three general positions toward the proposal for a new constitution. One group still wanted to extend democracy, one group still wanted a planters' oligarchy, and one wanted to turn the whole problem of Jamaica's future over to Great Britain. Before the rebellion, this last group had been very small, but the rebellion brought the planters a new and striking realization of their failure to manage the country, and it also brought a renewed fear of the demagogues. As a result, the great majority of the planters swung over to the position taken by H. A. Whitelocke:

I believe that if the British Government take over the island, they will be guided by the land-owners, and that they are not going to put the government into the hands of irresponsible men. I have no such fears. Parliament will always control the Ministry, and will never allow the island to be placed in the hands of those who have no property rights.[49]

A constitution act was passed with a handsome majority, but its only important provision was this:

. . . it shall be lawful for her Majesty the Queen to create and constitute a government for this island, in such form, and with such powers, as to Her Majesty may best seem fitting, and from time to time to alter or amend such government.[50]

The final opposition was only a handful — the small group of demagogues who had been led throughout the session by Robert Osborn and S. Constantine Burke, and, at the very end, Wellesley Bourke, author of numerous plans for a restrictive constitution, the last defender of oligarchy.[51] The majority of the Assembly, who had walked the narrow balance between democracy and oligarchy, now gave up hope and left the oligarchs and democrats as the only supporters of representative government. This was more than "immolation" of their constitutional privileges on the "altar of patriotism" — it was surrender in their attempt to solve Jamaica's problems. The rebellion at Morant Bay had finally shifted the balance between England and Jamaica in the minds of the white class. The prestige of Great Britain now outweighed the desire for Jamaican autonomy. When William Hosack rewrote his long poem on Jamaica in the 1870's, the love of the island remained, but the burden of responsibility for her future lay with Great Britain.

> Slav'ry, and Freedom! both enforced have been —
> Hence, doubly bound is England to provide
> Bridges of Gold to span the gulph between!
> But woe to Liberty, should she decide
> To pluck the unripe glory — or confide
> Her mighty plan to weak hands to unroll. —
> Work, is the Freeman's Capital! and Pride!
> But Freedom unemployed spurns all control —
> Breaks into Anarchy; risking both life and soul.
>
> . . . .

Queen of the Caribbean Sea farewell!
No hurricane can long obliterate
Thy beauty, nor destroy its magic spell —
Around thee guardian angels ever wait
Thy loveliness unique, to renovate. —
Long, over thee, and thine, have I revolved:
And fain would cleave to thee, and share thy fate,
When e'er by Albion it is nobly solved —
Or I, from mortal cares, for ever, am absolved.[52]

Conclusion

THE DECLINE OF JAMAICA could be discussed from several points of view. This study has used a form of analysis approaching what is sometimes called "history without names." The chief actors have appeared as social groups, institutions, or ideas. The same events might be seen with equal validity as a series of individual acts, decisions, or thoughts. Economic failure, the separation of the two Jamaicas, or the events leading to the surrender of self-government might then appear as a series of individual errors of omission or commission. In choosing one approach rather than the other, I do not mean to imply that men are puppets in the hands of such major forces as intellectual background or social structure. "Institutions" are, after all, only the habits of individuals, and "ideas" are no more than abstractions from the thoughts of men.

The general failure of the European Jamaicans to achieve success on their own terms, nevertheless, appears to rest more decidedly with their lack of a common and workable set of ideas for reconstructing their society than with individual decisions. And there are clear reasons why they lacked such a basis in ideas. Most obvious is the fact that the revolution was forced on Jamaica from outside. The beneficiaries of the revolution remained politically submerged, while the old ruling class took over the day-to-day control of a new order it had never desired. This odd situation resulted from Jamaica's position as a colonial dependent, and it explains many aspects of the failure of the planting class. But this situation was essentially unstable, depending on the willingness of the planting class to accept their defeat while keeping a large part of their former power. Its persistence for twenty-seven years is a problem requiring further explanation. Part of this explanation can be found in another condition of colonial life — the psychological membership of the planting class in two incompatible societies, that of their exile in Jamaica and that of their "home" in Britain. This division weakened resistance to revolution and made possible a relatively peaceful and sincere transition to the "free system." It brought about a sufficient acceptance of British political liberalism and a fair enough treatment of the ex-slaves to satisfy the British government.

The intellectual behavior of the European Jamaicans — their acceptance or rejection of British suggestions — also has a bearing on the problem of the origin and transfer of ideas. We can dismiss the Marxist claim that the ideas of any society grow only from the relations of classes and the mode of production. English ideas were readily transmitted to Jamaica — perhaps too readily for the good of that country — in spite of the vastly different milieu in which these ideas originated. And among ideas of Jamaican origin, it was often the class relations of the slave era that most influenced Jamaican attitudes after emancipation. This is not to deny that the conditions of Jamaican society were an important factor in making Jamaicans accept or originate a course of action, but current social structure was only one of a number of determinants, among which past social relations, outside influences, and individual choices all had a place.

The more crucial problem is to find what determinants led the Jamaicans to British sources for some solutions, and to their own background for others. No general answer is completely satisfactory, since a great deal depended upon the choices and attitudes of key individuals who were in a position to gain general acceptance for their own views. William Burge, for example, helped formulate interpretations of economic decline. Principal churchmen and missionaries, editors of journals and newspapers, and the political leaders of the House of Assembly were in a similar position as opinion-formers within the colony.

Nevertheless, Jamaicans seemed to choose ideas of English origin for solving some kinds of problems and ideas of Jamaican origin for others. And this pattern is not clearly traceable to the decisions of a few opinion-makers. Some of the post-emancipation problems were similar to those of the slave system. Others were new and unexpected. It was quite natural, then, that the planting class should treat the old problems according to Jamaican precedent and look to England for advice and assistance with the new. Most obviously, they kept the old plantation system, though it badly needed reform. And with it they kept their ideas about their position as "planters," the optimum size of a planting "property," and most of the old manufacturing and agricultural techniques. The principal area of economic innovation concerned the changed status of labor. This was forced on the planters by the revolution, and in this area they turned to Britain and the classical economists. Wage problems, the land-labor ratio, immigration policies, and the operation of the labor market were widely discussed. Perhaps the enforced acceptance of emancipation discouraged further change; at any rate, there was little further innovation.

A similar pattern emerged from the Jamaican treatment of legal and political problems. Potential rebellion was an old danger, and it was handled in the Police Acts of 1833 and again after the rising of 1865 by trying to strengthen the quasi-military colonies of the maroon Negroes. Similarly, Justices of the Peace were given powers appropriate to the slaveholder in order to control the labor force, both domestic and imported. But in matters that were new to Jamaican experience, the British precedent weighed more heavily. The reform of legislation was necessary in the forties, and it was carried out in the spirit of Benthamite doctrine. Although it was not entirely the desire of the planters, Jamaican representative government took on something of the spirit of English liberalism, and the precedent of increasing English and Canadian democracy had an influence till the eve of the rising.

In social thought and policy the process was only slightly different. In this case, the English ideas joined with older Jamaican ideas to block a need that was clearly recognized by many intelligent Jamaicans. If the Negroes were to be made full members of European Jamaica, education and religious training and public health measures would have been necessary. But the prevailing English attitude of *laissez faire* was supported by the slaveholders' objection to religion and education for his workers, and little was done. The objection was often made that these measures were desirable, but too expensive. They were expensive, but no more so than the support of the Establishment or induced immigration.

Another problem in the transmission of ideas is the question of time lag between the appearance of an idea or an intellectual movement in Great Britain and its acceptance in Jamaica. It has sometimes been said that colonial life, like provincial life, is backward or out of fashion in ideas and social customs. This view can be made to seem plausible, especially if European Jamaica alone is taken into account. For example, the Church of England in Jamaica had no evangelical movement in the early nineteenth century. It became evangelical after 1870 when it revived under Archbishop Enos Nuttall, and it has kept his evangelical stamp ever since. Similarly, Jamaican men of the upper class were very slow to accept British standards of decorum in their sexual behavior outside of marriage, but the creole whites of the late nineteenth century eventually became just as "Victorian" as the English.

Both of these examples are the kind of intellectual movement that must be spread generally among the population. In other matters the time lag was sometimes negligible, especially when the interest of only a few people had to be aroused. Thus, the doctrinal disputes of the Church of England rocked the Church in Jamaica, though they rarely spread beyond the clergy and a few interested laymen. In the forties baptismal regeneration and the Oxford movement were widely discussed, as they were also widely discussed among the English clergy, and Richard Hill, a colored layman, answered Dr. Colenso's book on the Pentateuch in 1863, only a year after its first publication.[1] Dissenters also showed a quick interest in British happenings, as we have seen in the simultaneous appearance of an Anti-State-Church Convention in Britain and Jamaica and the rapid imitation of the religious revival of 1859.

It would be convenient to attribute these differences in time lag to differences in the number of individuals concerned with various kinds of ideas, and this is, indeed, a partial explanation. It obviously affects less people and takes less time to produce a religious controversy among the clergy than it does to change the outlook of an entire church or the mores of an entire social class. This explanation, however, is far too simple to be satisfactory. Even in the examples cited to show relatively slow transmission, the eventual acceptance in Jamaica was not merely a matter of time but also of changed social conditions in the colony. The Church became evangelical after 1870 not only because the English Church had done so a half-century earlier but also because disestablishment forced the Jamaican Church to clean house. In a slightly different case, the upper-class whites of the later nineteenth century could dispense with their old alliances with colored women because there were now enough white women to go around. And it should not be forgotten that several of the ideas which were transmitted most rapidly to Jamaica were transformed just as rapidly into new patterns differing greatly from their British origins — or that some British ideas were not received at all in the colony. In the end, the question of time lag comes to involve so many different factors that it can be answered only by reference to specific determinants in an individual instance.

There is, however, one further factor of importance both to the time-lag problem and the problem of selection from different sources of ideas. It is the simple but basic fact that people are more interested in some things than in others. The African Jamaicans were most interested in religion, and the European Jamaicans were most interested in economic success. Whether or not this phenomenon is discussed in terms of the Herskovits' "focus of culture," some of their ideas are borne out by the history of Jamaica — more strikingly, perhaps, by the more advanced European Jamaicans than by those of African origin. The adaptations of either cultural group — from any source — were greater and more rapid in those fields that interested them, as, indeed, might be expected. Among the European Jamaicans there was little response to change in the style of British art and literature and little mention of art and literature in their writings. The greater bulk of the preceding sections on economics reflects the greater interest of the Jamaicans themselves. Because of their interest in economic success, they borrowed more from Britain in this field. But also because of their concentration on economics, their own preconceptions were stronger in this area than in others. Therefore, the borrowings had to be made compatible with a number of tenacious ideas already present in Jamaica. Borrowings were therefore reinterpreted to fit the preconceptions. In much the same way, the African Jamaicans found in the provision ground a satisfactory and traditional economic form. There was no pressing economic problem and very little borrowing of economic ideas from the ruling class or from Europe. Emancipation, however, was a mass religious movement as well as a grant of economic freedom. Religion was the Negroes' area of special interest and coincidentally the area in which European ideas were most readily available. They borrowed, therefore, in order to find a satisfactory religious solution, and in borrowing they reinterpreted the new ideas to fit them congenially into their religious inheritance. Ideas rarely move without being transformed in the process; like the chameleon, they change to fit their background.

APPENDIXES

BIBLIOGRAPHY

NOTES

INDEX

APPENDIX A

THE GOVERNORS OF JAMAICA

1829	Governor	Somerset Lowry, Earl of Belmore
1832	(President of Council)	George Cuthbert
1832	Governor	C. Henry, Earl of Mulgrave
1834	(President of Souncil)	George Cuthbert
1834	(Lieutenant-Governor)	Sir Amos Norcot
1834	Governor	Howe Peter, Marquis of Sligo
1836	Governor	Lieutenant-General Sir Lionel Smith
1839	Governor	Sir Charles Theophilus Metcalfe
1842	Governor	James, Earl of Elgin
1846	(Lieutenant-Governor)	Major-General Berkeley
1846	Governor	Sir Charles Edward Grey
1853	Governor	Sir Henry Barkly
1856	(Lieutenant-Governor)	Major-General E. Wells Bell
1857	Governor	Charles Henry Darling
1862	(Lieutenant-Governor)	Edward John Eyre
1864	Governor	Edward John Eyre
1866	Governor	Sir Henry Storks
1866	Governor	Sir John Peter Grant

APPENDIX B

THE COLONIAL OFFICE

Although the Secretary of State responsible for Colonial Affairs signed the dispatches, "The Colonial Office" as a personification meant, in the middle of the nineteenth century, the Permanent Under-Secretaries of State for the Colonies as much as the temporary head of the office. For West Indian policy, it also meant Sir Henry Taylor, the member of the permanent staff who was principally concerned with these colonies from the mid-thirties till his retirement in 1872.

SECRETARIES OF STATE

1828	Sir George Murray
1830, Nov. 22	Frederick John, Viscount Goderich (afterward Earl of Ripon)
1833, April 3	E. G. S. Stanley (afterward Lord Stanley and Earl of Derby)
1834, June 5	Thomas Spring Rice (afterward Lord Monteagle)

1834, Nov. 15	George, Earl of Aberdeen
1835, April 18	Charles Grant (afterward Lord Glenelg)
1839, Feb. 20	Constantine, Marquis of Normanby
1839, Aug. 30	Lord John Russell (afterward Earl Russell)
1841, Sept. 3	Lord Stanley (afterward Earl of Derby)
1845, Dec. 23	William Ewart Gladstone
1846, July 3	Henry, Earl Grey
1852, Feb. 27	Sir John S. Pakington, Bart. (afterward Lord Hampton)
1854, Dec. 8	Henry, Duke of Newcastle
1854, June 10	Sir George Grey, Bart.
1855, Feb. 8	Sidney Herbert (afterward Lord Herbert of Lea)
1855, Feb. 23	Lord John Russell (afterward Earl Russell)
1855, July 21	Sir William Molesworth, Bart.
1855, Nov. 17	Henry Labouchere (afterward Lord Taunton)
1858, Feb. 26	Lord Stanley (afterward Earl of Derby)
1858, May 31	Sir Edward Bulwer Lytton, Bart. (afterward Lord Lytton)
1859, June 18	Henry, Duke of Newcastle
1864, April 4	Edward Cardwell (afterward Viscount Cardwell)
1866, July 6	Earl of Carnarvon

PERMANENT UNDER-SECRETARIES OF STATE FOR THE COLONIES

1825	Robert William Hay
1836	Sir James Stephen
1847	Herman Merivale
1859–71	Sir Frederic Rogers, Bart. (afterward Lord Blachford)

APPENDIX C

THE CONTOURS OF DECLINE

1

QUANTITY AND VALUE OF SUGAR EXPORTED FROM JAMAICA 1831–1866

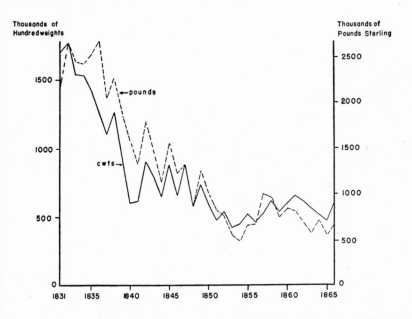

SOURCES: PP, 1867–8, xlviii [C. 3995], p. 9; PP, 1884, lxxiv (325), pp. 58–59; PP, 1865, lv [C. 3508], pp. 58–59; A. Sauerbeck, "On the Prices of Commodities and Precious Metals," *Journal of the Statistical Society* (London, 1886), XLIX, 592, 648.

2

JAMAICAN EXPORTS OF RUM, COFFEE, AND PIMENTO

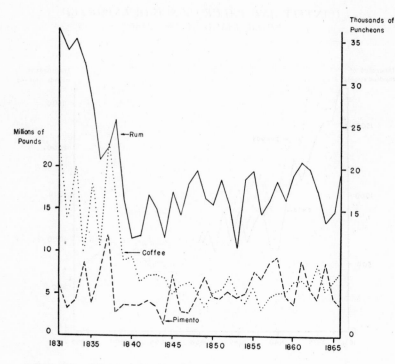

SOURCE: PP, 1867–68, xlviii [C. 3995], p. 9.

3

PRODUCTION OF SUGAR IN JAMAICA 1824–1866

ANNUAL AVERAGE SUGAR PRODUCTION IN JAMAICA

	Tons	*% decrease*
1824–33	68,465	
1839–46	33,431	51.5%
1857–66	25,168	24.8%

APPROXIMATE NUMBER OF SUGAR ESTATES IN JAMAICA

	Number	*% decrease*
1833	653	
1847	413	36.8%
1866	300	27.4%

APPROXIMATE AVERAGE PRODUCTION PER ESTATE

1833	105 tons
1847	81 tons
1866	84 tons

SOURCES: Deerr, *History of Sugar*, II, 377; PP, 1847–48, xxiii (167), p. 375; PP, 1867, xlviii [C. 3812], p. 9.

4

CHANGES IN SUGAR PRODUCTION BETWEEN 1839–1846 AND 1857–1866

Kind of sugar or area of production	*Percentage change in annual average production*
World total — beet sugar	+793.0
Barbados — cane sugar	+132.0
World total — all sugar	+ 98.2
Demerrara — cane sugar	+ 92.5
Trinidad — cane sugar	+ 77.1
St. Kitts — cane sugar	+ 59.5
World total — cane sugar	+ 56.4
Total British West Indies and British Guiana — cane sugar	+ 45.4
Antigua — cane sugar	+ 12.2
St. Vincent — cane sugar	+ 8.1
Grenada — cane sugar	− 7.2
Jamaica — cane sugar	− 24.7

SOURCE: Deerr, *History of Sugar*, II, 377, 490.

BIBLIOGRAPHY

A bibliography for a study of this type has no clear limits; potentially, anything written in Jamaica is a source of information about ideas, attitudes, or ways of thinking. Research in this field depends on sampling, rather than accumulating all available information. Its bibliography is therefore "select" by its very nature.

The existence of several good bibliographies on Jamaican history in general also helps to remove the obligation of listing all works that might be helpful to future scholarly work in an adjacent field. Lowell J. Ragatz's monumental *Guide for the Study of British Caribbean History* (Washington, 1932) covers every aspect of the subject from 1763 to 1834. Standard bibliographical guides for the later nineteenth century are supplied by Frank Cundall, *Bibliographia Jamaicensis* (Kingston, 1902 and supplement 1908) and by the printed catalogues of specialized collections, such as the *Catalogue of Books, Manuscripts, Etc. in the Caribbeana Section (Specializing in Jamaicana) of the Nicholas M. Williams Memorial Ethnological Collection* (Chestnut Hill, Mass., 1932) published by Boston College Library, the *Catalogue of the Library of the West India Committee* (London, 1941), or E. Lewin's *Subject Catalogue of the Library of the Royal Empire Society*, 4 vols. (London, 1930–1937). The second volume of *The Cambridge History of the British Empire* (Cambridge, 1940) contains, in addition, an excellent guide to the manuscript sources at the Public Records Office and to the printed sources in the *Parliamentary Papers*.

The lists below, therefore, emphasize works especially useful in the study of social and intellectual history.

I. MANUSCRIPT SOURCES

REFERENCE LIBRARY OF THE WEST INDIES, INSTITUTE OF JAMAICA, KINGSTON (IJ):

Baptist Missionary Papers:

Dendy Papers. Letters, etc. to the Baptist Missionary Society from Rev. Walter Dendy, 1847–1853.

Henderson Papers. Letters from J. E. Henderson, Baptist Missionary in Falmouth and Montego Bay, to the Baptist Missionary Society, 1841–1863.

Jamaica Baptist Union, Extract from the Minutes of the Annual Meeting of the Baptist Union, St. Ann's Bay, February 20–27, 1861.

Diaries and Unpublished Literary Works:

Nuttall, Rev. Enos, Diary, February 1866–1916, 19 bound volumes.

Freeman, W. G., *Pickwick Jamaica,* bound manuscript copy of part of a

novel about the adventures of Pickwick and Sam Weller in Jamaica
during the apprenticeship period.

Jingle, Jack (pseud.), *The Omnibus or Jamaica Scrap Book. A Thing
of Shreds and Patches*. A large bound copybook, compiled between the
early 1820's and about 1831. Contains original verse, Jamaican anec-
dotes, historical sketches, and copies of contemporaneous British
poetry.

Official Documents:

Commissioners of Correspondence. Letter Books, 17 December 1794 to 13
December 1833. (Copies of outgoing letters, mainly to the Jamaica
Agent in London.)

ARCHIVES OF THE DIOCESE OF JAMAICA (CHURCH OF ENGLAND), CHURCH HOUSE, CROSS-ROADS, KINGSTON (ADJ):

Letter Book of the Bishop's Registry Office, September 1828 to November
1832.

ARCHIVES OF THE WEST INDIA COMMITTEE, 40, NORFOLK STREET, LONDON:

Minute Books of the Acting Committee 1860–1866.

II. PRINTED SOURCES

A. PARLIAMENTARY PAPERS

The papers presented to Parliament contain a vast body of information
of all kinds about nineteenth-century Jamaica. For many periods of crisis
almost the entire body of dispatches between the Colonial Office and the
Governor of Jamaica were included. The series is indexed annually, and
there are further check lists of papers appropriate to Jamaica and to the
West Indies in the second volume of the *Cambridge History of the British
Empire*.

B. OTHER OFFICIAL AND SEMIOFFICIAL DOCUMENTS

Bell, K. N., and W. P. Morrell (eds.), *Select Documents on British Colonial
Policy, 1830–60* (Oxford, 1928).

Jamaica. House of Assembly. *Votes of the Honourable House of Assembly
1784–1866*, 82 vols. (Jamaica, 1785–1866).

Jamaica. Legislative Council. *Report of the Committee Appointed to
Enquire into the Prevalence of Concubinage and the High Rate of
Illegitimacy* (Kingston, 1941).

Jamaica. Laws. *Chronological Table of Statutes and Laws to the End of
1872 Session* (Kingston, 1873).

Jamaica. Laws. *The Statutes and Laws of the Island of Jamaica . . . 1681 to 1888,* 12 vols. (Kingston, 1889).

Jamaica Almanack. Published annually by various publishers in Kingston and Spanish Town from 1751 to 1880.

Judah, Abraham and A. C. Sinclair (comps.), *Debates of the Honourable House of Assembly of Jamaica, Commencing from the Fourth Session of the First General Assembly under the New Constitution,* 13 vols. (Kingston and Spanish Town, 1856–1866). A private publication, with changes in compilers and printers during the period of publication. Thirteen volumes in fourteen.

Minot, James, *A Digest of the Laws of Jamaica, from 33 Charles II to 28 Victoria* (Jamaica, 1865).

Royal Gazette (Kingston).

St. Jago de la Vega Gazette (Spanish Town).

C. TRAVELERS' AND OTHER DESCRIPTIVE ACCOUNTS

Baird, Robert, *Impressions of Experiences of the West Indies and North America in 1849,* 2 vols. (Edinburgh and London, 1850).

Belisario, I. M., *Sketches of Character in Illustration of the Habits, Occupation and Costume of the Negro Population in the Island of Jamaica,* 3 parts (Kingston, 1837–38).

Bigelow, John, *Jamaica in 1850* (New York, 1851).

Bourne (Miss), *The British West India Colonies in Connection with Slavery, Emancipation, Etc., by a Resident in the West Indies for Thirteen Years* (London, 1853).

[Bourne, Stephen], *The Uncle Toms and St. Clares of Jamaica. By a Stipendiary Magistrate* (London, 1853).

Brooke-Knight, Captain, *The Captain's Story; or Jamaica Sixty Years Since* (London [1890?]).

Candler, John, *The West Indies. Extracts from the Journal of John Candler, Whilst Travelling in Jamaica* (London, 1840).

De la Beche, Sir Henry, *Notes on the Present Condition of the Negroes in Jamaica* (London, 1825).

De Lisser, H. C., *Jamaica and Cuba* (Kingston, 1910).

Dennys, N. B., *An Account of the Cruise of the St. George on the North American and West Indian Station* (London, 1862).

Duperly, Adolphe, *Daguerian Excursions in Jamaica* (Kingston, [1840?]).

Emery, Robert, *About Jamaica* (London [1859]).

Foulks, Theodore, *Eighteen Months in Jamaica, with Recollections of the Late Rebellion* (London, 1833).

Gosse, Philip Henry, *A Naturalist's Sojourn in Jamaica* (London, 1851).

Gurney, Emilia Russell, *Letters of Emilia Russell Gurney,* 2nd ed. (London, 1903).

Gurney, Joseph John, *A Winter in the West Indies* (London, 1840).

Hakewill, James, *Picturesque Tour of the Island of Jamaica* (London, 1825).

Harvey, Thomas and William Brewin, *Jamaica in 1866. A Narrative of a Tour through the Island, with Remarks on its Social Educational and Industrial Condition* (London, 1867).

Hawkes, John, *A Steam Trip to the Tropics* (London, 1864).

Hovey, Sylvester, *Letters from the British West Indies* (New York, 1838).

Hubbard, Gardiner Green, "The Late Insurrection in Jamaica," *The New Englander* (New Haven, January 1867), pp. 53–69.

Kidd, Joseph B., *Illustrations of Jamaica* (London and Jamaica, 1840).

King, Rev. David, *The State and Prospects of Jamaica* (London, 1850).

[Leigh, John], *Jamaica (Being the First Part of) a Series of Letters Written from Jamaica to a Friend in England* (London, 1842).

Lewis, Matthew Gregory, *Journal of a West-India Proprietor, Kept During Residence in the Island of Jamaica* (London, 1834). Other editions use a different title.

Lloyd, William, *Letters from the West Indies during a Visit in the Autumn of MDCCCXXXVI, and the Spring of MDCCCXXXVII* (London [1837]).

Lorne, The Marquis of, *A Trip to the Tropics and Home through America* (London, 1867).

Lynch, Theodora Elizabeth (Mrs. Henry), *The Wonders of the West Indies* (London, 1856).

Madden, Richard Robert, *The Memoires from 1798 to 1886 of Richard Robert Madden* (London, 1891). Edited by T. M. Madden.

Madden, Richard Robert, *Twelve Months' Residence in the West Indies during the Transition from Slavery to Apprenticeship*, 2 vols. (London, 1835).

North, Marianne, *Recollections of a Happy Life*, 2 vols. (London, 1892).

Nugent, Maria, *Lady Nugent's Journal. Jamaica One Hundred and Thirty-Eight Years Ago*. 3rd ed. (London, 1939). Edited by Frank Cundall.

Park, Mungo, *Travels in the Interior Districts of Africa; Performed under the Direction and Patronage of the African Association in the Years 1795, 1796, and 1797* (New York, 1800).

Prince, Mrs. Nancy, *The West Indies: Being a Description of the Islands, Progress of Christianity, Education, and Liberty among the Colored Population Generally* (Boston, 1841).

Pringle, Hall, *The Fall of the Sugar Planters of Jamaica* (London, 1869).

Rampini, Charles, *Letters from Jamaica* (Edinburgh, 1873).

[Senior, Bernard Martin], *Jamaica as It Was, as It Is, and as It May Be . . . by a Retired Military Officer* (London, 1835). Authorship sometimes attributed to B. Martin, Sr.

Sewell, William Grant, *The Ordeal of Free Labor in the West Indies* (New York, 1861).

Sturge, Joseph and Thomas Harvey, *The West Indies in 1837* (London 1838).

Thome, James A. and J. Horace Kimball, *Emancipation in the West Indies* (New York, 1838).

Trollope, Anthony, *The West Indies and the Spanish Main* (New York, n.d.). First published London, 1859.

Truman, George, John Jackson and Thomas B. Longstreth, *Narrative of a Visit to the West Indies in 1840 and 1841* (Philadelphia, 1844).

Underhill, Edward Bean, *The West Indies* (London, 1862).

Williams, Cynric R., *A Tour through the Island of Jamaica from the Western to the Eastern End, in the Year 1823* (London, 1826).

D. MISSIONARY MEMOIRS AND RELIGIOUS TRACTS

Abbott, Thomas F., *Narrative of Certain Events Connected with the Late Disturbances in Jamaica* (London, 1832).

Banbury, T., *Jamaica Superstitions or The Obeah Book; a Complete Treatise of the Absurdities Believed in by the People of the Island, by the Rector (Native) of St. Peter's Church, Hope Bay, Portland* (Jamaica, 1894).

"Baptismal Regeneration, A Doctrine of the Church of England–Review," *The Jamaica Magazine* (Kingston, October 1844), I, 389–397.

"Baptist Missionary Churches in Jamaica," *The Evangelical Magazine and Missionary Chronicle* (London, March 1842), XX, 112–116.

Bleby, Henry, *Death Struggles of Slavery: Being a Narrative of Facts and Incidents which Occurred in a British Colony during Two Years Immediately Preceding Negro Emancipation* (London, 1853).

Bleby, Henry, *Scenes in the Caribbean Sea: Being Sketches from a Missionary's Note-Book* (London, 1868).

Blyth, Rev. G., *Reminiscences of Missionary Life* (Edinburgh, 1851).

Buchner, J. H., *The Moravians in Jamaica* (London, 1854).

Callender, Thomas P., *Memoir of the late Rev. Thomas P. Callender, Missionary to Jamaica* (Edinburgh, 1850).

Campbell, Rev. D. H. and Rev. Enos Nuttall, *Suggestions for the Better Selecting, Preparing, and Appointing the Catechists of the Church of England in Jamaica* (Kingston, 1869).

[Carlile, Edward], *Thirty-Eight Years of Mission Life in Jamaica* (London, 1884).

The Church in Jamaica, or Corespondence between the Society for the Propagation of the Gospel and the Bishop of Kingston (Kingston, 1868).

Church Patronage, as Dispensed in The Diocese of Jamaica Brought to a Test by the Incumbent of Trinity Chapel, Montego Bay (Montego Bay, 1860).

Clark, John, Walter Dendy, and J. M. Phillippo, *The Voice of Jubilee* (London, 1865).

Clarke, John, *Memorials of Baptist Missionaries in Jamaica* (London, 1869).

Courtenay, Reginald, *The Operations of the Spirit* (Kingston, 1861).

Courtenay, Reginald, *A Primary Charge Delivered at the Convocation of the Clergy of Jamaica Holden in Spanish Town, on 15th April, 1858* (Kingston [1858]).

Courtenay, Reginald, *Three Pastoral Charges: Addressed to the Clergy of the Diocese of Jamaica in the Years 1858, 1862, and 1868* (Kingston, 1868).

Courtenay, Reginald, *To the Clergy of the Diocese* (Kingston, 1866).

Duncan, Peter, *Narrative of the Wesleyan Mission to Jamaica; with Occasional Remarks on the State of Society in that Colony* (London, 1849).

Duncan, Peter and William Knibb, *Religious Persecution in Jamaica,* 3rd ed. (London, 1832).

Fletcher, Rev. Duncan, *Personal Recollections of the Honourable George W. Gordon, Late of Jamaica* (London, 1867).

Foster, Rev. Henry B., *The Rise and Progress of Wesleyan-Methodism in Jamaica* (London, 1881).

Green, Samuel, *Baptist Mission in Jamaica. A Review of Rev. W. G. Barrett's Pamphlet, Entitled: A Reply to the Circular of the Baptist Missionary Committee* (London, 1842).

Hill, Richard, *Address Delivered at the Baptist Jubilee on Tuesday, the 19th July, 1864, at the Baptist Chapel, St. Jago de la Vega* (Jamaica, 1864).

Hill, Richard, *The Book of Moses, How Say You, True or Not True? Being a Consideration of the Critical Objections in Dr. Colenso's Review of the Books of Moses and Joshua* (Kingston, 1863).

[Hill, Richard], *Correspondence Relating to a Sermon Preached in the Cathedral Church, Saint Jago de la Vega, on the Evening before Good Friday, April 8th, 1852* (Jamaica, 1852).

Jamaica Baptist Union, *Distress in Jamaica* (Montego Bay, 1865).

Kerr, David, *An Answer to the Objections of the Reverend Thomas Pennock, against "Methodism as it is;" as Published in the Jamaica Watchman* (Montego Bay, 1838).

[Knibb, William], *Facts and Documents Connected with the Late Insurrection in Jamaica* (London, 1832).

[Knibb, William], *Speech of the Rev. William Knibb before the Baptist Missionary Society, in Exeter Hall, April 28th, 1842* (London [1842]).

Magrath, Rev. John, *The Inseparability of External Baptism and Internal Regeneration* (Jamaica, 1844).

Marwick, William (ed.), *William and Louisa Anderson* (Edinburgh, 1897).

Middleditch, Rev. T. (comp.), *The Youthful Female Missionary,* 2nd ed. (London, 1840).

Minutes of Proceedings of the First Annual Congress of Clergy and Laity of the Diocese of Jamaica, Held in Kingston on Wednesday and Thursday, the 13th and 14th of May, 1868, with Papers Read before the Congress (Kingston, 1868).

A Pastoral Issued by the Bishops of the West Indian Dioceses, at Their

Conference Held in Georgetown, Demerara, 1873 (Georgetown, Demerara, 1873).

Phillippo, James M., Jamaica: Its Past and Present State (London, 1843).

Radcliffe, Rev. John, The Falmouth Kirk: A Series of Facts, Historically Arranged, Illustrative, Explanatory, and Confimatory of the Statements,
in the Petition on Behalf of the Claims of the Church of Scotland, now
Before the Honorable House of Assembly, in a Letter to the Members
of the Honorable House of Assembly (Jamaica, 1863).

Radcliffe, Rev. John, Lectures on Negro Proverbs (Kingston, 1869).

Radcliffe, Rev. John, Lord Palmerston's Letter to the Presbytery of Edinburgh Examined: a Sermon Preached in the Scotch Church, Kingston,
April 2nd, 1854 (Kingston, 1854).

Radcliffe, Rev. John, Samuel — A National Reformer (Kingston, 1853).

Radcliffe, Rev. John, A Sermon in Aid of Funds for the Relief of the Jews
Suffering in Jerusalem, Preached in the Scotch Church, Kingston,
July 16th, 1854 (Jamaica, 1854).

Retrospect of the History of the Mission of the Brethren's Church in
Jamaica, for the Past Hundred Years (London, 1855).

Robb, Rev. Alexander, The Gospel to the Africans (Edinburgh and London, 1861).

Samuel, Rev. Peter, The Wesleyan-Methodist Missions in Jamaica and
Honduras Delineated (London, 1850).

Spencer, Aubrey George, A Charge Delivered at the Primary Visitation of
the Clergy of the Archdeaconry of Jamaica in the Cathedral Church of
St. Jago de la Vega, 12th Dec. 1844 (Jamaica, 1845).

The Standing Committee of the Society for the Propagation of the Gospel
in Foreign Parts, and the Jamaica Clergy (Kingston, 1867).

"Tractarianism. Newman, Keble, and Pusey," The Jamaica Monthly
Magazine (Kingston, January 1846), II, 1–10.

Vindication of the "Declaration" of which the Rev. John Radcliffe so
Bitterly Complains (Kingston, n.d.).

"Voluntaryism," The Jamaica Magazine (Kingston, June 1844), I, 224–235.

Waddell, Rev. Hope Masterton, Twenty-nine Years in the West Indies and
Central Africa (London, 1863).

Watson, Rev. James, Christian Duties Viewed as Social, Religious, and
Civil (Kingston, 1866).

Young, Robert, A View of Slavery in Connection with Christianity: Being
the Substance of a Discourse Delivered in the Wesleyan Chapel, Stoney-
Hill, Jamaica, Sept. 19, 1824 (Jamaica, 1824).

E. CONTEMPORANEOUS WORKS OF LITERATURE

Allen, Grant, In All Shades, 3 vols. (London, 1886).

"The Baptist," The Jamaica Monthly Magazine (Kingston, January and
February 1847), II (new series), 18–32, 102–112.

Hosack, William, Isle of Streams: or the Jamaica Hermit and Other Poems
(Edinburgh, 1876).

[Hosack, William], "Jamaica: A Poem," *The Jamaica Monthly Magazine* (Spanish Town, September and October 1833, January 1834), Nos. X, XI, XII.

Lynch, Theodora Elizabeth (Mrs. Henry), *The Cotton-Tree* (London, 1847).

Lynch, Theodora Elizabeth (Mrs. Henry), *The Family Sepulchre* (London [1848]).

Lynch, Theodora Elizabeth (Mrs. Henry), *Lays of the Sea and Other Poems* (London, 1850).

Lynch, Theodora Elizabeth (Mrs. Henry), *Maude Effingham* (London, 1849).

Lynch, Theodora Elizabeth (Mrs. Henry), *The Mountain Pastor* (London, 1852).

Marly; Or, The Life of a Planter in Jamaica, 2nd ed. (Glasgow, 1828).

Scott, Michael, *Tom Cringle's Log* (London, 1915). First published in 1829.

F. POLITICAL AND ECONOMIC WORKS

Barclay, Alexander, *A Practical View of the Present State of Slavery in the West Indies* (London, 1827).

Barclay, Alexander, *Remarks on Emigration to Jamaica: Addressed to the Coloured Class of the United States* (New York, 1840).

[Barret], *A Reply to the Speech of Dr. Lushington in the House of Commons, on the 12th June 1827 on the Condition of the Free-Coloured People of Jamaica* (London, 1828).

Beaumont, Augustus H., *The Jamaica Petition for Representation in the British House of Commons, or for Independence* ([London], 1831).

Bickell, Rev. R., *The West Indies as They Are; or a Real Picture of Slavery: but More Particularly As It Exists in the Island of Jamaica* (London, 1825).

Bowerbank, Lewis Quier, *Letters of Mr. Alexander Fiddes Considered and Refuted . . .* (Kingston, 1865).

"The Brazils — The Late Debate," *The Jamaica Magazine* (Kingston, May 1844), I, 173–190.

Bridges, Rev. George Wilson, *A Call to His Parishioners* (Falmouth, 1837).

Bridges, Rev. George Wilson, *Dreams of Dulocracy, or the Puritanical Obituary* (Jamaica, 1824).

Bridges, Rev. George Wilson, *Emancipation Unmask'd* (London, 1835).

Bridges, Rev. George Wilson, *A Voice from Jamaica,* 4th ed. (London, 1824).

Burge, William, *Reply to the Letter by the Marquis of Sligo to the Marquis of Normanby, Relative to the Present State of Jamaica* (London, 1839).

Burge, William, *The Speech of W. Burge, Esq., Q.C., Agent for Jamaica, at the Bar of the House of Commons, Against the Bill Intituled "An Act to make Temporary Provision for the Government of Jamaica." Monday, 22nd April 1839* (London, 1839).

Burge, William, *The Speech of W. Burge, Esq. Q.C., Agent for Jamaica, at the Bar of the House of Commons, Against The Bill Entituled "An Act to Provide for the Enactment of Certain Laws in the Island of Jamaica." Friday, 7th June, 1839* (London, 1839).

[Campbell, Mrs. (nèe Bourne)], *Suggestions Relative to the Improvement of the British West Indian Colonies by Means of Instruction . . . By a Resident in the West Indies for Thirteen Years . . .* (London, 1853).

[Carlyle, Thomas], "Occasional Discourse on the Nigger Question," *Fraser's Magazine* (London, December 1849), XL, 670–679.

The Case of the Free-Labour British Colonies Submitted to the British Legislature & British Nation for an Impartial Re-Hearing (London, 1852).

Clarkson, Thomas, *Not a Labourer Wanted for Jamaica* (London, 1842).

[Davis, Anthony], *Copy of a Letter Addressed to a Member of the Legislative Assembly of Jamaica, by One of Its Members Now in England* (London, 1832).

Eight Practical Treatises on the Cultivation of the Sugar Cane (Jamaica, 1843).

"The Elections — The Franchise," *The Jamaica Magazine* (Kingston, October 1844), I, 481–492.

Evelyn, Lyndon Howard, *The Sketch of a Plan, for the Effectual Abolition of Slavery, on the Principles of Justice to Every Colonial Interest, and in Full Accordance with Every Temperate Desire of the British Philanthropists* (Montego Bay, 1832).

Facts and Documents Relating to the Alleged Rebellion in Jamaica and the Measures of Repression; Including Notes of the Trial of Mr. Gordon (London, 1866).

Farewell Addresses of the Inhabitants of Jamaica to the Rt Hon. Sir Charles Theophilus Metcalfe (Kingston, 1842).

Gurney, Joseph John, *Reconciliation, Respectfully Recommended to All Parties in the Colony of Jamaica in a Letter Addressed to the Planters* (Kingston, 1840).

Hibbert, George, *Correspondence between Mr. George Hibbert and the Society of Friends* (London [1833]).

Hildreth, Richard, *The "Ruin" of Jamaica* ([New York, 1855]).

Jamaica, Addresses to His Excellency E. J. Eyre, 1865, 1866 ([Kingston], 1866).

Jamaica Chamber of Commerce, *Report of the Jamaica Chamber of Commerce on the Sugar Duties Question in England* (Kingston, 1846).

"Jamaica Fashions in 1831. By a Johnny Newcome of Twelve Months' Experience," *Jamaica Monthly Magazine* (Kingston, April 1847), II (new series), 348–352. Reprinted from a newspaper of 1831.

Jamaica Insurrection, or the Proceedings of the Anti-Slavery Society Exposed and Refuted (London, 1832).

"Jamaica — Its Past and Present State," *Jamaica Monthly Magazine* (Kingston, April 1844), I, 62–82.

Jamaica, Its State and Prospects; with an Exposure of the Proceedings of the Freed-man's Aid Society, and the Baptist Missionary Society (London, 1867).

Jamaica; Who is to Blame? by a Thirty Years' Resident (London [1866]).

Jelly, Thomas, *A Brief Inquiry into the Condition of Jamaica* (London, 1847).

Jelly, Thomas, *A Cursory Glance at the Past and Present Condition of Great Britain; Intended as a Beacon to the British Sugar Colonies* (London, 1848).

[Lindo, Abraham], *Dr. Underhill's Testimony on the Wrongs of the Negro in Jamaica, Examined* (Falmouth [1866]).

Long, Charles Edward, *Letter to Viscount St. Vincent, on the Jamaica House of Assembly's Abandonment of its Legislative Functions* (London, 1839).

McMahon, Benjamin, *Jamaica Plantership* (London, 1839).

Merewether, Henry Alworth, *The Speech of Mr. Serjeant Merewether, at the Bar of the House of Commons, Against the Bill Intituled "An Act to Make Temporary Provision for the Government of Jamaica." Tuesday, 23d April 1839* (London, 1839).

Merivale, Herman, *Lectures on Colonisation and Colonies*, 2 vols. (London, 1841–42).

Milner, Thomas Hughes, *The Present and Future State of Jamaica Considered* (London, 1839).

"The Ministry and the Sugar Duties. Better Prospects for Jamaica." *The Jamaica Magazine* (Kingston, July 1844), I, 376–388.

Morris, M. O'Connor, "Jamaica," *Eclectic Magazine* (New York, March 1866), III (new series), 284–291.

Morson, Henry, *The Present Condition of the West Indies, Their Wants and the Remedy for Them* (London, 1841).

A Narrative of Recent Events Connected with the Baptist Mission in This Island (Kingston, 1833).

"Natural Death of Slavery," *Edinburgh Review* (Edinburgh, October 1827), XLVI, 490–497.

Negro Emancipation No Philanthropy, a Letter to the Duke of Wellington by a Jamaica Landed Proprietor (London, 1830).

"Official Jottings in 1845 and 1846," *The Jamaica Monthly Magazine* (Kingston, January 1847), II (new series), 56–57.

Ogilby, John, *A Description and History of the Island of Jamaica* (Kingston, 1851). Edited by William Wemyss Anderson.

Oughton, Rev. Samuel, "The Influence of Artificial Wants on the Social, Moral, and Commercial Advancement of Jamaica," *West India Quarterly Magazine* (Kingston, May 1862), I, 474–483.

Oughton, Rev. Samuel, *Jamaica: Why It Is Poor, And How It May Become Rich* (Kingston, 1866).

[Paterson, Robert], *Observations on the System by which Estates Have Been and Are Still Managed in Jamaica; and on the Apprenticeship Introduced by the Recent Abolition Act. By a Proprietor* (Edinburgh, 1836).

Paterson, Robert, *Remarks on the Present State of Cultivation in Jamaica;
    the Habits of the Peasantry; and Remedies Suggested for the Improve-
    ment of Both* (Edinburgh, 1843).
Pim, Bedford, *The Negro and Jamaica* (London, 1866).
"The Present Policy of Great-Britain, with Respect to Jamaica," *Jamaica
    Monthly Magazine* (Kingston, April 1847), II (new series), 285-290.
Price, George, *Jamaica and the Colonial Office. Who Caused the Crisis?*
    (London, 1866).
"The Result of Emancipation in the British West Indies," *The Jamaica
    Monthly Magazine* (Kingston, April 1847), II (new series), 341-348.
Ricardo, David, *The Principles of Political Economy and Taxation* (Lon-
    don, 1911). First published 1817.
Rodgers, John H., *A Lecture Delivered in Wolmer's School Room on Mon-
    day Evening, 6th October, 1862* (Jamaica, 1862).
Roughley, Thomas, *The Jamaica Planter's Guide* (London, 1823).
Roundell, Charles Savile, *England and Her Subject-Races with Special Ref-
    erence to Jamaica* (London, 1866).
Scotland, George, *A Letter Addressed to the Public of Jamaica on the Polit-
    ical and Financial State of the Colony* (Jamaica, 1847).
[Sligo, Howe Peter, Marquis of], *Jamaica under the Apprenticeship. By a
    Proprietor* (London, 1838).
Sligo, Lord, *Letter to the Marquess of Normanby Relative to the Present
    State of Jamaica* (London, 1839).
Smith, Adam, *An Inquiry Into the Nature and Causes of the Wealth of
    Nations* (New York, 1937). First published 1776.
Solomon, George, *Population and Prosperity; or, Free vs. Slave Production*
    (Kingston, 1859).
Statement of the [Jamaica] Committee and Other Documents (London,
    1866).
Sterne, Henry, *A Statement of Facts . . .* (London, 1837).
Stewart, John, *A View of the Past and Present State of the Island of
    Jamaica; With Remarks on the Moral and Physical Condition of the
    Slaves, and on the Abolition of Slavery in the Colonies* (Edinburgh,
    1823).
Stewart, Rev. Samuel H., "On the Defects of the Agricultural System Hith-
    erto Pursued in Jamaica," *The Jamaica Magazine* (Kingston, July
    1844), I, 317-325.
"The Sugar Question, and the Prospects for Jamaica," *The Jamaica Maga-
    zine* (Kingston, June 1844), I, 279-287.
Thompson, Edward, William Smith, and William Girod, *Statement of Facts
    Relative to Jamaica* (London, 1852).
Trew, Rev. J. M., *Hints Briefly Suggestive of Jamaica's Future* (London,
    1866).
[Turnbull, David (ed.)], *The Jamaica Movement for Promoting the En-
    forcement of The Slave-Trade Treaties and the Suppression of the
    Slave Trade* (London, 1850).
Underhill, Edward Bean, *A Letter Addressed to the Rt. Honourable E.*

Cardwell, with Illustrative Documents on the Condition of Jamaica and an Explanatory Statement (London [1866]).

"Underhill's West Indies — A Visit to a Ruined Colony," *Eclectic Review* (London, March 1862), II (new series), 245–260.

Valpy, Leonard Rowe and others, *Jamaica. Its Existing Condition with a Few Suggestions for its Amelioration* (London, 1856).

The Voice of the West Indies, and the Cry of England; or, Compensation or Separation Considered, 2nd ed. (London, 1832).

Wakefield, Edward Gibbon, *England and America* (London, 1833).

Wakefield, Edward Gibbon, *A Letter from Sydney the Principal Town of Australasia* (London, 1929). First published 1829.

West India Association [Glasgow], *Case of the British West Indies Stated* (Glasgow, 1852).

"What is the Matter with Jamaica?", *West India Quarterly Magazine* (Kingston, August 1861), I, 61–70.

[Whitehouse, W. F.], *Agricola's Letters and Essays on Sugar Farming in Jamaica* (London, 1845).

Whiteley, Henry, *Three Months in Jamaica in 1832: Comprising a Residence of Seven Weeks on a Sugar Plantation* (London, 1833).

Wray, Leonard, *The Practical Sugar Planter* (London, 1848).

G. CONTEMPORANEOUS HISTORIES AND MEMOIRS

Blachford, Frederick, Lord, *Letters of Frederick Lord Blachford* (London, 1896). Edited by George Eden Marindin.

Bleby, Henry, "The Results of West India Emancipation," *Methodist Quarterly Review* (New York, January and April 1860), XLII, 33–55, 201–228.

Bridges, George Wilson, *The Annals of Jamaica,* 2 vols. (London, 1828).

[Bridges, Rev. George Wilson], *Outlines and Notes of Twenty-Nine Years, 1834–1862* (n.p. [1862]).

Bridges, Rev. George Wilson, *The Statistical History of the Parish of Manchester* (Kingston, 1824).

Clerk, James Otway, *An Abridged History of Jamaica* (Falmouth, 1859).

Edwards, Bryan, *The History, Civil and Commercial, of the British Colonies in the West Indies,* 2nd ed., 2 vols. (London, 1794).

Gardner, William James, *A History of Jamaica From Its Discovery by Christopher Columbus to the Year 1872* (London, 1873).

Grey, Henry George, 3rd Earl, *The Colonial Policy of Lord John Russell's Administration,* 2 vols. (London, 1853).

Hill, Richard, *Lights and Shadows of Jamaica History* (Kingston, 1859).

Kaye, Sir J. W. (ed.), *Selections from the Papers of Lord Metcalfe* (London, 1885).

[Luckock, Benjamin], *Jamaica: Enslaved and Free* (London [1846]).

Moister, Rev. William, *The West Indies, Enslaved and Free* (London, 1883).

Sinclair, Augustus Constantine, *Political Life of the Hon. Charles Hamilton Jackson* (Kingston, 1878).

Taylor, Henry, *Autobiography of Henry Taylor 1800–1875*, 2 vols. (London, 1885).

Walrond, Theodore (ed.), *Letters and Journals of James, Eighth Earl of Elgin* (London, 1872).

H. NEWSPAPERS AND PERIODICALS

Christian Record (Kingston), 1831–32.[1]

Colonial Standard (Kingston), January 1866.

Daily Advertiser (Kingston), February–April 1851.

Evangelical Magazine and Missionary Chronicle (London), 1830–1860.

Falmouth Post, January–February 1848, April–December 1862.

The First Fruits of the West, and Monthly Jewish Magazine (Kingston), 1844.

The Gleaner (Kingston).

Jamaica Baptist Herald and Friend of Africa (Falmouth).

Jamaica Daily Guardian (Kingston).

Jamaica Despatch (Kingston).

Jamaica Journal of Arts, Sciences, and Literature (Kingston).

Jamaica Magazine (Kingston), 1844.

Jamaica Monthly Magazine (Spanish Town and Kingston), 1833–34, 1846–1848.

Jamaica Quarterly Journal of Medicine, Science, and Arts (Kingston), 1860–1861.

Jamaica Society of Arts, *Transactions* (Kingston), 1855–1857.

Royal Society of Arts, *Transactions* (Kingston), 1867–68.

Jamaica Standard and Royal Gazette (Kingston), January–April 1842.

Jamaica Tribune and Daily Advertiser (Kingston), March–April 1865.

Jamaica Watchman and People's Free Press (Kingston), August–December 1830.

Kingston Chronicle and City Advertizer, January 1830.

Morning Journal (Kingston), March–April 1865.

The Missionary Herald (London), 1819–1855.

The Pioneer and Jamaica Literary Miscellany (Kingston), 1858–59.

The Sentinel (Kingston), March–April 1865.

The Struggler (Montego Bay).

Sheridan's Jamaica Monthly Magazine (Kingston), 1832–33.

Wesleyan Missionary Notices (London), 1820–1853, 1862–1866.

The Report of the Wesleyan-Methodist Missionary Society (London, annual), 1840–1863.

West India Quarterly Magazine (Kingston), 1861–62.

[1] Dates indicate thorough coverage. Otherwise the material was used for occasional references only.

III. SELECT BIBLIOGRAPHY OF SECONDARY
AUTHORITIES

Beckwith, Martha W., *Black Roadways: A Study of Jamaican Folk Life* (Chapel Hill, 1929).

Burn, W. L., *The British West Indies* (London, 1951).

Burn, W. L., *Emancipation and Apprenticeship in the British West Indies* (London, 1937).

Burns, Alan, *The History of the British West Indies* (London, 1954).

Cambridge History of the British Empire. Volume II, *The Growth of the New Empire 1783–1870* (Cambridge, 1940). Edited by J. Holland Rose, A. P. Newton, and E. A. Benians.

Coupland, Reginald, *The British Anti-Slavery Movement* (London, 1933).

Cumper, G. E., "Labour Demand and Supply in the Jamaican Sugar Industry, 1830–1950," *Social and Economic Studies* (Jamaica, March 1954), II, No. 4, 37–86.

Cumpston, I. M., *Indians Overseas in British Territories 1834–1854* (London, 1953).

[Cundall, Frank], "Literature, Science and Art in Jamaica: a Retrospect," *Journal of the Institute of Jamaica* (Kingston, 1894), I, 200–208.

Deerr, Noel, *The History of Sugar*, 2 vols. (London, 1949–50).

Ellis, John B., *The Diocese of Jamaica* (London, 1913).

Erickson, Edgar L., "The Introduction of East Indian Coolies into the British West Indies," *Journal of Modern History* (Chicago, June 1934), VI, 127–146.

Findlay, G. G. and W. W. Holdsworth, *A History of the Wesleyan Methodist Missionary Society*, 5 vols. (London, 1921–1924).

Herskovits, Melville J., *The Myth of the Negro Past* (New York, 1941).

Herskovits, Melville J. and Frances S., *Trinidad Village* (New York, 1947).

Hinton, John H., *Memoir of William Knibb, Missionary in Jamaica* (London, 1847).

Klingberg, Frank Joseph, *The Anti-Slavery Movement in England: A Study of English Humanitarianism* (New Haven, 1926).

Knaplund, Paul, *James Stephen and the British Colonial System 1813–1847* (Madison, Wisconsin, 1953).

Knorr, Klaus Eugen, *British Colonial Theories (1570–1850)* (Toronto, 1944).

Livingstone, William Pringle, *Black Jamaica* (London, 1900).

Ludlow, J. M., *A Quarter Century of Jamaica Legislation* (London, 1866).

Martin, R. Montgomery, *History of the West Indies*, 2 vols. (London, 1836–1837).

Mathieson, William Law, *British Slave Emancipation, 1838–1849* (London, 1932).

Mathieson, William Law, *British Slavery and its Abolition 1823–1838* (London, 1926).

Mathieson, William Law, *The Sugar Colonies and Governor Eyre, 1849–1866* (New York, 1936).

Mellor, George R., *British Imperial Trusteeship 1783–1850* (London, 1951).

Morrell, W. P., *British Colonial Policy in the Age of Peel and Russell* (Oxford, 1930).

Olivier, Sydney Haldane, Lord, *Jamaica the Blessed Island* (London, 1936).

Olivier, Sydney Haldane, Lord, *The Myth of Governor Eyre* (London, 1933).

Ragatz, Lowell J., *The Fall of the Planter Class in the British Caribbean 1763–1833* (New York, 1928).

Roberts, W. Adolphe, *Six Great Jamaicans* (Kingston, 1951).

Sires, Ronald V., "Negro Labor in Jamaica in the Years Following Emancipation," *Journal of Negro History* (Washington, October 1940), XXV 484–497.

Sires, Ronald V., "Sir Henry Barkly and the Labor Problem in Jamaica, 1853–1856," *Journal of Negro History* (Washington, April 1940), XXV 216–235.

Underhill, Edward Bean, *The Life of J. M. Phillippo* (London, 1881).

Underhill, Edward Bean, *The Tragedy of Morant Bay: a Narrative of the Disturbances in the Island of Jamaica in 1865* (London, 1895).

Williams, Eric, *Capitalism and Slavery* (Chapel Hill, 1944).

Wrong, Hume, *The Government of the West Indies* (Oxford, 1923).

NOTES

PREFACE

1. A. Trollope, *The West Indies and the Spanish Main* (New York, n.d.), p. 104. First published in 1859.

CHAPTER I   A PLANTING ECONOMY

1. See R. L. Schuyler, *The Fall of the Old Colonial System* (New York, 1945) for the gradual dissolution of the old order, and L. J. Ragatz, *The Fall of the Planter Class in the British Caribbean 1763–1833* (New York and London, 1928) for the decline of the West Indian component of the system.

2. Between 1702 and 1807, over 400,000 slaves had been imported for use in Jamaica. Yet the slave population in 1807 was only 319,351 (N. Deerr, *The History of Sugar*, 2 vols. [London, 1951], II, 278).

3. Ragatz, *Planter Class*, pp. 81–107; E. Williams, *Capitalism and Slavery* (Chapel Hill, 1944), pp. 51–84.

4. For general statistical tables covering the sugar trade in the early nineteenth century, see *Parliamentary Papers* (cited hereafter as PP), 1856, lv (209), 2–3.

5. M. G. Lewis, *Journal of a West-India Proprietor, Kept During Residence in the Island of Jamaica* (London, 1834), p. 95.

6. [B. M. Senior], *Jamaica as It Was, as It Is, and as It May Be . . . by a Retired Military Officer* (London, 1835), p. 168.

7. G. W. Bridges, *The Annals of Jamaica*, 2 vols. (London, 1828), II, 397.

8. *Marly; or, the Life of a Planter in Jamaica*, 2nd edition (Glasgow, 1828), p. 317.

9. Lewis, *Journal*, p. 162.

10. R. R. Madden, *Twelve Months' Residence in the West Indies During the Transition from Slavery to Apprenticeship*, 2 vols. (London, 1835), II, 78–79.

11. See PP, 1831, xix (260), 2–3.

12. H. Merivale, *Lectures on Colonisation and Colonies*, 2 vols. (London, 1841–42), I, 222–223. The estimate is for the year 1836.

13. T. Jelly, *A Brief Inquiry into the Condition of Jamaica* (London, 1847), pp. 24–25; W. J. Gardner, *A History of Jamaica from its Discovery by Christopher Columbus to the Year 1872* (London, 1873), p. 414.

14. There was no official census in Jamaica until 1844, but the population may be estimated by taking the slave registration for June 1829 (322,421) and adding an estimated 40,000 free colored and black people and 15,000 whites. The total is about 370,000. (See PP, 1845, xxxi (426), 4 for census returns; PP, 1831–32, xx (381), 318 for slave registration.) This is about 89 people per square mile, a low population density for the tropics

even taking into account the lower technological level of the early nine-teenth century. The present population density is 314 per square mile (1952 estimate).

15. By 1839, 3,493,349 acres had been patented to private owners, from a total area now estimated by the Jamaican government to be 2,823,174 acres. In 1839 a Jamaican government Commission of Quit-Rent Inquiry thought they had another 590,000 acres of Crown Lands to be given away (PP, 1840, xxxv [C. 212], 67).

16. Measured in the "official" values used at the time, sugar and rum together accounted for 71 per cent of Jamaican exports in 1831. Although "official" values are not accurate for this date, the proportion was still 63 per cent in 1850, the first year in which declared values of exports were used. (PP, 1867–68, xlviii [C. 2995], 9–10; PP, 1872, lxiii [C. 616], 72.)

17. In Jamaican usage, an "estate" referred only to a sugar property. All properties growing staples were "plantations." Others were distin-guished as a cattle "pen" or a coffee "mountain." Smaller properties were often called "settlements" rather than "plantations." Hence a man farming a few acres of provisions, or even minor products like pimento, was a "settler" or a "small settler," rather than a "planter." At the same time, the term "planter" referred to all the people in plantation management, dis-tinguished from the "proprietor." (Memorial of the House of Assembly, 24 December 1847, PP, 1847–48, xxiii (167), 375; Lord Olivier, *Jamaica: the Blessed Island* [London, 1936], p. 69.)

18. By 1928, with a much larger population, only 278,000 acres were under cultivation. (R. N. Whitbeck, "The Agricultural Geography of Jamaica," *Annals of the Association of American Geographers,* XXII [March, 1932] 17.) Recent cane acreage has tended to be slightly more than 100,000. (International Bank of Reconstruction and Development, *The Economic Development of Jamaica* [Baltimore, 1952], pp. 164–165.)

19. This was the land use on Golden Grove, St. Thomas-in-the-East, then regarded as one of the finest estates on the island (PP, 1842, xiii (497), 338–339).

20. Madden, *Twelve Months,* II, 155–156; Bigelow, *Jamaica in 1850,* pp. 90–97; C. W. Guillebaud, "The Development of the Crown Colonies, 1815–45," *Cambridge History of the British Empire* (Cambridge, 1940), II, 485–487.

21. Jelly, *Brief Inquiry,* p. 62. The minimum number needed to oper-ate the sugar works on a two-hundred-slave estate is given by A. Davis, *Copy of a Letter Addressed to a Member of the Legislative Assembly of Jamaica, by One of Its Members now in England* (London, 1832), pp. 37–38, as follows: three men as cane carriers, two strong women as feeders, one woman to turn trash, six young women as trash carriers, one stocker-man, one pan-man, three boiler-men, one boatswain to superintend. These were all slaves. In addition was a white bookkeeper on duty constantly in the boiling house to keep track of the sugar produced and prevent thefts. This calls for nineteen slaves and one white on duty twenty-four hours a day. The total manpower needed would be a little less than twice this num-

ber, since working hours were usually more than twelve a day for this sort of work.

22. Senior, *Jamaica as It Was*, pp. 50–51; W. L. Burn, *Emancipation and Apprenticeship in the British West Indies* (London, 1937), pp. 41–44; Charles Royes's Report on his Management of Seville Estate, St. Ann, PP, 1946, xxviii (691–I), 10.

23. P. H. Gosse, *A Naturalist's Sojourn in Jamaica* (London, 1851), pp. 155–156; Lewis, *Journal*, pp. 84–85.

24. R. Pares, *A West-India Fortune* (London, 1950) is a very valuable study of the Pinneys of Nevis and Bristol, showing the process of fortune-building and absenteeism in the eighteenth-century West Indies.

25. Absentees owned a much higher proportion of the total land area than they owned of cultivated land, since almost all the uncultivated land was absentee-owned. Perhaps as much as 90 per cent of the land area was absentee-owned, but the figure has little meaning. Most of the land was unoccupied. For nineteenth-century absenteeism see Guillebaud, *Cambridge British Empire*, II, 481–482; L. J. Ragatz, "Absentee Landlordism in the British Caribbean," *Agricultural History*, V, 7–24 (January 1931).

26. Burn, *Emancipation*, pp. 28–30.

27. This, and most other monetary sums having to do with the internal economy of the island, are given in pounds currency, rather than pounds sterling. In the Jamaican monetary system of the early nineteenth century, 100 pounds sterling was about equal to 140 pounds currency at par; but, since most business was done through bills drawn on London, the actual ratio between the two varied with the discount rate. The price of bills in Kingston in the early 1830's varied between a premium of 20 per cent and a discount of 10 per cent. This situation was further complicated by the fact that the coins in circulation were not pounds, shillings, and pence, but Spanish doubloons and gold dollars. In the case of the dollar, the most common coin, par was taken to be 6 s. 8 d. currency (R. M. Martin, *History of the West Indies*, 2 vols. [London, 1836], I, 124–125.)

In any event, it is almost impossible to translate Jamaican pay scales into pounds sterling to arrive at a comparison between Jamaican and British real incomes of the period. The Jamaican price structure was quite different from the contemporaneous British price structure. The only valid generalization is that Jamaican prices translated into pounds sterling tended to be about one-third or more higher than British prices. This was true until 1865 and later.

28. J. Stewart, *A View of the Past and Present State of the Island of Jamaica; with Remarks on the Moral and Physical Condition of the Slaves, and on the Abolition of Slavery in the Colonies* (Edinburgh, 1823), pp. 184–187; B. McMahon, *Jamaica Plantership* (London, 1830), pp. 136–177; Burn, *Emancipation*, pp. 35–36; Senior, *Jamaica as It Was*, p. 90.

29. T. Roughley, *The Jamaica Planter's Guide* (London, 1823), p. 72; Senior, *Jamaica as It Was*, p. 61.

30. Burn, *Emancipation*, pp. 37–38; P. Duncan, *Narrative of the Wesleyan Mission to Jamaica; with Occasional Remarks on the State of Society*

in That Colony (London, 1849), pp. 367–368; B. McMahon, *Jamaica Plantership* (London, 1830), pp. 185–212; *Marly, passim.*

31. Stewart, *Past and Present*, p. 194.

32. In Jamaica the deficiency tax was repealed shortly before emancipation. In the 1820's it had been 20 s. per slave, which could be written off at the rate of £50 for each white man resident on the estate and registered in the militia (Setwart, *Past and Present*, p. 128).

33. Duncan, *Narrative*, p. 367.

34. For the position of the bookkeeper see: Senior, *Jamaica as It Was*, p. 62; Duncan, *Narrative*, p. 367; Burn, *Emancipation*, pp. 38–39; Stewart, *Past and Present*, pp. 189 ff. For the bitterness of the bookkeeper and the "walking buckra," see McMahon, *Jamaica Plantership, passim.*

35. Gardner, *History of Jamaica*, p. 380; Madden, *Twelve Months*, I, 91; *Marly*, p. 56; H. Whiteley, *Three Months in Jamaica in 1832; Comprising a Residence of Seven Weeks on a Sugar Plantation* (London, 1833), pp. 16–17.

36. Roughley, *Planter's Guide*, p. 81.

37. Roughley, *Planter's Guide*, pp. 99–107; Senior, *Jamaica as It Was*, p. 59; Burn, *Emancipation*, p. 40.
The breakdown of the labor force for a 100-hogshead, 150-slave estate might be expected to be about as follows: old people, 30; infants, 25; first gang, 40; second gang, 30; third gang, 25. (L. H. Evelyn, *The Sketch of a Plan, for the Effectual Abolition of Slavery, on the Principles of Justice to Every Colonial Interest, and in Full Accordance with Every Temperate Desire of the British Philanthropists* [Montego Bay, 1832], p. 61.)

38. Roughley, *Planter's Guide*, p. 85.

39. Stewart, *Past and Present*, pp. 261–264.

40. Senior, *Jamaica as It Was*, p. 59. Estimate of proportionate amount of land in estates and pens is based on B. Edwards, *The History, Civil and Commercial, of the British Colonies in the West Indies*, 2 vols., 2nd edition (London, 1794), I, 194.

41. During the decade of the 1820's production had averaged more than 20 million pounds annually. After 1840 it never reached 10 million. For statistical tables, see PP, 1867–68, xlviii [C. 3995], 9. See also, Olivier, *Jamaica*, pp. 137–138.

42. Although the original decision was, perhaps, unconscious, the nature of the decision that had been made was clear to at least some commentators of the 1830's. An anonymous "Jamaica proprietor" wrote; "Instead of becoming, as we might have become, a colony of English, increasing in population, with smaller gains but greater stability, with more of an agricultural and less of a commercial character; we have concentrated a dense population in one spot, and the rest of our estates is waste. The labour of 300 Negroes is brought to bear on a portion of land, which in ordinary cultivation of the richest European soils would require but ten or twelve efficient labourers. The prospect of high gains from sugar checked the cultivation of minor products." (*Negro Emancipation No Philanthropy, a Letter to The Duke of Wellington by a Jamaica Landed Proprietor* [London, 1830], pp. 4–5.)

CHAPTER II   AFRICAN JAMAICA

1. M. J. Herskovits, *The Myth of the Negro Past* (New York, 1941), *passim*.

2. A sampling of slave population in twelve Jamaican estates showed a population of 1,764 Africans and 3,325 creoles in 1817 reduced to 1,021 Africans and 3,720 creoles in 1829 (PP, 1831–32, xx (721), 567, 575). For statistical table of annual imports of slaves, see N. Deerr, *The History of Sugar*, 2 vols. (London, 1949–50), II, 278.

3. W. J. Gardner, *A History of Jamaica From Its Discovery by Christopher Columbus to the Year 1872* (London, 1873), pp. 174–175; J. Stewart, *A View of the Past and Present State of the Island of Jamaica; with Remarks on the Moral and Physical Condition of the Slaves, and on the Abolition of Slavery in the Colonies* (Edinburgh, 1823), pp. 250–251; see also Herskovits, *Negro Past*, pp. 33–39, 50.

4. Herskovits, *Negro Past*, pp. 61–85.

5. *Memoir of the Late Rev. Thomas P. Callender, Missionary to Jamaica* (Edinburgh, 1850), p. 42; J. M. Phillippo, *Jamaica: Its Past and Present State* (London, 1843), p. 218. For a contemporaneous description of Afro-Jamaican culture in the late eighteenth century see Bryan Edwards, *The History, Civil and Commercial, of the British Colonies in the West Indies*, 2 vols., 2nd ed., (London, 1794), II, 34–192.

6. [B. M. Senior], *Jamaica as It Was, as It Is, and as It May Be . . . by a Retired Military Officer* (London, 1935), p. 43; H. De la Beche, *Notes on the Present Condition of the Negroes of Jamaica* (London, 1825), pp. 17–18.

7. Jamaica. Legislative Council. *Report of the Committee Appointed to Enquire into the Prevalence of Concubinage and the High Rate of Illegitimacy* (Kingston, 1941).

8. M. G. Lewis, *Journal of a West-India Proprietor, Kept During Residence in the Island of Jamaica* (London, 1834), pp. 187, 190, 345; Stewart, *Past and Present*, p. 251.

9. H. M. Waddell, *Twenty-nine Years in the West Indies and Central Africa* (London, 1863), p. 107; Lewis, *Journal*, p. 350.

10. Phillippo, *Jamaica*, pp. 243–244; Gardner, *History of Jamaica*, p. 384; De la Beche, *Negroes of Jamaica*, pp. 41–42; Lewis, *Journal*, pp. 53–55.

11. Phillippo, *Jamaica*, p. 243; Gardner, *History of Jamaica*, p. 385; Lewis, *Journal*, p. 51.

12. M. W. Beckwith, *Black Roadways: A Study of Jamaican Folk Life* (Chapel Hill, 1929), pp. 150–155.

13. Phillippo, *Jamaica*, pp. 241–242. See also Stewart, *Past and Present*, pp. 269–272; Lewis, *Journal*, pp. 80–81.

14. Herskovits, *Negro Past*, p. 84.

15. M. J. and F. S. Herskovits, *Trinidad Village* (New York, 1947), p. 6.

16. Later in the century they were legally defined as one and the same thing. See Chapter VIII.

17. Herskovits, *Negro Past*, p. 73.

18. Phillippo, *Jamaica*, pp. 247–248; T. Banbury, *Jamaica Superstitions, or the Obeah Book; a Complete Treatise of the Absurdities Believed in by the People of the Island, by the Rector (Native) of St. Peter's Church, Hope Bay, Portland* (Jamaica, 1894), p. 6 and *passim*.

19. Herskovits, *Negro Past*, pp. 69–72.

20. H. M. Waddell, *Twenty-nine Years*, p. 137; J. J. Williams, *Voodoos and Obeahs: Phases of West Indian Witchcraft* (New York, 1932), pp. 155–159.

21. This is the Ceiba tree, or *Eriodendoron anfractuosum,* a near biological relative of *Bombax pentandrum,* which was held sacred in West Africa (P. H. Gosse, *A Naturalist's Sojourn in Jamaica* [London, 1851], p. 275).

22. For accounts of early nineteenth-century myal ceremonies, see Phillippo, *Jamaica*, pp. 248–249; Waddell, *Twenty-nine Years*, pp. 137–138; Lewis, *Journal*, pp. 345–355; Banbury, *Obeah Book,* pp. 19–23. For some of the later developments and variations see Beckwith, *Black Roadways,* pp. 142–149, 157.

23. For Negro funeral ceremonies see Gardner, *History of Jamacia,* pp. 386–387; Stewart, *Past and Present,* pp. 274–276; Phillippo, *Jamaica,* pp. 244–246; M. Scott, *Tom Cringle's Log* (London, 1915), pp. 128, 143–144; A. Barclay, *A Practical View of the Present State of Slavery in the West Indies* (London, 1827), pp. 134–137.

24. L. H. Evelyn, *The Sketch of a Plan, for the Effectual Abolition of Slavery, on the Principles of Justice to Every Colonial Interest, and in Full Accordance with Every Temperate Desire of the British Philanthropists* (Montego Bay, 1832), p. 52; Barclay, *A Practical View,* pp. 39–40.

25. De la Beche, *Negroes of Jamaica,* p. 27; R. Bickell, *The West Indies as They Are; or a Real Picture of Slavery: but More Particularly as It Exists in the Island of Jamaica* (London, 1825), pp. 89–91.

26. Gardner, *History of Jamaica,* p. 344; J. Clark, W. Dendy, and J. M. Phillippo, *The Voice of Jubilee* (London, 1865), pp. 30–31.

27. J. Clarke, *Memorials of Baptist Missionaries in Jamaica* (London, 1869), pp. 12–14.

28. Clark, *et al., Jubilee,* pp. 32–33; F. A. Cox, *History of the Baptist Missionary Society from 1792 to 1842,* 2 vols. (London, 1842), II, 17; Phillippo, *Jamaica,* p. 395.

29. For Gibb's doctrine see A. Robb, *The Gospel to the Africans* (Edinburgh and London, 1861), pp. 34–35; for Baker's version see Waddell, *Twenty-nine Years,* pp. 26–27, 35–36; G. Blyth, *Reminiscences of Missionary Life* (Edinburgh, 1851), pp. 50–51. See also Gardner, *History of Jamaica,* pp. 344–348. There were, in addition, Native Wesleyans, who had split off from the European missionaries in the 1820's. See Barclay, *A Practical View,* pp. 187–188.

30. Waddell, *Twenty-nine Years,* p. 112; Barclay, *A Practical View,* pp. 39–40.

31. J. B. Ellis, *The Diocese of Jamaica* (London, 1913), p. 66; Bishop

Lipscomb to Rev. James H. Archer, Spanish Town, 29 March 1832, Letter
Book of the Bishop's Registry Office, Archives of the Diocese of Jamaica,
Church House, Cross-Roads, Jamaica (cited hereafter as ADJ); Waddell,
Twenty-nine Years, p. 23.

32. Waddell, *Twenty-nine Years,* pp. 80–82.

33. For a general history of Methodism to emancipation, see C. G. Findlay and W. W. Holdsworth, *A History of the Wesleyan Methodist Missionary Society,* 5 vols. (London, 1921–24), II, 63–132. See also Gardner, *History
of Jamaica,* p. 361; P. Duncan, *Narrative of the Wesleyan Mission to
Jamaica; with Occasional Remarks on the State of Society in that Colony*
(London, 1849), p. 158.

34. Findlay and Holdsworth, *Wesleyan Methodist Missionary Society,*
II, 301–302, 358–359; "Instructions to Missionaries," printed annually in
the first pages of *The Report of the Wesleyan-Methodist Missionary So-
ciety* (London). These instructions remained unchanged from the 1830's to
the 1850's. R. Young, *A View of Slavery in Connection with Christianity:
Being the Substance of a Discourse Delivered in the Wesleyan Chapel,
Stoney-Hill, Jamaica, Sept. 19, 1824* (Jamaica, 1824), p. 10; J. Sturge and
T. Harvey, *The West Indies in 1837* (London, 1838), p. 157.

35. Gardner, *History of Jamaica,* p. 361; Cox, *Baptist Missionary Society,*
pp. 17–25.

36. Cox, *Baptist Missionary Society,* p. 69.

37. Waddell, *Twenty-nine Years,* pp. 25–26; Blyth, *Missionary Life,*
p. 159; Gardner, *History of Jamaica,* 360–361; Burchell, "Statement to the
Missionary Society," quoted in Cox, *Baptist Missionary Society,* pp. 69–74.

38. M. Park, *Travels in the Interior Districts of Africa: Performed under
the Direction and Patronage of the African Association in the Years 1795,
1796, and 1797* (New York, 1800), pp. 52–53. M. J. and F. S. Herskovits,
Trinidad Village, pp. 136, 152, indicate survivals of a similar attitude
in modern Trinidad.

39. [W. Knibb], *Speech of the Rev. William Knibb before the Baptist
Missionary Society, in Exeter Hall, April 28th, 1842* (London [1842]), p. 23
shows a replica of the type of ticket then in use.

40. H. Bleby, *Scenes in the Caribbean Sea: being Sketches from a Missionary's Note-book* (London, 1868), p. 32; A. Caldecott, *The Church in
the West Indies* (London, 1898), p. 107; Waddell, *Twenty-nine Years,*
pp. 111–114.

41. Senior, *Jamaica as It Was,* p. 280.

42. Phillippo, *Jamaica,* pp. 188–189.

43. Herskovits, *Negro Past,* pp. 89–95; E. Williams, *Capitalism and
Slavery* (Chapel Hill, 1944), pp. 197–208.

44. Senior, *Jamaica as It Was,* p. 168; Waddell, *Twenty-nine Years,*
pp. 67–68; Gardner, *History of Jamaica,* pp. 272–273; H. Bleby, *Death
Struggles of Slavery: Being a Narrative of Facts and Incidents which Occurred in a British Colony, during the Two Years Immediately Preceding
Negro Emancipation* (London, 1853), pp. 131–133; Blyth, *Missionary Life,*
p. 57; Report of a Committee of the House of Assembly, 1824, quoted in

Barclay, *Practical View*, pp. 246–248; Barclay, *Practical View*, pp. 243–244; Bickell, *The West Indies as They Are*, p. 143.

45. Lewis, *Journal, passim*.

46. [W. Hosack], "Jamaica: A Poem," *Jamaica Monthly Magazine*, XI, 286 (Spanish Town, October 1833).

47. G. W. Bridges, *The Annals of Jamaica*, 2 vols. (London, 1828), II, 400–401.

48. G. W. Bridges, *A Voice from Jamaica*, 4th ed. (London, 1824), p. 18.

CHAPTER III   EUROPEAN JAMAICA

1. The first census, in 1844, listed the following racial totals: white, 15,776; black, 293,128; colored, 68,549 (PP, 1845, xxxi (426), 4). There were perhaps 40,000 free colored people in 1830.

The racial criterion of the census-taker, however, has only a limited meaning for historical purposes. Racial distinctions in Jamaican history are important for their social, and not for their biological meaning. Thus, some people classified as "colored" were more nearly "white" in their outlook and position. Others in the same group were more nearly "black."

2. The common distinctions of racial mixture within the brown class were as follows: white with black produces mulatto; mulatto with white produces quadroon; quadroon with white produces mestee; mestee with white is legally white and free by law; mulatto with black produces sambo. (J. Stewart, *A View of the Past and Present State of the Island of Jamaica; with Remarks on the Moral and Physical Condition of the Slaves, and on the Abolition of Slavery in the Colonies* [Edinburgh, 1823], p. 324).

3. PP, 1831–32, xxxi (59), 10. See also F. Cundall, "Jamaica Worthies: Richard Hill," *Journal of the Institute of Jamaica*, II, 223–230 (Kingston, 1894), and W. A. Roberts, *Six Great Jamaicans* (Kingston, 1951), pp. 4–15.

The racial statistics of Wolmer's Free School, the principal school in Kingston, show the educational advancement of the colored people.

Date	White Students	Colored Students
1815	111	3
1820	116	78
1825	89	185
1830	88	194

From a letter of E. Reid, headmaster, quoted in A. Barclay, *Remarks on Emigration to Jamaica: Addressed to the Coloured Class of the United States* (New York, 1840), pp. 10–11.

4. Barrett, *A Reply to the Speech of Dr. Lushington in the House of Commons, on the 12th of June 1827 on the Condition of the Free-Coloured People of Jamaica* (London, 1828), p. 29.

5. *Christian Record*, I, 24 (Kingston, September 1831).

6. R. Bickell, *The West Indies as They Are; or a Real Picture of Slavery: but More Particularly as It Exists in the Island of Jamaica* (London, 1825),

pp. 104–113; Stewart, *Past and Present,* pp. 173–175, 325–339; W. J. Gardner, *A History of Jamaica from Its Discovery by Christopher Columbus to the Year 1872* (London, 1873), p. 378; J. Sturge and T. Harvey, *The West Indies in 1837* (London, 1838), p. 163; *Marly; or, The Life of a Planter in Jamaica,* 2nd ed. (Glasgow, 1828), pp. 193–194.

7. C. R. Williams, *A Tour through the Island of Jamaica, from the Western to the Eastern End, in the Year 1823* (London, 1826), pp. 152–153, 310; Protest of the House of Assembly, June 1838, quoted in K. N. Bell and W. P. Morrell, *Select Documents on British Colonial Policy,* 1830–60 (Oxford, 1928), p. 404. See also "Jamaica Fashions in 1831. By a Johnny Newcome of Twelve Months' Experience," *Jamaica Monthly Magazine,* II (new series), 349, (Kingston, April 1847).

8. Stewart, *Past and Present,* pp. 329–330.

9. Stewart, *Past and Present,* p. 324; Commissioners of Correspondence to William Burge, 21 June 1831, Commission of Correspondence Letter Books, Reference Library of the West Indies, Kingston, Jamaica (hereafter cited as IJ); P. Duncan, *Narrative of the Wesleyan Mission to Jamaica: with Occasional Remarks on the State of Society in that Colony* (London, 1849), p. 337.

10. *Marly,* pp. 183–203.

11. T. Roughley, *The Jamaica Planters' Guide* (London, 1823), pp. 68–69, 50–51; *Marly,* pp. 73–75. See B. McMahon, *Jamaica Plantership* (London, 1830), for the bitterness of the underdog toward his "betters."

12. See W. G. Freeman, *Pickwick Jamaica,* MSS. IJ, chapter xi for a fictional treatment of the rise to prominence in Jamaican society from humble British origins.

13. Stewart, *Past and Present,* pp. 199–201; [B. M. Senior], *Jamaica as It Was, as It Is, and as It May Be . . . by a Retired Military Officer* (London, 1835), pp. 124–125; Gardner, *History of Jamaica,* p. 379.

14. L. J. Ragatz, *The Fall of the Planter Class in the British Caribbean, 1763–1833* (New York, 1928), pp. 17–18; Stewart, *Past and Present,* pp. 195–197; Senior, *Jamaica as It Was,* pp. 87–88; E. B. Underhill, *The West Indies* (London, 1862), p. 419.

15. Senior, *Jamaica as It Was,* p. 131; Stewart, *Past and Present,* p. 198.

16. Freeman, *Pickwick Jamaica,* ch. xi.

17. G. W. Bridges, *The Annals of Jamaica,* 2 vols. (London, 1828), I, 561. For the history of the Church of England in Jamaica see A. Caldecott, *The Church in the West Indies* (London, 1898), and J. B. Ellis, *Diocese of Jamaica* (London, 1913).

18. Bridges, *Annals of Jamaica,* II, 495; Ellis, *Diocese of Jamaica,* pp. 62–65, 78–79; Bishop Lipscomb to Robert Banks Pitman, 5 November 1831; Lipscomb to Rev. George Pinnock, 5 December 1831; Lipscomb to Viscount Goderich, 6 April 1832; Letter Book of the Bishop's Registry Office, ADJ.

19. Senior, *Jamaica as It Was,* p. 125; R. R. Madden, *Twelve Months' Residence in the West Indies During the Transition from Slavery to Apprenticeship,* 2 vols. (London, 1835), I, 82.

20. "Slave Law of 1828," art. 84, quoted in Duncan, *Wesleyan Mission,* p. 178; Commissioners of Correspondence to George Hibbert, 2 January 1829; Commissioners of Correspondence to William Burge, 25 February 1831, IJ; PP, 1831–32, xxi (59).

21. A. H. Beaumont, *The Jamaica Petition for Representation in the British House of Commons, or for Independence* ([London], 1831), pp. 14–15.

22. [A. Davis], *Copy of a Letter Addressed to a Member of the Legislative Assembly of Jamaica, by One of Its Members in England* (London, 1832), p. 11; *Marly,* p. 23. See also R. Pares, *A West India Fortune* (London, 1950), especially pp. 141–159, for a study of similar tensions between Nevis and Great Britain in the eighteenth century.

23. Madden, *Twelve Months,* I, 96.

24. Duncan, *Wesleyan Mission,* p. 365; Madden, *Twelve Months,* I, 81; J. M. Phillippo, *Jamaica: Its Past and Present State* (London, 1843), pp. 121–122. See also Mrs. H. Lynch, *The Family Sepulchre* (London, [1848]), p. 82.

25. W. Hosack, *Isle of Streams: or the Jamaica Hermit and Other Poems* (Edinburgh, 1876), p. 28. This is a new edition, with many changes, of the poem that first appeared in the *Jamaica Monthly Magazine* in 1833 and 1834 under the title, "Jamaica: A Poem."

26. Stewart, *Past and Present,* pp. 216–218; Gardner, *History of Jamaica,* p. 381.

27. Freeman, *Pickwick Jamaica,* ch. i.

28. Stewart, *Past and Present,* pp. 170–172; Gardner, *History of Jamaica,* p. 377.

29. Madden, *Twelve Months,* I, 81. See also *Marly,* p. 211; Phillippo, *Jamaica,* pp. 121–122.

30. *Jack Jingle. The Omnibus or Jamaica Scrap Book. A Thing of Shreds and Patches,* p. 239, MSS. IJ. See also Mrs. Lynch, *Family Sepulchre,* p. 231, where the authoress laments that ". . . those who have resided between the tropics, know that death and sorrow are there familiar guests; that members of one family follow each other in quick succession to the grave."

31. [W. Hosack], "Jamaica: a Poem," *Jamaica Monthly Magazine,* XII, 66 (Spanish Town, January 1834).

32. Memorandum of October 1831, quoted from the Howick Papers in Bell and Morrell, *Documents of British Colonial Policy,* p. 373.

33. Stewart, *Past and Present,* p. 205; F. C. Cundall, "Literature, Science, and Art in Jamaica: A Retrospect," *Journal of the Institute of Jamaica,* I, 200–208 (Kingston, 1894).

34. W. L. Burn, *Emancipation and Apprenticeship in the British West Indies* (London, 1937), p. 273.

35. Duncan, *Wesleyan Mission,* pp. 373–374.

36. Duncan, *Wesleyan Mission,* pp. 365–368; B. McMahon, *Jamaica Plantership* (London, 1830), p. 215; H. Whiteley, *Three Months in Jamaica*

in 1832: Comprising a Residence of Seven Weeks on a Sugar Plantation (London, 1833), *passim.*

37. "Jamaica Fashions in 1831," *Jamaica Monthly Magazine,* II (n.s.), 350.

CHAPTER IV DEFENSES AGAINST REVOLUTION

1. Coupland, *Anti-Slavery Movement,* pp. 124–125; G. B. Mellor, *British Imperial Trusteeship 1783–1850* (London, 1951), pp. 87–89.

2. G. W. Bridges, *The Annals of Jamaica,* 2 vols. (London, 1828). For Bridges' proslavery activities in general, see L. J. Ragatz, *The Fall of the Planter Class in the British Caribbean 1763–1833* (New York, 1928), pp. 430, 436–439; F. Cundall, "The Rev. George Wilson Bridges," *Journal of the Institute of Jamaica,* III, 101 ff. (April 1895).

3. W. L. Burn, *Emancipation and Apprenticeship in the British West Indies* (London, 1937), p. 51.

4. A. H. Beaumont, *The Jamaica Petition for Representation in the British House of Commons, or for Independence* ([London], 1831), pp. 12–13. For the Assembly subsidy of this work, see Commissioners of Correspondence to William Burge, 5 August 1832 and 1 February 1833, Commission of Correspondence Letter Books, IJ.

5. G. W. Bridges, *Dreams of Dulocracy, or the Puritanical Obituary* (Jamaica, 1824), p. 41.

6. [B. M. Senior], *Jamaica as It Was, as It Is, and as It May Be . . . by a Retired Military Officer* (London, 1835), pp. 296–297; *Marly, or, the Life of a Planter in Jamaica,* 2nd ed. (Glasgow, 1828), p. 250; J. Stewart, *A View of the Past and Present State of the Island of Jamaica . . .* (Edinburgh, 1823), p. 244; A. Barclay, *A Practical View of the Present State of Slavery in the West Indies* (London, 1827), pp. xii–xiii.

7. *Negro Emancipation No Philanthropy, a Letter to the Duke of Wellington by a Jamaica Landed Proprietor* (London, 1830), pp. 26, 30.

8. Bridges, *Annals of Jamaica,* II, 407–408.

9. Bridges, *Annals of Jamaica,* II, 275–276.

10. Bridges, *Annals of Jamaica,* I, 453–457, 470–471. See also *Dreams of Dulocracy,* p. 42.

11. This corresponds to the phenomenon that Lyford P. Edwards and Crane Brinton have pointed out in connection with European revolutions as "the desertion of the intellectuals." Here, of course, the intellectuals who deserted were not Jamaican, but British. In spite of this, the end result was much the same: it weakened the will of the old ruling class to resist. See L. P. Edwards, *The Natural History of Revolution* (Chicago, 1927), ch. iv; C. Brinton, *The Anatomy of Revolution,* 2nd ed. (New York, 1952), pp. 45–53.

12. [Barrett], *A Reply to the Speech of Dr. Lushington in the House of Commons, on the 12th of June 1827 on the Condition of the Free-Coloured People of Jamaica* (London, 1828), pp. 3–4.

13. Stewart, *Past and Present*, pp. 242–244; *Negro Emancipation No Philanthropy*, pp. 15–21, 37–39; *Marly*, pp. 312–317.

14. A. H. Beaumont, *The Jamaica Petition*, p. 13.

15. [A. Davis], *Copy of a Letter Addressed to a Member of the Legislative Assembly of Jamaica, by One of its Members Now in England* (London, 1832), *passim*; C. R. Williams, *A Tour Through the Island of Jamaica, from the Western to the Eastern End, in the Year 1823* (London, 1826), pp. 74–75; "Solemn Declaration of the General Meeting of the Colonial Church Union," Falmouth, Jamaica, 28 July 1832, quoted in H. Bleby, *Death Struggles of Slavery* (London, 1853), p. 224; *Negro Emancipation No Philanthropy*, pp. 8–15; H. Whiteley, *Three Months in Jamaica in 1832: Comprising a Residence of Seven Weeks on a Sugar Plantation* (London, 1833), pp. 2–3; *Marly*, p. 92.

16. Stewart, *Past and Present*, pp. 241–242; *Negro Emancipation No Philanthropy*, pp. 6–8; *Marly*, p. 93.

17. *Marly*, pp. 250–251; see also Stewart, *Past and Present*, pp. 241–242; L. H. Evelyn, *The Sketch of a Plan, for the Effectual Abolition of Slavery . . .* (Montego Bay, 1832), pp. 1–2.

18. Williams, *Tour of Jamaica*, p. 75.

19. *Negro Emancipation No Philanthropy*, p. 6. See also the statements cited in note 20, below. This particular piece of foolishness had its most famous rendering some years later in Thomas Carlyle's "Occasional Discourse on the Nigger Question," *Fraser's Magazine*, XL, 670–679 (London, December 1849).

20. Williams, *Tour of Jamaica*, p. 224; *Marly*, pp. 92–93, 247–249; Bridges, *Annals of Jamaica*, I, 510–511.

21. Burn, *Emancipation*, pp. 94–95.

22. Complaints of this sort abound in the missionary literature. For secular corroboration see PP, 1831–32, xlvii (480), *passim*; Whiteley, *Three Months*, pp. 13–14; H. De la Beche, *Notes on the Present Condition of the Negroes of Jamaica* (London, 1825), p. 28.

23. Bridges, *Dreams of Dulocracy*, p. 26, and *Annals of Jamaica*, II, 294–298.

24. Quoted in P. Duncan, *Narrative of the Wesleyan Mission to Jamaica . . .* (London, 1849), p. 238, from House of Assembly, *Votes, 1828*, Appendix.

25. Beaumont, *Jamaica Petition*, p. 11. See also Barrett, *Reply to Lushington*, p. 48.

26. Burn, *Emancipation*, pp. 151–152 and 156–159; R. M. Martin, *History of the British West Indies*, 2 vols. (London, 1836–37), I, 109.

27. PP, 1845, xxxi (623), 3; PP, 1842, xiii (479), p. 316. See also L. M. Penson, *The Colonial Agents of the British West Indies* (London, 1924), for a general study of the institution.

28. The Letter Books of the Commissioners of Correspondence at the Institute of Jamaica in Kingston are a detailed record of Burge's many activities in the cause of slavery during these years.

29. Duncan, *Wesleyan Mission*, pp. 369–370.

30. PP, 1839, xxxv (107), 175–176, 187–188. In this election there was a ratio of one qualified voter for each 40 members of the class that had been free before emancipation, or one voter for each 125 of the total population. Even after the Reform Act of 1832, the similar ratio for Great Britain was 1 to 30, and it was 1 to 200 for France under the July Monarchy.

31. PP, 1839, xxxv (107), 187–188; Burn, *Emancipation,* p. 153.

32. Burn, *Emancipation,* pp. 160–163; [Lord Sligo], *Jamaica Under the Apprenticeship. By a Proprietor* (London, 1838), pp. 1–3; J. M. Phillippo, *Jamaica: Its Past and Present State* (London, 1843), pp. 101–104; Martin, *West Indies,* I, 104–109.

33. Martin, *West Indies,* I, 109; Burn, *Emancipation,* p. 165; Phillippo, *Jamaica,* p. 110.

34. Quoted in W. Burge, *The Speech of W. Burge, Esq., Q.C., Agent for Jamaica, at the Bar of the House of Commons, against the Bill Intituled "An Act to Make Temporary Provision for the Government of Jamaica." Monday, 22nd April, 1839* (London, 1839), p. 31.

35. Resolution at a meeting of the freeholders and inhabitants of the parish of St. Thomas-in-the-East, Morant Bay, 8 August 1831, quoted in PP, 1831–32, xlvii (285), 8.

36. Resolutions of the Magistrates and Vestry of the Parish of St. Ann, 14 May 1830, *The Watchman,* 3 July 1830; Letter to the *Jamaica Courant* signed "Sergius Umbratus" (attributed to Rev. G. W. Bridges), 30 July 1831, quoted in Bleby, *Death Struggles,* pp. 121–122.

37. Resolutions of a meeting for the Parish of Manchester, 2 August 1831, in PP, 1831–32, xlvii (285), 11. See also the resolutions of St. Mary, 23 July 1831, and of St. Ann, 6 August 1831, PP, 1831–32, xlvii (285), 10, 12; Beaumont, *Jamaica Petition,* pp. 4–24.

38. Letter to the *Jamaica Courant,* signed "Sergius Umbratus" (attributed to Rev. G. W. Bridges), 11 August 1831, quoted in Bleby, *Death Struggles,* p. 123.

39. Commissioners of Correspondence to William Burge, 17 December 1831, Commission of Correspondence Letter Books, IJ.

40. *Jack Jingle. The Omnibus or Jamaica Scrapbook,* MSS. IJ, p. 345.

CHAPTER V THE JAMAICAN REVOLUTION

1. For a more detailed treatment of the Jamaican revolution, see W. L. Burn, *Emancipation and Apprenticeship in the British West Indies* (London, 1937). L. J. Ragatz, *The Fall of the Planter Class in the British Caribbean 1763–1833* (New York, 1928) is valuable for the period to 1833, while W. L. Mathieson, *British Slavery and its Abolition 1823–1838* (London, 1926) presents another view. For the emancipation movement as a whole G. B. Mellor, *British Imperial Trusteeship 1783–1850* (London, 1951); E. Williams, *Capitalism and Slavery* (Chapel Hill, 1944); R. Coupland, *The British Anti-Slavery Movement* (London, 1933); and F. J. Klingberg, *The Anti-Slavery Movement in England* (New Haven, 1926) present a variety of recent interpretations.

2. E. Halevy, *The Triumph of Reform 1830–1841,* 2nd ed. (London, 1950), pp. 3–15.

3. W. L. Mathieson, in *Cambridge History of the British Empire* (Cambridge, 1940), II, 324–326.

4. William Knibb, evidence before Select Committee on the Extinction of Slavery, PP, 1831–32, xx (721), 244, q. 3283; Rev. H. M. Waddell, *Twenty-nine Years in the West Indies and Central Africa* (London, 1863), pp. 66–68; Rev. G. Blyth, *Reminiscences of Missionary Life* (Edinburgh, 1851), p. 57; Rev. H. Bleby, *Death Struggles of Slavery* (London, 1853), pp. 127–133. See also Jamaica House of Assembly, Report of the Committee on the Causes of the Rebellion, PP, 1831–32, xlvii (561), 3–4.

5. [B. M. Senior], *Jamaica as It Was, as It Is, and as It May Be . . . by a Retired Military Officer* (London, 1835), pp. 170–173.

6. Bleby, *Death Struggles,* pp. 3–8.

7. Bleby, *Death Struggles,* pp. 9–14.

8. Bleby, *Death Struggles,* pp. 14–16.

9. Bleby, *Death Struggles,* pp. 17–25; Rev. H. Bleby, *Scenes in the Caribbean Sea* (London, 1868), pp. 56–107; B. McMahon, *Jamaica Plantership* (London, 1839), pp. 90–109.

10. Burn, *Emancipation,* p. 94; Bleby, *Death Struggles,* p. 37.

11. These reports are most careless in the names given the various rebel leaders. For example, Samuel Sharp, John Sharp, John Thorp Lawrence, John Tharp, Samuel Tharp, and "Daddy Ruler" Tharp all occur with a certain amount of confusion. Some reporters have the impression that these are all aliases of the same person. Actually they describe at least three different people, and perhaps four.

12. Bleby, *Death Struggles,* pp. 109–119; [Rev. W. Knibb], *Facts and Documents Connected with the Late Insurrection in Jamaica* (London, 1832), pp. 10–13; William Knibb, evidence before Select Committee on the Extinction of Slavery, PP, 1831–32, xx (721), 245–246, 271–273; Confessions of Negro Leaders, PP, 1831–32, xlvii (561), 29–35.

13. Blyth, *Missionary Life,* p. 58; Knibb, *Facts and Documents,* pp. 10–11.

14. Waddell, *Twenty-nine Years,* p. 79.

15. T. F. Abbott, *Narrative of Certain Events Connected with the Late Disturbances in Jamaica* (London, 1832), pp. 10–12; J. H. Buchner, *The Moravians in Jamaica* (London, 1854), pp. 90–96; Bleby, *Death Struggles,* p. 98.

16. Quoted in Bleby, *Death Struggles,* p. 140.

17. Burn, *Emancipation,* pp. 93–95; Bleby, *Death Struggles,* pp. 175–176, 215, 224; *A Narrative of Recent Events Connected with the Baptist Mission in this Island* (Kingston, 1833), Appendix V, pp. 7–9; *Christian Record* (Kingston, March 1832), I, 63–64; *Jamaica Courant,* 3 March 1832, quoted in Knibb, *Facts and Documents,* pp. 17–18.

18. Burn, *Emancipation,* p. 96; Bleby, *Death Struggles,* pp. 150, 196–208; Abbott, *Narrative of Certain Events,* pp. 16–38; *Narrative of Recent Events* (Kingston), 114–117; Knibb, *Facts and Documents,* p. 8.

19. Bleby, *Death Struggles,* pp. 79–93, 192–195; PP, 1833, xxvi (541), 481 ff.

20. Bleby, *Death Struggles,* pp. 200–201, 239–246; Abbott, *Narrative of Events,* p. 38; *Christian Record,* I, 87 (April 1832).

21. William Knibb and Peter Duncan, evidence before Select Committee on the Extinction of Slavery, PP, 1831–32, xx (721), qq. 1577–1579, 3284–3286.

22. Bleby, *Death Struggles,* pp. 133–135; W. A. Roberts, *Six Great Jamaicans* (Kingston, 1952), pp. 10–15.

23. Waddell, *Twenty-nine Years,* p. 77; P. Duncan, *Narrative of the Wesleyan Mission to Jamaica; with Occasional Remarks on the State of Society in that Colony* (London, 1849), p. 337; Bleby, *Death Struggles,* pp. 252–281.

24. H. Taylor, *Autobiography of Henry Taylor 1800–1875,* 2 vols. (London, 1885), I, 124; Howick, Memorandum of 31 December 1832, quoted in Bell and Morrell, *Select Documents of British Colonial Policy, 1830–60* (Oxford, 1928), pp. 383–389; Burn, *Emancipation,* pp. 110–111.

25. Taylor, *Autobiography,* I, 128.

26. Taylor, *Autobiography,* I, 125–128.

27. Burn, *Emancipation,* pp. 114–117.

28. Burn, *Emancipation,* pp. 118–119, 166–167.

29. Commissioners of Correspondence to William Burge, 13 December 1833, Commission of Correspondence Letter Books, IJ.

30. Quoted in R. M. Martin, *History of the West Indies,* 2 vols. (London, 1836), I, 132.

31. [Lord Sligo], *Jamaica under the Apprenticeship. By a Proprietor* (London, 1838), p. ii; Burn, *Emancipation,* pp. 166–169.

32. Sligo, *Apprenticeship,* p. 75; Burn, *Emancipation,* pp. 196–266; H. S. Cooper to Sir Lionel Smith, St. Thomas-ye-Vale, 25 July 1837, PP, 1837–38, xlix (154–I), 282.

33. Sligo, *Apprenticeship, passim;* Burn, *Emancipation,* pp. 148–160, 290–318.

34. Sligo, *Apprenticeship,* pp. 88 ff.; Burn, *Emancipation, passim,* especially pp. 175–178.

35. Sligo, *Apprenticeship,* pp. 20–32; PP, 1836, xv (560), 86–88; PP, 1835 [C. 278–I], pp. 294–300.

36. Burn, *Emancipation,* pp. 319, 332–357; W. L. Mathieson in *Cambridge British Empire,* II, 332 ff.

37. Burn, *Emancipation,* pp. 359–360.

38. Protest of the Assembly of Jamaica, June 1838, quoted in Bell and Morrell, *Select Documents,* p. 403.

39. Protest of the Assembly of Jamaica, June 1838, quoted in Bell and Morrell, *Select Documents,* p. 405.

40. W. J. Gardner, *A History of Jamaica from its Discovery by Christopher Columbus to the Year 1872* (London, 1873), pp. 400–404; Mathieson, *British Slavery and its Abolition,* pp. 310–313.

41. Taylor, *Autobiography*, I, 249–261, especially Taylor's memorandum quoted on I, 254; Halevy, *Triumph of Reform*, p. 240.

42. W. P. Morrell, *British Colonial Policy in the Age of Peel and Russell* (Oxford, 1930), p. 152; James Stephen to G. W. Hope, 15 September 1841, quoted in Bell and Morrell, *Select Documents*, pp. 418–421.

CHAPTER VI   THE TWO ECONOMIES

1. Robert Osborn, Address to the St. Andrew Anti-Slave-Trade Meeting, 19 June 1849, quoted in [D. Turnbull, ed.], *The Jamaica Movement for Promoting the Enforcement of the Slave-Trade Treaties and for the Suppression of the Slave Trade* (London, 1850), p. 187.

2. J. J. Gurney, *Reconciliation, Respectfully Recommended to All Parties in the Colony of Jamaica in a Letter Addressed to the Planters* (Kingston, 1840), pp. 5–6.

3. [W. Hosack], "Jamaica: a Poem," *Jamaica Monthly Magazine* (Spanish Town, January 1834), XII, 66.

4. Address of the House of Assembly to Lord Sligo, 4 August 1835, PP, 1847, xxxviii (160), 5.

5. Jamaican annual average sugar production 1824–1833 was 68,465 tons. In 1839–1846 it was only 33,431 tons. N. Deerr, *The History of Sugar*, 2 vols. (London, 1949–50), II, 377.

6. See Appendix C.

7. Deerr, *History of Sugar*, II, 377.

8. Memorial of the Jamaica College of Physicians and Surgeons, April 1852, PP, 1852–53, lxvii (76), 142.

9. Memorial of the House of Assembly, 24 December 1847, PP, 1847–48, xxiii (167), 375; Census of 1844, PP, 1845, xxxi (426), 4; PP, 1854, lxiii [C. 1848], 55; PP, 1867, xlviii [C. 3812], 9. See Appendix C.

10. W. G. Sewell, *The Ordeal of Free Labor in the West Indies* (New York, 1861), p. 175.

11. Sewell, *Free Labor*, p. 169.

12. "The Baptist," *Jamaica Monthly Magazine*, II (new series), 18 (Kingston, February 1847).

13. Lord Olivier, *Jamaica the Blessed Island* (London, 1936), pp. 135–136; William Hosack, in the House of Assembly, February 1861, Judah and Sinclair, *Debates of the Honourable House of Assembly of Jamaica*, 13 vols. (Kingston and Spanish Town, 1856–66), V, 395; *Jamaica; Who is to Blame? by a Thirty Years' Resident* (London [1866]), pp. 34–38; Barkly to Newcastle, 26 May 1854, PP, 1854, lxiii [C. 1848], 52–53; G. Solomon, *Population and Prosperity; or, Free vs. Slave Production* (Kingston, 1859), pp. 5–6; J. Bigelow, *Jamaica in 1850* (New York, 1851), pp. 113–114; Sewell, *Free Labor*, pp. 236–237.

14. These were the steps of the process in outline:

1825 Sugar from Mauritius entered on the same terms as British West India sugar. All other sugar paid prohibitive duties.

1835 East India empire sugar received the West India rate.

1844 Foreign free-labor sugar rate was lowered, but still well above the West India rate.

1846 All foreign sugar immediately received equalization with foreign free-labor sugar. Commenced a gradual equalization of all sugar duties to reach full equality in 1851.

1848 Eventual equalization of all sugar duties put off till 1854.

(C. R. Fay in *Cambridge History of the British Empire* [Cambridge, 1940], II, 396–397; G. R. Mellor, *British Imperial Trusteeship 1783–1850* [London, 1951], p. 141; W. L. Mathieson, *British Slave Emancipation 1838–1849* [London, 1932], pp. 151–158, 184; R. L. Schuyler, *The Fall of the Old Colonial System* [New York, 1945], pp. 132–158). For a general discussion of the problem of sugar duties, see Philip D. Curtin, "The British Sugar Duties and West Indian Prosperity," *Journal of Economic History*, XIV, 157–164 (Spring, 1954).

15. For an annual series of British and foreign sugar prices, see PP, 1856, lv (209), 2–3 and PP, 1863, lxvii (272), 3. For the comparative sugar production of Jamaica and the competing British sugar colonies, see PP, 1884, lxxiv (325), 58–59 and Deerr, *History of Sugar*, II, 377. See also Appendix C.

16. Alexander Heslop, evidence before the Jamaica Royal Commission of 1866 (hereafter cited as JRC), PP, 1866, xxxi [C. 3683–I], pp. 330–331, qq. 16438, 16470.

17. John Daughtrey to Sligo, St. Elizabeth, July 1836, PP, 1837, liii (521–I), 119; Edmund Lyons to C. H. Darling, Palmetto River, St. Thomas-ye-East, 31 December 1836, PP, 1837 (521–I), 264; Report of J. W. Grant, Manchester and Clarendon, 10 June 1836, PP, 1840, xxxv [C. 212], 9.

18. Alexander Geddes and William Christie, evidence before Select Committee on the West Indies, PP, 1842, xiii (479), 467–468, 498, qq. 6685–6688 and 7170–7175. Report of the Hanover Society of Industry, 1860, PP, 1861, xl [C. 2841], pp. 8–9.

19. E. B. Underhill, *A Letter Addressed to the Rt. Honourable E. Cardwell, with Illustrative Documents on the Condition of Jamaica and an Explanatory Statement* (London, [1866]), pp. 77–82; T. Harvey and W. Brewin, *Jamaica in 1866. A Narrative of a Tour Through the Island, with Remarks on its Social Educational and Industrial Condition* (London, 1867), p. 9.

20. T. Carlyle, "Occasional Discourse on the Nigger Question," *Fraser's Magazine*, XL, 672 (London, December 1849).

21. Olivier, *Jamaica*, pp. 158–163.

22. E. B. Underhill, *The West Indies* (London, 1862), p. 258; Charles Lake to Hugh W. Austin, 10 January 1854, PP, 1854, xliii [C. 1848], 13–14; A. G. Fyfe to H. W. Austin, Portland, July 1858, PP, 1859, Sess. 2, xx (31), 262; Report of the Hanover Society of Industry, 1860, PP, 1861, xl [C. 2841], 8–9.

23. The following returns and estimates, while quite inaccurate, give some idea of the pace of growth in the settlement movement. The number of small freeholds was reported as:

2,014 in 1838   22,703 in 1844
7,848 in 1840   50,000 in 1860

(C. T. Metcalfe to Lord John Russell, 14 December 1840, PP, 1841, Sess. 2, iii [C. 344], 228; Census of 1844, PP, 1845, xxxi (426), 4; Sewell, *Free Labor,* p. 244; Harvey and Brewin, *Jamaica in 1866,* p. 18.) See also W. M. Macmillan, *Warning from the West Indies* (London, 1936), pp. 87–88 for the difficulties involved in small settlement calculations.

24. The evidence of Alexander Geddes before the Select Committee on Sugar and Coffee Planting is one indication of the importance of Jamaican training rather than the simple fact of unused land or African inheritance. Geddes complained that Jamaicans deserted the estates for provision farming; while post-emancipation immigrants from Africa were willing to work on the estates, since they did not know how to grow West Indian root crops. PP, 1847–48, xxiii (184), 5, q. 8953.

25. Lord Olivier, *White Capital and Coloured Labor* (London, 1906), p. 82.

26. Rev. John Thorp, evidence before Select Committee on the Extinction of Slavery, PP, 1831–32, xx (721), 168, qq. 2039–2040; Elgin to Stanley, 4 August 1845, quoted in K. N. Bell and W. P. Morrell, *Select Documents on British Colonial Policy,* 1830–1860 (Oxford, 1928), p. 424; Underhill, *West Indies,* p. 259; Sewell, *Free Labor,* p. 284.

27. Hall Pringle, Special Magistrates' Report, Clarendon, 26 January 1839, PP, 1839, xxxv (107–II), 10. For British surprise at the lack of deference shown them by Jamaican Negroes, see A. Trollope, *The West Indies and the Spanish Main* (New York, n.d.), pp. 25–26; G. Allen, *In All Shades,* 3 vols. (London, 1886), II, 245–247.

28. Richard R. Madden, evidence before Select Committee on the Apprenticeship System, PP, 1836, xx (560), 76; Lord Olivier, *The Myth of Governor Eyre* (London, 1933), p. 176 ff. For accounts of two of these incidents see E. B. Underhill, *The Life of J. M. Phillippo* (London, 1881), pp. 348–356; Alexander Heslop, evidence before JRC, PP, 1866, xxxi [C. 3683–I], 330, q. 16438.

29. Rev. Richard Harding to Wesleyan-Methodist Committee, Falmouth, 8 August 1839, *Wesleyan Missionary Notices,* I (new series), 187 (London, December 1839); *Jamaica; Who is to Blame?,* pp. 64–65.

30. Rev. William Seccombe to Wesleyan-Methodist Committee, Lucea, 11 September 1838 and Rev. Isaac Whitehouse to Wesleyan-Methodist Committee, Mount Ward, 4 September 1838, *Wesleyan Missionary Notices,* I (new series), 57–58 (London, April 1839); H. Bleby, "The Results of West India Emancipation," *Methodist Quarterly Review,* XLII, 51 (New York, January 1860).

31. H. M. Waddell, *Twenty-nine Years in the West Indies and Central Africa* (London, 1863), pp. 149, 152–153, 170; G. Blyth, *Reminiscences of Missionary Life* (Edinburgh, 1851), p. 115.

32. [W. Knibb], *Speech of the Rev. William Knibb before the Baptist Missionary Society, in Exeter Hall, April 28th, 1842* (London [1842]), p. 45.

33. Rev. Walter Dendy to E. B. Underhill, Salters' Hill, 4 May 1852, MSS. Baptist Missionary Correspondence, IJ.

34. William Knibb to Joseph Sturge, 14 September and 2 October 1839, quoted in F. J. Klingberg, "Lady Mico Charity Schools in the British West Indies, 1835–1842," *Journal of Negro History*, XXIV, 293. See also J. H. Hinton, *Memoir of William Knibb, Missionary in Jamaica* (London, 1847), pp. 283–287.

35. Jamaica Baptist Union to Eyre, 1865, quoted in Underhill, *Letter to Cardwell*, p. 37.

36. Trollope, *West Indies*, p. 109. See also J. P. Grant to Buckingham, 24 October 1868, PP, 1868–69, xliii [C. 4090], 16; Allen, *In All Shades*, II, 4–5; J. Bigelow, *Jamaica in 1850* (New York, 1851), p. 105.

37. Carlyle, "Nigger Question," *Fraser's Magazine*, XL, 674–675.

38. See, for example, Anthony Davis to Richard Hill, St. Mary and Metcalfe, 31 December 1853, PP, 1854, xliii [C. 1848], 32.

39. "Report of the State of the Labouring Population and Sugar Cultivation in Hanover Parish by a Committee of Planters of that Parish," PP, 1839, xxxv (107–III), 14.

40. R. Paterson, *Remarks on the Present State of Cultivation in Jamaica; the Habits of the Peasantry; and Remedies Suggested for the Improvement of Both* (Edinburgh, 1843), p. 4; C. E. Grey to Pakington, 10 June 1852, PP, 1852–53, xlvii (76), 153–154.

41. *Colonial Standard* (Kingston), 16 May 1865.

42. T. H. Milner, *The Present and Future State of Jamaica Considered* (London, 1839), pp. 20–21, 30–32.

43. H. Merivale, *Lectures on Colonisation and Colonies*, 2 vols. (London, 1841–42), I, 312–313, 326.

44. E. Halevy, *The Age of Peel and Cobden* (London, 1948), p. 111.

45. Cardwell to Eyre, Downing Street, 14 June 1865, quoted in Underhill, *Letter to Cardwell*, pp. 5–6. Cardwell was mistaken about the Jamaican cost of living. It was higher than in Britain — not lower.

46. Hall Pringle, Special Magistrate's Report, Clarendon, 26 January 1839, PP, 1839, xxxv (107–II), 10; Sir Charles Metcalfe to Lord John Russell, 30 March 1840, quoted in J. W. Kaye (ed.), *Selections from the Papers of Lord Metcalfe* (London, 1885), p. 334.

47. C. H. Darling to Newcastle, 26 December 1860, PP, 1861, xl [C. 2841], 7.

48. T. Witter Jackson to H. W. Austin, St. Thomas-in-the-Vale, 31 January 1854, PP, 1854, xliii [C. 1848], 30. See also W. W. Anderson, "The Condition and Prospects of Jamaica," Appendix E, Harvey and Brewin, *Jamaica in 1866*.

CHAPTER VII THE "FREE SYSTEM"

1. L. H. Evelyn, *The Sketch of a Plan, for the Effectual Abolition of Slavery, on the Principles of Justice to Every Colonial Interest, and in Full*

Accordance with Every Temperate Desire of the British Philanthropists
(Montego Bay, 1832), pp. i–ii.

2. Evelyn, *Sketch of a Plan, passim,* especially pp. 1–2.

3. Evelyn, *Sketch of a Plan,* pp. 7, 15, 34–37.

4. Evelyn, *Sketch of a Plan,* pp. 51–57.

5. Evelyn tried to raise money in Jamaica in 1831 and 1832, but he gave up because of local opposition after raising some £5000. He was removed from his official position for political activity in 1839 and disappeared as a voice in Jamaican public affairs. See PP, 1856, xliv (108).

6. Thome and Kimball, *Emancipation in the West Indies* (New York, 1838), p. 432; W. W. Anderson and Edward Barrett, evidence before Select Committee on East India Produce, PP, 1840, vii (527), 439–440.

7. Quoted by Thome and Kimball, *Emancipation,* p. 453. See also John Doughtrey, Special Magistrate's Report, St. Elizabeth, 24 February 1839, PP, 1839, xxxv [C. 272], 25.

8. Alexander Geddes, evidence before Select Committee on the West Indies, PP, 1842, xiii (479), 474, q. 6792; T. Jelly, *A Brief Inquiry into the Condition of Jamaica* (London, 1847), p. 34; D. King, *The State and Prospects of Jamaica* (London, 1850), p. 149; Report of the House of Assembly Committee to Investigate the Causes of Distress, PP, 1847–48, xxiii (167), 375.

9. William Hosack to Pilgrim, 27 August 1850, PP, 1852–53, lxvii (76), 43; T. Dickon, evidence before Select Committee on Sugar and Coffee Planting, 1847–48, xxiii (167), 172–174; Richard Hill to Bruce, 23 December 1845, PP, 1846, xxviii (691–I), 44; Alexander Geddes, evidence before Select Committee on Sugar and Coffee Planting, PP, 1847–48, xxiii (184), 4–5, qq. 8951–8956; Charles Royes, evidence before JRC, PP, 1866, xxxi [C. 3683–I], 807.

10. Sir Lionel Smith to Glenelg, 3 December 1838, quoted in Bell and Morrell, *Select Documents on British Colonial Policy, 1830–60* (Oxford, 1928), p. 407; C. E. Grey to Earl Grey, 26 February 1851, PP, 1852–53, lxvii (76), 48.

The contract legislation was strict at first, and then more lenient, but the damage had already been done. In summary, the important acts were:

5 Will IV, c. 2 (Jamaica), 1834, which provided that a worker could be sentenced for up to three months at hard labor merely for being "neglectful" of his work. (Expired 1840.)

6 Will. IV, c. 32 (Jamaica), 1836, which provided that a worker under oral or written contract could be fined 5 pounds or sentenced for thirty days in gaol for any refusal to work.

5 Vict., c. 43 (Jamaica), 1842, provided a reduced fine of 3 pounds or sentence of thirty days for a servant breaking contract, but allowed him to break the contract for ill-usage. Master also could break the contract for "misconduct" or "ill-behavior." This is more liberal, but breach of contract was legal only at the discretion of two justices, which is to say two planters.

11. Sir Lionel Smith to Normanby, 7 September 1839, PP, 1840, xxxv [C. 212], 53; *Eight Practical Treatises on the Cultivation of the Sugar*

THE "FREE SYSTEM" 253

Cane (Jamaica, 1843), pp. 25–43; J. Bigelow, *Jamaica in 1850* (New York, 1851), p. 118; Harvey and Brewin, *Jamaica in 1866* (London, 1867), p. 43; *Jamaica: Who Is to Blame?* by a *Thirty Years' Resident* (London [1866]), p. 24.

12. Augustus Hardin Beaumont, evidence before Select Committee on the Apprenticeship System in the Colonies, PP, 1836, xv (560), 373, 387, qq. 4270, 4404; [J. Leigh], *Jamaica (Being the First Part of) a Series of Letters Written from Jamaica to a Friend in England* (London, 1842), p. 77.

13. Smith to Glenelg, 10 September 1838, PP, 1839, xxxv (107), 83 and (107), *passim*; Lord Sligo, *Letter to the Marquess of Normanby Relative to the Present State of Jamaica* (London, 1839), p. 16; Metcalfe to Normanby, 16 October 1839, PP, 1840, xxxv [C. 212], 71–72; T. H. Milner, *The Present and Future State of Jamaica Considered* (London, 1839), pp. 32–33; PP, 1842, xxix [C. 374], 24–25; [W. F. Whitehouse], *Agricola's Letters and Essays on Sugar Farming in Jamaica* (London, 1845), p. 12.

14. Report of Charles Royes, PP, 1846, xxviii (691–I), 13.

15. Estimated maximum value of a house and grounds, 12 pounds. Rents in most areas, 1/8 and 2/6 per person per week. E. D. Baynes to Sir Lionel Smith, Aylmer's, St. John, 13 October 1836, PP, 1837, liii (521–I), 221. Thomas Abbott, Special Magistrate's report, Westmoreland, 1839, PP, 1839, xxxv (107), 197–198.

16. Richard Hill to Bruce, 23 December 1845, PP, 1846, xxviii (691–I), 45.

17. Arthur Welch, Special Magistrate's report, Manchester, 29 June 1836, PP, 1837, liii (521–I), 33; P. Pryce to C. H. Darling, Trelawney, 10 October 1836, PP, 1837, liii (521–I), 224; PP, 1841, Sess. 2, iii [C. 344], 9, 13, and Appendix, pp. 9–11; PP, 1837–38, xlix (154–I), 17–25.

18. J. M. Ludlow, *A Quarter Century of Jamaica Legislation* (London, 1866), pp. 14–27.

19. James Stephen, who was permanent under-secretary of the Colonial Office until 1847, was opposed to this kind of tax and was often able to make his influence felt, although his political superiors could overrule his objection if they saw fit. He was able to prevent the renewal of a Jamaican act of 1843, which laid a tax of 4s. annually on all able-bodied males for the purpose of improving the roads (6 Vict., c. 47 [Jamaica]; P. Knaplund, *James Stephen and the British Colonial System 1813–1847* [Madison, Wisconsin, 1953]).

20. Earl Grey to Sir Charles Grey, 15 February 1851, PP, xxxvi (104), 26–35; Earl Grey, *The Colonial Policy of Lord John Russell's Administration,* 2 vols. (London, 1853), I, 76–79.

21. Grey, *Colonial Policy,* I, 88–91.

22. Henry Laidlaw to H. W. Austin, Mandeville, 30 January 1854, PP, 1854, xliii [C. 1848], 36; Ludlow, *Legislation,* p. 86.

23. C. E. Grey, Governor's Report for 1847, February 1849, PP, 1849, xxxiv [C. 1126], 93.

24. "The Ministry and the Sugar Duties. Better Prospects for Jamaica," *The Jamaica Magazine* (Kingston, July 1844), I, 376–388.

25. A. Smith, *An Inquiry into the Nature and Causes of the Wealth of Nations* (New York, 1937), pp. 531–532 (Bk. III, Ch. vii, Pt. 2).

26. E. G. Wakefield, *A Letter from Sydney the Principal Town of Australasia* (London, 1929), pp. 68–82; E. G. Wakefield, *England and America* (London, 1833), p. 22.

27. W. L. Burn, *Emancipation and Apprenticeship in the British West Indies* (London, 1937), p. 290.

28. [Lord Sligo], *Jamaica under the Apprenticeship. By a Proprietor* (London, 1838), p. 107; C. T. Metcalfe, evidence before Select Committee on the West Indies, PP, 1842, xiii (479), 512, q. 7310; Report of the Select Committee on the West Indies, PP, 1842, xiii (497), iv; Elgin to Gladstone, 6 May 1846, PP, 1846, xxxix [C. 428], 23–24; Barkly to Newcastle, 26 May 1854, PP, 1854, xliii [C. 1848], 54; C. H. Darling, Address to the Legislature, 9 November 1858, Judah and Sinclair, *Debates of the Honourable House of Assembly of Jamaica*, 13 vols. (Spanish Town, 1856–66), III, 2–3.

29. J. M. Phillippo, *Jamaica: Its Past and Present State* (London, 1843), p. 95; William Knibb, evidence before Select Committee on the West Indies, PP, 1842, xiii (497), 449; Rev. J. Clarke, evidence before Select Committee on the Slave Trade, PP, 1847–48, xxii (536), 130, qq. 7406–7410; Memorial of the Anti-Slavery Society, 1868, quoted in R. Emery, *About Jamaica* (London [1859]), pp. 19–20.

30. Alexander Geddes and William Christie, evidence before Select Committee on the West Indies, PP, 1842, xiii (479), 481, 500.

31. K. Smith, *The Malthusian Controversy* (London, 1951), p. 284; D. Ricardo, *The Principles of Political Economy and Taxation* (London, 1911), p. 52 (Ch. v); Wakefield, *Letter from Sydney*, pp. 84, 78.

32. Alexander Geddes, evidence before Select Committee on the West Indies, PP, 1842, xiii (479), 481.

33. Thompson, Girod, and Smith, "A Statement of Facts Relative to the Island of Jamaica," PP, 1852–53, lxvii (76), 307.

34. G. Solomon, *Population and Prosperity; or Free Vs. Slave Production* (Kingston, 1859), p. 40.

35. Glenelg to the Governors of the West Indian Colonies, 30 January 1836, PP, 1846, xxx (514), 3–4. See also W. L. Burn, *Emancipation,* pp. 305–308.

36. Report of the Colonial Land and Emigration Commissioners to Lord John Russell, 9 July 1840, PP, 1841, Sess. 2, iii [C. 344], 102–104.

37. Lord Olivier, *The Myth of Governor Eyre* (London, 1933), pp. 176–178; Judah and Sinclair, *Debates,* VII, 67–71.

38. E. L. Erickson, "The Introduction of East India Coolies into the British West Indies," *Journal of Modern History,* VI, 128 (June 1934); Burn, *Emancipation,* pp. 290–292.

39. The number of immigrants imported varied considerably from one year to the next. Between 1834 and 1865, immigrants came in these principal groups of years. No immigrants were reported for years not listed.

1834–37	2,462
1840–42	3,304
1843–49	9,543
1850–57	2,544
1860–63	6,482
Total	24,335

Neglecting Europeans, about half came from Africa and half from India in the period before 1843. After 1843, the Indian share was two-thirds and the African one-third. China did not become an important source until after 1865. See tables in PP, 1850, xxxix (228), 1, and PP, 1872, lxiii (202), 2. For a general account of Indian emigration, see I. M. Cumpston, *Indians Overseas in British Territories 1834–1854* (London, 1953).

40. Eyre to Cardwell, 25 September 1865, PP, 1866, xlix [C. 3719], 6; W. J. Gardner, *A History of Jamaica from Its Discovery by Christopher Columbus to the Year 1872* (London, 1873), p. 420.

41. Erickson, *Journal of Modern History*, VI, 132–138.

42. Barkly to Newcastle, 26 May 1854, quoted in Bell and Morrell, *Select Documents*, p. 446; Darling to Labouchere, 19 March 1858, PP, 1859, Sess. 2, xx (31), 210; Solomon, *Population and Prosperity*, pp. 47–48.

43. J. H. Berkley to Earl Grey, 21 November 1846, PP, 1847, xxxix (325), 20–21.

44. Memorial of the House of Assembly, 24 December 1847, PP, 1847–48, xxiii (167), 376; PP, 1849, xxxvii (280), 77–79, 128, 161–162.

45. Ludlow, *Legislation*, p. 73; 9 Vict., c. 17 (Jamaica); C. E. Grey, Governor's Report for 1847, PP, 1849, xxxiv [C. 1126], 84–87; PP, 1847, xxxix (325), 18.

The Indians were probably a more expensive labor force than Jamaicans, the planter paying a premium for the power to control the labor through indentures. Under this act, Indians were paid 6d. per day, six days a week, all year round. They also received housing, food, and medical care, and there was the annual 40s. toward the cost of importation. Indian workers had to be paid whether there was work to be done or not. Against this, the creole wage rate averaged 15d. per day at the time.

The relatively low Jamaican wages may explain why induced immigration was not so successful there as in Trinidad and British Guiana, where the local wage was 25d. and 20½d. respectively in 1848. In these two colonies, the planter taking immigrants probably got cheaper labor, as well as the ability to control it. See PP, 1849, xxxvii (280), 165.

46. Ludlow, *Legislation*, pp. 74–76; C. H. Darling to Sir E. B. Lytton, 26 November 1858, PP, 1859, Sess. 2, xx (31), 272. See also 21 Vict. c. 5 (Jamaica), the disallowed immigration act of 1857, for evidence of the rigorous controls the Assembly wanted, but was not allowed to have.

47. See Assembly debate on the Immigration Bill of 1861, Judah and Sinclair, *Debates*, V, 392–396.

48. Sligo, *Letter to Normanby*, pp. 25–26; J. W. Grant to Sir Lionel

Smith, August 1839, PP, 1841, Sess. 2, iii [C. 344], 205; Charles Royes, Report on Seville Estate for 1844, PP, 1846, xxviii (691–I), 14; Louis McKinnon, evidence before House of Assembly Committee on the Depressed State of Agriculture, 1848, PP, 1847–48, xxiii (245), 155.

49. Ricardo, *Principles,* p. 52 (ch. v).

50. Sligo, *Letter to Normanby,* pp. 6–7, 9–11.

51. R. Paterson, *Remarks on the Present State of Cultivation in Jamaica; the Habits of the Peasantry; and Remedies Suggested for the Improvement of Both* (Edinburgh, 1843), p. 10.

52. Evidence before the Select Committee on the West Indies, PP, 1842, xiii (479), 548, q. 7900.

53. Hall Pringle to Robert Bruce, Vere, 1 June 1845, PP, 1846, xxviii (691–I), 6–7; Solomon, *Population and Prosperity,* p. 38.

54. Sligo, *Letter to Normanby,* p. 11; Paterson, *Cultivation in Jamaica,* p. 3; W. W. Anderson, introduction to J. Ogilby, *A Description and History of the Island of Jamaica* (Kingston, 1851), p. 8; Solomon, *Population and Prosperity,* p. 38; G. Price, *Jamaica and the Colonial Office. Who Caused the Crisis?* (London, 1866), p. 7; S. Oughton, "The Influence of Artificial Wants on the Social, Moral, and Commercial Advancement of Jamaica," *West India Quarterly Magazine,* I, 474–483 (Kingston, May 1862); S. Oughton, *Jamaica: Why it is Poor, and How it May Become Rich* (Kingston, 1866).

55. Oughton, "Artificial Wants," p. 478.

56. Oughton, "Artificial Wants," p. 479.

57. H. Pringle, *The Fall of the Sugar Planters of Jamaica* (London, 1869), pp. 22–23; Jelly, *A Brief Inquiry,* pp. xiv–xv; Sligo, *Apprenticeship,* p. 105; Whitehouse, *Agricola's Letters,* p. 218; *Falmouth Post,* 18 January 1848; *Jamaica; Who Is to Blame?,* pp. 34–35.

58. Evelyn, *Sketch of a Plan,* pp. 56–57; Jelly, *Brief Inquiry,* pp. 71–72, 46–65; "The Present Policy of Great-Britain, with Respect to Jamaica," *Jamaica Monthly Magazine,* II, 288–289 (Kingston, April 1874).

59. "What is the Matter with Jamaica?," *West India Quarterly Magazine* (Kingston, August 1861), I, 68–69; Barkly to Newcastle, 26 May 1854, quoted in Bell and Morrell, *Select Documents,* pp. 445–446.

60. S. H. Stewart, "On the Defects of the Agricultural System Hitherto Pursued in Jamaica," *The Jamaica Magazine,* I, 317–323 (Kingston, July 1844); Jelly, *Brief Inquiry,* pp. 28–29; L. Wray, *The Practical Sugar Planter* (London, 1848), pp. 56–66.

61. G Scotland, *A Letter Addressed to the Public of Jamaica on the Political and Financial State of the Colony* (Jamaica, 1847), pp. 4–10; *Jamaica Monthly Magazine,* II, 287–288.

62. These appear in PP, 1838, xxv (158), (200), (290), (581), and (304). See Capt. R. Browne, evidence before Select Committee on the West Indies, PP, 1842, xiii (497), 465, q. 6641 for the non-spontaneous origin of the parish meetings.

63. Quoted in C. Rampini, *Letters from Jamaica* (Edinburgh, 1873), p. 69.

64. Quoted in Marquis of Lorne, *A Trip to the Tropics and Home through America* (London, 1867), pp. 128–129.

65. "The Brazils — The Late Debate," *The Jamaica Magazine* (Kingston, May 1844), I, 173. See also Thome and Kimball, *Emancipation*, p. 440; William Burge to Stanley, 28 May 1844, PP, 1844, xlv (341), 2–3; Thompson, Girod, and Smith, *Statement of Facts Relative to Jamaica* (London, 1852), pp. 3–4.

66. John S. Calchar to T. F. Pilgrim, Port Antonio, 25 July 1848 and G. M. Lawson to T. F. Pilgrim, St. James, 24 July 1848, PP, 1849, xxxvii (280), 4–5; C. H. Darling, quoted in PP, 1859, Sess. 2, xx (31), 270.

67. T. Carlyle, "Occasional Discourse on the Nigger Question," *Fraser's Magazine*, XL, 676–677 (London, December 1849); B. Pim, *The Negro and Jamaica* (London, 1866), pp. 16–17.

68. H. Merivale, *Lectures on Colonisation and Colonies*, 2 vols. (London, 1841–42), I, 201–202.

69. Commissioners of Correspondence to William Burge, 13 December 1833, Commission of Correspondence Letter Books, IJ.

70. For a summary of this argument see Report of the Committee on the Sugar Duties of the Jamaica Chamber of Commerce, 1 July 1846, PP, 1846, xliv (700), 8.

71. Scotland, *Letter to the Public*, p. 11.

72. T. Jelly, *A Cursory Glance at the Past and Present Condition of Great Britain; Intended as a Beacon to the British Sugar Colonies* (London, 1848), *passim,* especially pp. 65–66.

73. Milner, *Present and Future*, p. 93; Petition of the Parish of St. Thomas-in-the-East, PP, 1846, xxxviii (160), 10–11; Thompson, Girod, and Smith, *Statement of Facts*, pp. 26–27; J. O. Clark, *An Abridged History of Jamaica* (Falmouth, 1859), p. 95.

74. Paterson, *Cultivation in Jamaica*, p. 46.

75. Memorial of the House of Assembly, 12 January 1842, PP, 1842, xxix [C. 374], 51.

76. Merivale, *Lectures*, I, 297.

77. Memorial of the House of Assembly, 21 December 1844, PP, 1845, xxxi (66), 2; Petition of the Parish of St. George, July 1852, quoted in *The Case of the Free-Labour British Colonies Submitted to the British Legislature & British Nation for an Impartial Re-Hearing* (London, 1852), pp. 17–22.

78. C. W. Guillebaud in *Cambridge History of the British Empire* (Cambridge, 1940), II, 706; W. L. Mathieson, *British Slave Emancipation, 1838–49* (London, 1932), pp. 166–171.

79. See below, Chapter VIII, for the rise and fall of the missionary churches. The missionary fight against free trade also left its mark on missionary historiography of Jamaica. In retrospect, it was the Sugar Act of 1846, rather than the act of emancipation, that received major blame for the ruin of Jamaica. See J. O. Clark, *An Abridged History of Jamaica,* pp. 93–95; H. Bleby, "The Results of West India Emancipation," *Methodist Quarterly Review*, XLII, 52–53 (New York, January 1860).

80. [D. Turnbull, ed.], *The Jamaica Movement for Promoting the Enforcement of the Slave-Trade Treaties and for the Suppression of the Slave Trade* (London, 1850); PP, 1850, xxxix [C. 1139], 142–146; King, *State and Prospects*, p. 185.

81. Report quoted in PP, 1847–48, xxiii (245), 152–153.

82. G. R. Mellor, *British Imperial Trusteeship 1783–1850* (London, 1951), pp. 151–152; Report of the Select Committee on Sugar and Coffee Planting, PP, 1847–48, xxiii (361–II), iii–iv.

83. C. E. Grey to Earl Grey, 19 June 1848 and 27 March 1849, PP, 1847–48, xliv (685), 1–7, 163–168.

84. PP, 1850, xxxix [C. 1139], *passim;* Earl Grey, *Colonial Policy,* pp. 189–190; C. E. Grey to Newcastle, 10 May 1853, PP, 1852–53, lxv [C. 1655], 7–9; Resolutions of the House of Assembly, 16 February 1852, PP, 1852–53, lxvii (76), 138–139; Guillebaud in *Cambridge British Empire,* II, 710–711; W. L. Mathieson, *The Sugar Colonies and Governor Eyre, 1849–1866* (New York, 1936), pp. 123–125.

85. Americans like John Bigelow, for example, saw Jamaica from a background in which small farms were predominant. This was a factor in making Bigelow's analysis of Jamaica very different from that of his English contemporaries. See J. Bigelow, *Jamaica in 1850* (New York, 1851).

CHAPTER VIII   RACE, RELIGION, AND SOCIAL ADJUSTMENT

1. Harris to Earl Grey, Trinidad, 19 June 1849, PP, 1847–48, xlvi (749), 323.

2. William Burge to Normanby, 20 February 1839, PP, 1839, xxxv (158), 8.

3. Edward Jordon, Address to the Kingston Anti-Slave-Trade Meeting, 25 June 1849, quoted in [D. Turnbull, ed.], *The Jamaica Movement for Promoting the Enforcement of the Slave-Trade Treaties . . .* (London, 1850), p. 238.

4. Anthony Davis to Richard Hill, St. Mary, 31 December 1853, PP, 1854, xliii [C. 1848], 32. See also *Jamaica Standard,* 14 February 1842; E. R. Gurney, *Letters of Emilia Russell Gurney* (London, 1903), p. 307.

5. G. B. Mellor, *British Imperial Trusteeship 1783–1850* (London, 1951), pp. 146–147.

6. E. B. Underhill, *The Life of J. M. Phillippo* (London, 1881), pp. 277–278.

7. Jamaican educational statistics tend to be tremendously inflated, since they were gathered by asking for returns from the religious societies and others keeping schools. A thorough investigation in 1837 showed 38,754 students on the books, but only 9,789 actually attending day-schools. In 1864 the total enrollment was 30,514. (PP, 1837–38, xlviii (113), 72–73; Eyre to Cardwell, 25 September 1865, PP, 1866, xlix [C. 3719], 7.)

8. T. Jelly, *A Brief Inquiry into the Condition of Jamaica* (London, 1847), pp. 39–40; Earl Grey to C. E. Grey, 15 February 1851, PP, 1851, xxxvi (104), 26–35; Henry Laidlaw to H. W. Austin, Mandeville, 30 Jan-

uary 1854, PP, 1854, xliii [C. 1848], 36; C. E. Grey to Newcastle, 23 September 1853, PP, 1854, xliii (235), 114; E. B. Underhill, *The West Indies* (London, 1862), p. 419.

9. C. E. Grey to Earl Grey, 31 December 1851, PP, 1852, xxxi [C. 1539], 30; Dr. Gavin Milroy to Pakington, July 1852, PP, 1854, xliii (235).

10. C. E. Grey to Newcastle, 23 September 1853, PP, 1854, xliii (235), 114.

11. J. M. Ludlow, *A Quarter Century of Jamaica Legislation* (London, 1866), pp. 4–5, 9–11; J. W. Kaye, *The Life and Correspondence of Charles, Lord Metcalfe,* revised edition, 2 vols. (London, 1858), II, 275, 284; C. T. Metcalfe, Address to the House of Assembly, 28 October 1840, PP, 1841, Sess. 2, iii [C. 344], 226.

12. The maximum penalty for petty theft, for example, climbed from ten days' imprisonment in 1841 through three intermediate increases till it reached ninety days in 1856. Ludlow, *Legislation,* pp. 11–12.

13. Address to the Legislature, Judah and Sinclair, *Debates of the Honourable House of Assembly of Jamaica,* 13 vols. (Spanish Town, 1856–66), XII, 2.

14. Rev. John G. Manly to Wesleyan-Methodist Committee, Clarendon, 20 August 1844, *Wesleyan Missionary Notices,* III (new series), 11–12 (London, January 1845).

15. Rev. J. M. Phillippo, *Jamaica: Its Past and Present State* (London, 1843), p. 253.

16. See below, Chapter IX.

17. Quoted from a Baptist letter to Metcalfe in Kaye, *Life of Metcalfe,* II, 268–269.

18. "The Baptist," *Jamaica Monthly Magazine,* II, 19 (Kingston, January 1847).

19. *Falmouth Post,* 11 January 1848. See also John Salmon to W. R. Myers, Malvern, 6 January 1866, PP, 1866, xxx [C. 3682], 113–114.

20. J. H. Hinton, *Memoir of William Knibb, Missionary in Jamaica* (London, 1847), p. 397; Jamaica Presbytery to Association of Baptist Missionaries in Jamaica, Goshen, 14 July 1841, quoted in H. M. Waddell, *Twenty-nine Years in the West Indies and Central Africa* (London, 1863), Appendix I, pp. 661–663; "Baptist Missionary Churches in Jamaica," *The Evangelical Magazine and Missionary Chronicle* (London, March 1842), XX, 112–116.

21. William Knibb to W. B. Gurney, 24 August 1841, quoted in Hinton, *Knibb,* p. 402.

22. Hinton, *Knibb,* pp. 416–419; Underhill, *Phillippo,* pp. 198–200.

23. G. G. Findlay and W. W. Holdsworth, *A History of the Wesleyan Methodist Missionary Society,* 5 vols. (London, 1921–24), II, 329–335; W. J. Gardner, *A History of Jamaica from its Discovery by Christopher Columbus to the Year 1872* (London, 1873), p. 465. For the doctrinal controversy, see D. Kerr, *An Answer to the Objections of the Reverend Thomas Pennock, Against "Methodism as It Is"; as Published in the Jamaica Watchman* (Montego Bay, 1838).

24. Findlay and Holdsworth, *Wesleyan Methodist Missionary Society*, II, 360–368.

25. A. Trollope, *The West Indies and the Spanish Main* (New York, n.d.), p. 28.

26. Sir J. P. Grant to Granville, 23 July 1869, PP, 1871, xlviii (269), 5–6; E. Stock, *The History of the Church Missionary Society*, 4 vols. (London, 1899–1917), I, 342–347.

27. George W. Gordon brought in bills to disestablish the Church in Jamaica in 1863 and 1864. They lost by a vote of 16 to 1 and 20 to 5, respectively. Judah and Sinclair, *Debates*, IX, 94–96; XII, 267–274.

28. *The Standing Committee of the Society for the Propagation of the Gospel in Foreign Parts, and the Jamaica Clergy* (Kingston, 1867), p. 30.

29. J. B. Ellis, *The Diocese of Jamaica* (London, 1913), pp. 108–110.

30. Rev. Robert A. Johnson to Wesleyan-Methodist Committee, Mandeville, 5 January 1846, *Wesleyan Missionary Notices*, IV (new series), 75 (London, May 1846); E. B. Underhill, *West Indies*, p. 191.

31. J. H. Buchner, *The Moravians in Jamaica* (London, 1854), pp. 146–147; H. B. Foster, *The Rise and Progress of Wesleyan-Methodism in Jamaica* (London, 1881), pp. 100–101; Phillippo, *Jamaica*, pp. 243–244; Rev. Edward J. Thompson to Wesleyan-Methodist Committee, Duncans, 28 June 1850, *Wesleyan Missionary Notices*, VIII, 168 (London, October 1850).

32. Officially, the baptism of any child brought forward by a communicant could not be prohibited, but the baptism of illegitimates was discouraged and sometimes refused in practice (R. Courtenay, Bishop of Kingston, "A Pastoral Charge Addressed to the Clergy of the Diocese of Jamaica in the Year 1862," *Three Pastoral Charges* . . . [Kingston, 1868], p. 26; Rev. J. W. Sloan to W. R. Myers, Golden Grove, St. Thomas-in-the-East, 1866, PP, 1866, xxx [C. 3682], 93).

See also Lewis Quier Bowerbank, "The Bastardy Law," *Minutes of Proceedings of the First Annual Congress of Clergy and Laity of the Diocese of Jamaica . . . May 1868, with Papers Read before the Congress* (Kingston, 1868), p. 39; Jamaica. Legislative Council, *Report of the Committee Appointed to Enquire into the Prevalence of Concubinage and the High Rate of Illegitimacy* (Kingston, 1941), pp. 3–4.

33. 6 Will. IV, c. 32 (Jamaica); 7 Vict. c. 14 (Jamaica); 11 Vict. c. 14 (Jamaica); Kaye, *Life of Metcalfe*, II, 282.

34. Underhill, *West Indies*, pp. 191–192; Rev. Joshua Tinson to S. M. Peto, Calabar, 1850, *Missionary Herald*, VIII, 106 (London, July 1850).

35. Myalism and obeah were considered a single offense. In 4 Vict. c. 42 (1840) they were included in the terms of the vagrancy act and only lightly punished. In 19 Vict. c. 30 (1856) the penalty was increased to a maximum of three months at hard labor, if convicted before two justices, or twelve months and seventy-eight lashes, if bound over for a criminal court. Finally, 21 Vict. c. 24 (1857) made even the consultation of an obeah man punishable at hard labor to a maximum of three months.

36. Gardner, *History of Jamaica,* p. 461; Waddell, *Twenty-nine Years,* pp. 188–192; T. Banbury, *Jamaica Superstitions or the Obeah Book* . . .

(Jamaica, 1894), p. 20; Rev. John Vaz to Wesleyan-Methodist Committee, Manchester, 19 January 1847, *Wesleyan Missionary Notices*, V, 91 (London, May 1847); *Daily Advertiser* (Kingston), 26 February 1857; PP, 1862, xxxvi [C. 2955], 7–8.

37. Buchner, *Moravians*, pp. 139–140.

38. Phillippo, *Jamaica*, pp. 263–264; Buchner, *Moravians*, p. 142; The Bishop of Kingston to Sir J. P. Grant, 12 November 1866, PP, 1866, xlix [C. 3903], p. 42; Waddell, *Twenty-nine Years*, p. 192; Rev. John Vaz to Wesleyan-Methodist Committee, Manchioneal, January 1846, *Wesleyan Missionary Notices* (London, May 1846), IV, 76.

39. Underhill, *Phillippo*, pp. 302–313; D. Fletcher, *Personal Recollections of the Honourable George W. Gordon, Late of Jamaica* (London, 1867), p. 60; [E. Carlile], *Thirty-eight Years of Mission Life in Jamaica* (London, 1884), pp. 113–121.

40. R. Courtenay, *The Operations of the Spirit* . . . (Kingston, 1861), p. 3; Report of the Annual Jamaica District Meeting, January 1861, *The Report of the Wesleyan Methodist Missionary Society* (London, 1861), p. 101; Jamaica Baptist Union, Minutes of the Annual Meeting of 1861, MSS. Baptist Missionary Correspondence, IJ.

41. Gardner, *History of Jamaica*, p. 467.

42. Carlile, *Mission Life*, pp. 115–116; Rev. George Truman, evidence before JRC, PP, 1866, xxxi [C. 3683–I], 415–416.

43. Rev. William Tyson to Wesleyan-Methodist Committee, Browns Town, 23 April 1861, *Wesleyan Missionary Notices*, VIII (third series), 153 (London, 25 June 1861).

44. For twentieth-century Revivalism, see M. W. Beckwith, *Black Roadways: a Study of Jamaican Folk Life* (Chapel Hill, 1929), pp. 158–164.

45. P. Duncan, *Narrative of the Wesleyan Mission to Jamaica; with Occasional Remarks on the State of Society in That Colony* (London, 1849), pp. 394–395; Rev. Walter Dendy, Address to the Montego Bay Anti-Slave-Trade Meeting, 29 June 1849, quoted in Turnbull, *Jamaica Movement*, p. 300; Rev. D. King, *The State and Prospects of Jamaica* (London, 1850), pp. 132, 212–213. See also R. Hill, *Lights and Shadows of Jamaica History* (Kingston, 1859), pp. 104–105.

46. Duncan, *Wesleyan Mission*, pp. 395–396.

47. Quoted by W. W. Anderson, "Introduction," to J. Ogilby, *A Description and History of the Island of Jamaica* (Kingston, 1851), p. 6. See also A. Barclay, *Remarks on Emigration to Jamaica: Addressed to the Coloured Class of the United States* (New York, 1840).

48. G. Allen, *In All Shades*, 3 vols. (London, 1886), III, 124–126.

49. "The Baptist," *Jamaica Monthly Magazine*, II, 121 (Kingston, February 1847).

50. Augustus Hardin Beaumont, evidence before Select Committee on the Apprenticeship System in the Colonies, PP, 1836, xv (560), 388; John Daughtrey, Special Magistrate's report, 24 February 1839, PP, 1839, xxxv [C. 272], 25.

The white population at various dates was as follows:

| 1788 | — | 18,347 | | 1861 | — | 13,816 |
| 1844 | — | 15,776 | | 1871 | — | 13,101 |

(L. J. Ragatz, *The Fall of the Planter Class in the British Caribbean* [New York, 1928], p. 30; PP, 1845, xxxi (426), 4; PP, 1874, lxx [C. 1038], 492.)

51. G. G. Hubbard, "The Late Insurrection in Jamaica," *The New Englander* (New Haven, January 1867), p. 56; T. Harvey and W. Brewin, *Jamaica in 1866. A Narrative of a Tour through the Island, with Remarks on its Social Educational and Industrial Condition* (London, 1867), p. 51 ff.; PP, 1866, xxxi [C. 3683–I], *passim*; Rev. David R. Morris to W. R. Myers, Montego Bay, 1 January 1866, PP, 1866, xxx [C. 3682], 85.

52. A survey in 1852 showed the following balance of resident as against absentee proprietors:

	Cultivated by:	
Type of Plantation	*Resident proprietor or lessee*	*Absentee*
Sugar estates	194	233
Coffee properties	199	49
Cattle pens	521	115

(PP, 1854, lxiii [C. 1848], 55.)

At the same time, the number of white men and white women was becoming more nearly equal:

	Men	*Women*
1844	9,289	6,487
1861	7,295	6,521
1871	6,909	6,192

(PP, 1845, xxxi (426), 4; PP, 1874, lxx [C. 1038], 492.)

53. Trollope, *West Indies,* pp. 86–89; Alexander Heslop, evidence before JRC, PP, 1866, xxxi [C. 3683–I], 332, qq. 16485–16486, 16494. Grant Allen's novel, *In All Shades,* is built on this theme.

54. Underhill, *West Indies,* p. 192; Rev. Henry Clarke to L. A. Chamerovzow, Grange-Hill, 6 January 1866, quoted in *Facts and Documents Relating to the Alleged Rebellion in Jamaica and the Measures of Repression; Including Notes of the Trial of Mr. Gordon* (London, 1866), pp. 31–34.

55. Robert Osborn, in House of Assembly, 2 December 1858, Judah and Sinclair, *Debates,* III, 141; Alexander Heslop, evidence before JRC, PP, 1866, xxxi [C. 3683–I], 332, q. 16495 ff.; J. Bigelow, *Jamaica in 1850* (New York, 1851), pp. 25–26.

56. *Falmouth Post,* 14 November 1862 (unsigned, but probably the work of John Castello, editor and member of the Assembly).

57. Robert Osborn, in House of Assembly, 3 November 1864, Judah and Sinclair, *Debates,* XII, 48.

58. Robert Osborn, in House of Assembly, 27 November 1860, Judah and Sinclair, *Debates,* V, 161.

59. Robert Osborn, in House of Assembly, 21 November 1865, Judah and Sinclair, *Debates*, XIII, 74. See also Barkly to Newcastle, 26 May 1854, PP, 1854, lxiii [C. 1848], 53–54.

60. T. H. Milner, *The Present and Future State of Jamaica Considered* (London, 1839), pp. 26–27.

CHAPTER IX   FAILURE OF SELF-GOVERNMENT

1. W. L. Burn, *Emancipation and Apprenticeship in the British West Indies* (London, 1937), pp. 192–193, 323; James Stephen, Memorandum of 22 February 1837, quoted from C.O. 323/52, ff. 292–300 in P. Knaplund, *James Stephen and the British Colonial System 1813–1847* (Madison, Wisconsin, 1953), p. 120.

2. Protest of the House of Assembly, June 1838, quoted in K. N. Bell and W. P. Morrell, *Select Documents on British Colonial Policy, 1830–60* (Oxford, 1928), p. 406. See also W. Burge, *The Speech of W. Burge, Esq. Q.C., Agent for Jamaica, at the Bar of the House of Commons, Against the Bill Intituled "An Act to Make Temporary Provision for the Government of Jamaica." Monday, 22nd April 1839* (London, 1839), pp. 76–77; H. A. Merewether, *The Speech of Mr. Serjeant Merewether, at the Bar of the House of Commons, Against the Bill Intituled "An Act to Make Temporary Provision for the Government of Jamaica." Tuesday, 23d April 1839* (London, 1839), *passim*; T. H. Milner, *The Present and Future State of Jamaica Considered* (London, 1839), pp. 25–26.

3. These provisions remained substantially unchanged until 1858, although an act of 1841 tightened the registration procedure against the interest of the small freeholder, and an act of 1852 lowered the requirement in the case of a tenant from 30 pounds to 20 pounds (4 Vict., c. 31; 5 Vict., c. 34; 15 Vict., c. 34 [Jamaica]).

4. Sir Henry Taylor, Minute of January 1839, quoted in H. Taylor, *Autobiography of Henry Taylor 1800–1875*, 2 vols. (London, 1885), I, 250–260; Lord Sligo, *Letter to the Marquess of Normanby Relative to the Present State of Jamaica* (London, 1839), pp. 29–31.

5. In the Assembly of 1865, which has been carefully analyzed by occupation and property, there were ten colored members and thirty-seven white members. Of this total, twenty-six were landholders, nine were merchants, three were in journalism and printing, seven were in the legal profession, three were in the medical profession, one a former banker, one a Crown surveyor, and one a civil engineer. (Those with two occupations were counted twice.) Of the forty-seven members, thirty-four had been educated in England, and forty were also Justices of the Peace (G. Price, *Jamaica and the Colonial Office. Who Caused the Crisis?* [London, 1866], pp. 118–119).

6. Each party had newspaper support. For the Country Party a succession of papers followed in the tradition of the old *Jamaica Courant*, first the *Jamaica Despatch* in 1832 and then the *Colonial Standard* in 1849. The last

two of these were edited by William Girod, who was the chief editorial spokesman for the party.

The *Morning Journal* succeeded the *Watchman* as the publication of Jordon and Osborn. It was then the chief organ of the City Party, although Jordon and Osborn dropped their connection with the paper in 1863.

The *Falmouth Post,* edited and published by John Castello from the 1830's to 1874, was the chief northside paper, generally Country Party, and equal to any of the Kingston papers in quality. Throughout the island, there were about a dozen smaller papers, mainly edited by colored men in the towns.

7. Resolutions of the Falmouth Public Meeting, 1 January 1839, PP, 1839, xxxv (107), 223.

8. For the English movement, see E. Halevy, *The Age of Peel and Cobden* (London, 1948), pp. 58–59.

9. "The Elections — the Franchise," *The Jamaica Magazine,* I, 481–492 (Kingston, October 1844); Lord Elgin, quoted in T. Walrond (ed.), *Letters and Journals of James, Eighth Earl of Elgin* (London, 1872), p. 25; J. L. Morison, *The Eighth Earl of Elgin — a Chapter in Nineteenth Century Imperial History* (London, 1928), pp. 55–57.

10. The bitterness of the City Party is clear enough in a poem that William Hosack (then a City-Party leader) published in the *Morning Journal* shortly before the rising (Quoted in PP, 1866, xxxi [C. 3683–I], 927).

George Gordon was a magistrate
Of scriptural renown,
For fifteen rural parishes
And eke for our old town.

Since George has battled for revenge
As Satan did when driven,
With flaming swords from Paradise
Down through the vaults of Heaven.

A pious loyal man seemed he,
Who served his God and Queen,
Until the Queen's lieutenant found
His spirit was unclean.

Wild, east and west, he roams and raves,
Against the church and State
Seeking to idolize the small,
And demonize the great.

11. Metcalfe to Russell, 12 February 1841, quoted in J. W. Kaye (ed.), *Selections from the Papers of Lord Metcalfe* (London, 1885), pp. 376–377.

12. 5 Vict., c. 34 (Jamaica); A. Judah and A. C. Sinclair, *Debates of the Honourable House of Assembly of Jamaica,* 13 vols. (Spanish Town, 1856–66), III, 93, 130.

13. Memorial of the House of Assembly, 2 March 1849, PP, 1849, xxxvii [C. 1065], 81–82; William Smith to Earl Grey, 12 August 1851, PP, 1852–53, lxvii (76), 229.

14. Barkly to Newcastle, 10 April 1854, PP, 1854, xliii [C. 1806], 92–93.

15. Newcastle to Barkly, 16 August 1853, PP, 1854, xliii [C. 1806], 121.

16. Although there are no reports of the debates of the Assembly for 1854, there are reflections of the earlier discussions in the debates of 1860, when the question of responsible government again arose. See the citations of note 22, below, and Judah and Sinclair, *Debates,* V, *passim.*

17. This act differed from the Franchise Act of 1840 (4 Vict., c. 31)

among other things by lowering the requirement as a payer or receiver of a rent-charge from 30 to 20 pounds, by lowering the requirement as a direct taxpayer from three pounds to one, and by adding two new requirements — receipt of a salary of 50 pounds annually or the possession of 100 pounds in cash or in a bank account (22 Vict., c. 18).

See the debates of the House of Assembly, 29 November and 2 December 1858, Judah and Sinclair, *Debates*, III; Edward Jordon, in the House of Assembly, 5 December 1860, Judah and Sinclair, *Debates*, V, 214–215; PP, 1865, xxxvii [C. 3423], 12.

18. Judah and Sinclair, *Debates*, III, 91, 107–108; VIII, 167.

19. Judah and Sinclair, *Debates*, VIII, 199.

20. Henry Westmorland, in Assembly, Judah and Sinclair, *Debates*, VIII, 202.

21. Henry Westmorland, in Assembly, Judah and Sinclair, *Debates*, VIII, 201.

22. Minute of Edward Jordon, George Price, and William Hosack to Darling, 25 September 1860, quoted in Judah and Sinclair, *Debates*, V, 23–24; Darling to Newcastle, 26 November 1861, PP, 1862, xxxvi [C. 2955], 6; Stephen Cave to William Hosack, 1 February 1861, Minute Books of the Acting Committee of the West India Committee, 1861, Part I, p. 76, Archives of the West India Committee, London (cited hereafter as WIC).

23. For a detailed account of Jamaican politics in the early 1860's, compare W. J. Gardner, *A History of Jamaica from its Discovery by Christopher Columbus to the Year 1872* (London, 1873); W. L. Mathieson, *The Sugar Colonies and Governor Eyre* (New York, 1936); and Lord Olivier, *The Myth of Governor Eyre* (London, 1933).

24. Burge to Normanby, 20 February 1839, PP, 1839, xxxv (158), 8.

25. Walrond (ed.). *Letters and Journals,* pp. 26–27.

26. G. B. Mellor, *British Imperial Trusteeship 1783–1850* (London, 1951), p. 163.

27. Police Acts of 1836 and 1838, PP, 1837–38, xlix (154–I), 334–338; 6 Will. IV, c. 32 (Jamaica); J. M. Ludlow, *A Quarter Century of Jamaica Legislation* (London, 1866), pp. 37–38.

28. 4 Will. IV, c. 30 (Jamaica).

29. Judah and Sinclair, *Debates*, III, 76–86.

30. Ludlow, *Legislation,* pp. 36–37; Henry Laidlaw to Bruce, Montego Bay, 1 December 1845, PP, 1846, xxviii (691–I), 56; Mr. Justice Ker, evidence before JRC, PP, 1866, xxxi [C. 3683–I], 286–288.

31. PP, 1866, xxxi [C. 3683–I], 1099–1100. The small freeholders of the parish petitioned the Governor on 5 September 1865, complaining of the injustice done them by the planter-magistrates and stating, "The island has been ruin consequently of the advantage that is taken of us by the managers of the estates" (PP, 1886, li [C. 3594–II], 17–18).

32. H. C. De Lisser, *Jamaica and Cuba* (Kingston, 1910), p. 113.

33. Report of the Jamaica Royal Commission, PP, xxx [C. 3683], especially pp. 10–18.

34. Report of the JRC, PP, 1866, xxx [C. 3683], 25.

35. See Olivier, *The Myth of Governor Eyre* and Mathieson, *The Sugar Colonies and Governor Eyre* for recent, though divergent, interpretations.

36. Report of the JRC, PP, 1866, xxx [C. 3683], 18.

37. Signed by Paul Bogle and nineteen others, quoted in JRC Report, PP, 1866, xxx [C. 3683], 14.

38. Address to the Legislature, 7 November 1865, Judah and Sinclair, *Debates*, XIII, 1–3.

39. Addresses of the Assembly and the Legislative Council, Judah and Sinclair, *Debates*, XIII, 11–13.

40. PP, 1866, xxx [C. 3682], *passim*, especially pp. 85 ff., 477–483; Rev. Johnathan Edmondson to Wesleyan-Methodist Committee, Kingston, 23 October 1865, *Wesleyan Missionary Notices*, XIII (3rd series), 3 (London, December 26, 1865); Price, *Jamaica and the Colonial Office*, pp. 32–33.

41. Eyre to Cardwell, 20 December 1865, PP, 1866, li [C. 3594–I], 3–4.

42. Rev. Henry Clarke, Island Curate, Trinity, Westmoreland, quoted in PP, 1866, xxx [C. 3682], 156.

43. PP, 1866, li [C. 3749], Part I.

44. Gardner, *History of Jamaica*, pp. 492–494; PP, 1866, xxx [C. 3682], 185–187.

45. *Jamaica; Who is to Blame?* by a *Thirty Years' Resident* (London [1866]), pp. iii–ix; West India Committee, Minutes of the Meeting of the Acting Committee on 10 November 1865, Minute Books, 1865, Part III, pp. 90–92, WIC.

46. Charles Royes to Eyre, Windsor, St. Ann, 31 March 1865, PP, 1866, li [C. 3595], 98.

47. A. Trollope, *The West Indies and the Spanish Main* (New York, n.d.), pp. 100–101.

48. Andrew Lewis, in House of Assembly, 14 December 1865, Judah and Sinclair, *Debates*, XIII, 168.

49. H. A. Whitelocke, in House of Assembly, 14 December 1865, Judah and Sinclair, *Debates*, XIII, 170.

50. Judah and Sinclair, *Debates*, XIII, 217–218.

51. Judah and Sinclair, *Debates*, XIII, 174.

52. W. Hosack, *Isle of Streams: or the Jamaica Hermit and Other Poems* (Edinburgh, 1876), pp. 52, 66.

CONCLUSION

1. R. Hill, *The Book of Moses, How Say You, True or Not True? Being a Consideration of the Critical Objections in Dr. Colenso's Review of the Books of Moses and Joshua* (Kingston, 1863).

INDEX